Praise for *The Intelligent REIT Investor Guide*

"The simple genius of public REITs is that they turn bricks and mortar into transparent and predictable liquid assets. Since they tend to pay high dividends, REITs can serve as a terrific addition to an investment portfolio. Thomas' book helps break down this asset class for the average person, making REITs more understandable and therefore more accessible to everyone."

Sam Zell
Founder and Chairman of Equity Group Investments

"In just 30 years, the REIT market has grown to a diverse $2 trillion global opportunity. Yet there remain a great number of misconceptions about the nature and behavior of equity REITs. Brad Thomas' book provides readers a wealth of tools and insights to appreciate – and potentially profit from – this asset class."

Joseph M. Harvey
President of Cohen & Steers

"Brad Thomas has been guiding REIT investors through many economic cycles. His common-sense, bottom-up approach identifies the financial, operational, and strategic characteristics that separate winners and losers over the long term. This book is an essential overview for anyone looking for the tools for success investing in REITs."

Paul E. Adornato
CFA, veteran REIT analyst

"In this book, Brad Thomas continues to display his in-depth knowledge and expertise of the REIT industry. Through several decades of interviews and discussions with the top management of many major REITs, detailed research into the industry. . . and his own experience as a commercial real estate developer, Brad brings a unique insight and perspective to the world of REITs."

Dave Henry
Board member of several large REITs, former Kimco CEO,
former ICSC chairman, former vice chair of Nareit

"By publishing this book, Brad Thomas is allowing the general public to have access to his many years of successful professional expertise in listed real estate. . . [that] will help generations of individual investors to profit from a very attractive and diversified class of stocks."

Eric Nemeth
Private equity investor, independent board member

"The structure of a REIT is generally and essentially simple: Collect rent and distribute rent after debt service and basic corporate expenses to equity owners as dividends. But the general simplicity and similarity of the REIT structure in some ways makes it harder to distinguish a good REIT from a mediocre REIT."

"To make those distinctions and thus to make the right investment decisions takes investigative work, historical knowledge, and actionable insight. Brad Thomas works the REIT field energetically and diligently, and anyone who follows his work acquires a big advantage in understanding America's REITs."

Edward B. Pitoniak
CEO of VICI Properties

"Brad has been a voice of reason in the REIT space for many years. This book provides a comprehensive guide to REIT investing."

Jonathan Litt
Founder and CIO at Land & Buildings Investment Management

"Brad has been a longtime follower of REITs and a contributor to the growth of the REIT industry. He has a broad knowledge of the industry, deep connections, and an intellectual curiosity that help shine a light on this often misunderstood investment vehicle. One of Brad's mentors, Ralph Block – to whom the book is dedicated – was not only one of the greatest gentlemen I've had the pleasure of knowing, but also a disciple and true visionary of the REIT industry."

Craig Robinson
CEO of GSI Capital Advisors

"*The Intelligent REIT Investor Guide* is the definitive and comprehensive resource for investing in real estate investment trusts. Brad uses his in-depth knowledge from his 25 years of experience in the business to offer unique insight and provide an invaluable resource for both novices as well as sophisticated professional investors."

Randy Blankstein
President of The Boulder Group

"Brad Thomas has once again delivered a highly accessible roadmap to investing in the REIT sector. In addition to the foundational overview of REIT valuation, performance measurement, and portfolio construction, this new volume tackles current innovations, including the growth of technology and specialized REITs and the pandemic's impact on real estate."

Sam Chandan
Silverstein chair and Dean of the NYU Schack Institute

"Brad Thomas' book provides a comprehensive overview of REIT investment, from the basic concepts of what REITs are and why they belong in investors' portfolios, to more advanced subjects like understanding REITs' financial statements. It's a highly useful source of information on REITs and the REIT marketplace for beginning and more advanced investors alike."

Steven A. Wechsler
President and CEO of Nareit

"Whether you're an experienced investor or a novice investor, this is a MUST READ book for anyone exploring REIT investing or education. As Ben Graham is known as an icon for value investing, Brad has become an icon in REIT investing."

Jonathan Hipp
Principal of U.S. Capital Markets,
head of U.S. Net Lease Group

"Brad Thomas has gained a well-deserved reputation as the preeminent REIT expert of our time and has compiled this comprehensive book on all aspects of investing in REITs. Whether you are new to REITS or well-versed in the sector, this is a must-read."

Alex Bossert
Founder and Portfolio Manager of Bossert Capital

"Brad is a dedicated and thorough REIT connoisseur who has been following the sector and companies [in it] for decades. His insight has helped Main Street investors navigate events."

Floris van Dijkum
Managing Director, REITs of Compass Point Research & Trading

"The world is fascinated by the opportunity to invest in real estate but is often overwhelmed by the world of REITs. Brad has been a leading resource in the REIT industry; and his *The Intelligent REIT Investor Guide* provides an incredibly useful roadmap for the benefits of REITs, the differences between REIT asset sectors, and the unique investment characteristics that REITs exhibit. REITs are a notable opportunity for diversified real estate investments within the stock market, and Brad's book is a must-read for anyone considering allocating a portion of their investment portfolio into REITs."

Michael Riopel
Assistant General Counsel at Northwestern Mutual

"*The Intelligent REIT Investor Guide* is a must-read for any investor who wants a great introduction and guide to REIT investing. A timely publication for those looking to REITs for income, an inflation hedge, and dedicated to REIT legend Ralph Block, to boot! Well done, Brad!"

Tom Lewis
Former CEO of Realty Income

"Brad has produced another excellent textbook on REITs for those seeking a solid foundation. The book provides a valuable resource, giving students the definitions and descriptions they need as we build from there."

J. Morris
Professor at Georgetown University, founder of REIT Academy

"Brad Thomas has taken the mystery out of investing in REITs. *The Intelligent REIT Investor Guide* is a timely and useful guide to navigating this often overlooked asset class."

Greg Morillo
Managing Partner at Lionbridge Capital, L.P.

"From the basics to how to think about analyzing and investing in REITs, this book offers a valuable perspective for investors of any experience level."

Brian Nelson
CFA, President of Valuentum Securities, Inc.

"Brad's skillful guide to the world of REIT investing is a must-read for anyone considering sustainable liquid real estate investments. His deep knowledge of commercial real estate combined with the constant study of REITs is a combination producing rich takeaways."

Michael Bull
CEO of Bull Realty

"I worked with Brad as a development partner in my firm and have always been awestruck by his creativity and grasp of capital and markets."

Ed Kobel
President of DeBartolo

"Brad Thomas is one of the most trusted voices in real estate investing. REIT investors who follow Brad's research and analysis have benefitted from consistent dividends and long-term value creation."

Brad Watt
President and managing partner at Petra Capital Properties

"There is a reason that Brad Thomas is among the most followed REIT analysts and writers. He harnesses his broad knowledge of the players and familiarity with various real estate businesses to make REIT investing accessible and simple. Brad has long believed that REIT investing is foundational to creating a solid personal long-term stock portfolio. This book shows you why."

Christopher Volk
Cofounder and Executive Chairman of STORE Capital

"I believe in and follow Brad Thomas, my go-to for REIT investing knowledge."

Prince Dykes
Veteran, host of *The Investor Show*,
and author of the *Wesley Learns* book series

The Intelligent REIT Investor Guide

HOW TO SLEEP WELL AT NIGHT WITH SAFE AND RELIABLE DIVIDEND INCOME

Brad Thomas

WILEY

Published by John Wiley & Sons, Inc., Hoboken, New Jersey.
Published simultaneously in Canada.

No part of this publication may be reproduced, stored in a retrieval system, or transmitted in any form or by any means, electronic, mechanical, photocopying, recording, scanning, or otherwise, except as permitted under Section 107 or 108 of the 1976 United States Copyright Act, without either the prior written permission of the Publisher, or authorization through payment of the appropriate per-copy fee to the Copyright Clearance Center, Inc., 222 Rosewood Drive, Danvers, MA 01923, (978) 750-8400, fax (978) 750-4470, or on the web at www.copyright.com. Requests to the Publisher for permission should be addressed to the Permissions Department, John Wiley & Sons, Inc., 111 River Street, Hoboken, NJ 07030, (201) 748-6011, fax (201) 748-6008, or online at http://www.wiley.com/go/permissions.

Limit of Liability/Disclaimer of Warranty: While the publisher and author have used their best efforts in preparing this book, they make no representations or warranties with respect to the accuracy or completeness of the contents of this book and specifically disclaim any implied warranties of merchantability or fitness for a particular purpose. No warranty may be created or extended by sales representatives or written sales materials. The advice and strategies contained herein may not be suitable for your situation. You should consult with a professional where appropriate. Neither the publisher nor author shall be liable for any loss of profit or any other commercial damages, including but not limited to special, incidental, consequential, or other damages.

For general information on our other products and services or for technical support, please contact our Customer Care Department within the United States at (800) 762-2974, outside the United States at (317) 572-3993 or fax (317) 572-4002.

Wiley also publishes its books in a variety of electronic formats. Some content that appears in print may not be available in electronic formats. For more information about Wiley products, visit our web site at www.wiley.com.

Library of Congress Cataloging-in-Publication Data

Names: Thomas, R. Brad, 1966- author.
Title: The intelligent REIT investor guide : how to sleep well at night with safe and reliable dividend income / Brad Thomas.
Description: Hoboken, New Jersey : Wiley, [2021] | Includes index.
Identifiers: LCCN 2021020641 (print) | LCCN 2021020642 (ebook) | ISBN 9781119750307 (cloth) | ISBN 9781119750352 (adobe pdf) | ISBN 9781119750376 (epub)
Subjects: LCSH: Real estate investment trusts. | Dividends.
Classification: LCC HG5095 .T46 2021 (print) | LCC HG5095 (ebook) | DDC 332.63/247—dc23
LC record available at https://lccn.loc.gov/2021020641
LC ebook record available at https://lccn.loc.gov/2021020642

Cover images: Front: © LRuthven/Getty Images; Back: © Domin_Domin/Getty Images
Cover design: Tony Merola

Set in 11/13pt ITC New Baskerville Std, Straive, Chennai, India
SKY1002889_082721

In many ways, my love of REITs can be correlated to my love for my five kids. That's why I dedicate this book to Lauren, Lexy, Nicholas, Riley, and A.J. They're always worth investing in.

"The true investor will do better if he forgets about the stock market and pays attention to his dividend returns and to the operation results of his companies."

– Benjamin Graham

Contents

Acknowledgments

Anyone who's written a book recognizes the time, energy, and effort it takes to turn an idea into a finished product. In bringing *The Intelligent REIT Investor Guide* to fruition, it took an army of individuals; and I'm honored and blessed to have collaborated with all of them.

Most importantly, I want to acknowledge my family for being patient and understanding in support of this project. It took me over eight months to complete the book, and that means spending almost every weekend away from home.

A very special thank you is in order for my editor, Jeannette DiLouie. She is an amazing and gifted professional, and I'm honored to have her on the Wide Moat Research team. I also want to thank other WMR teammates, such as Noah Blacker, Tony Merola, Stephen Hester, and Frances Popp, who were all helpful in the creation of this book.

My experienced team of contributors who are listed at the end of the book deserve special mention as well. They include Mark Decker, Sr., Scott Robinson, Jennifer Fritzsche, David Gladstone, Jay Hatfield, Eva Steiner, and Paul Smithers.

Also, special praise goes out to Nareit, FactSet, and Seeking Alpha, which all provided me with data. That third source deserves a second mention as well for being a terrific investment platform to work with over the years. Without the Seeking Alpha platform, I would have never been able to build my audience and become a global influencer in the world of real estate investing. In that regard, I would like to especially recognize the thousands of followers who trust me there, as well as Eli Hoffman, who worked at Seeking Alpha until he passed away in 2020.

In addition to Ralph Block, who was a mentor to me and inspired me to write this book, I want to thank others who were instrumental in my career as a real estate analyst, such as Tom Lewis (former CEO of

Realty Income), Norman Scarborough (my professor at Presbyterian College), and Chuck Carnevale (owner of FAST Graphs).

Perhaps one day I will write an entire book on my career in commercial real estate. But for now, I must highlight two friends who hired me when I graduated from college in 1988. Arthur Cleveland and Lewis White both took me under their wings and inspired me to get rich by owning real estate.

Finally, I want to thank my mother, Louise Thomas, who raised my brother and me while working tirelessly in real estate. I obtained my real estate license when I was 18 years old but, had it not been for her, I would have never become an intelligent REIT investor. Thank you, Mom!

A Building Block for REITs

Innovations in the world of finance tend to be incremental, rather than revolutionary, but every now and then one comes along that truly enhances societal value. Two that quickly come to mind are the introduction of the first mutual fund nearly 100 years ago and a refinement of that idea – the ETF – about 30 years ago. Both provided a means for investors of all sizes to efficiently gain access to diversified portfolios that otherwise would have been cumbersome and costly to construct. A similar quantum leap occurred with the formation of the first Real Estate Investment Trusts (REITs) in 1960, which, like mutual funds and ETFs, are non-taxable, pass-through entities. Whereas mutual funds and ETFs own stocks or bonds, REITs provide a comparable mechanism for investing in properties.

The primary appeal is obvious: Publicly traded REITs turn an asset class that is otherwise illiquid and hard to access into something that can be bought or sold with a few clicks on a keypad. In addition, today's REITs are best-in-class companies that own some of the highest-quality real estate. In most U.S. property sectors, REITs dominate the list of largest property owners, and they bring a level of managerial acumen and operational expertise that is often not found among smaller players. Their size also affords efficiency on overhead and borrowing costs, and their corporate governance practices provide reasonable alignment of interests between managers and investors.

As a result, the REIT model has thrived. In the United States, REITs now own more than $1.5 trillion of real estate. In addition to traditional property sectors such as retail, office, industrial, and apartments, REITs are dominant owners of cell towers, data centers, healthcare facilities, single-family rentals, and numerous niche sectors. This exposure to non-traditional property types poised to prosper in tomorrow's economy is impossible to replicate via other investment vehicles. Outside of the United States, the REIT template has now been adopted in 40 countries, and there are nearly 500 REITs scattered across the globe. Further expansion both domestically and globally is a certainty.

This growth has been accompanied by excellent returns. The industry reached adulthood about 25 years ago, and listed property-owning REITs have delivered total returns that are slightly better than those of either small- or large-cap stocks over that time frame. They have also delivered better risk-adjusted returns than private-market real estate investment vehicles. As important, REIT share prices often stray from the market herd, a trait that can soften the blow of broad market downturns. Their demonstrated propensity to enhance returns while reducing risk makes them a valuable addition to any broadly diversified portfolio. These attributes have been quantified and validated by reputable academics and investment consultants employing state-of-the-art portfolio allocation models, with most recommending a weighting of at least 10%.

Common sense also supports an allocation at least that large. Investors should have a roughly proportionate exposure to every asset class, and real estate is a very large asset class. Estimates of the size of this country's commercial property market run a wide gamut, but a credible midpoint that includes a broad array of property types is $17 trillion. That compares with capitalization for the U.S. stock market of $50 trillion, $11 trillion for corporate bonds, and $4 trillion for municipal bonds. Debt obligations backed by the U.S. Treasury tally $30 trillion, but with the Federal Reserve increasingly dictating prices in that market, it's fair to question whether a proportionate allocation is optimal for most investors. There is no "right" allocation for real estate, but portfolios lacking an explicit target of at least 10% are not as well diversified as they should be.

Investing in property, whether via private vehicles or publicly traded REITs, can seem daunting, as the arena is littered with jargon and valuation approaches that are often foreign even to trained investment professionals. Indeed, until the early 1990s, this issue served as an impediment to the acceptance of REITs into the mainstream. At about that time, however, a critical mass of sophisticated investors, analysts, and executives descended on the space, and they invented and popularized the specialized performance and valuation metrics that are ubiquitous today. Their contributions served as foundational building blocks for the subsequent growth and prosperity the industry has enjoyed.

Ralph Block, the author of *Investing in REITs*, was one of those pioneers. There weren't very many of us back then who took it as self-evident that publicly traded real estate was a transformative idea, but the vision had no more passionate adherent than Ralph. His enthusiasm for REITs (his email was REITnut@aol.com) was contagious, and his regular newsletters were both informative and fun to read. A quote from Samuel Johnson appeared above each edition: "No one but a blockhead ever wrote, except for money." As the newsletter was free, the quote was a clever, self-deprecating joke. And no one ever gleaned more investment insight from a golden retriever than Ralph, but his interviews with his beloved Sammy were classic. The newsletter, certainly a seed for this book, was perhaps a way for Ralph to give back to an investment sector that had given him so much in both financial and intellectual rewards.

Like its legendary namesake, *The Intelligent Investor* by Ben Graham, the book is full of common-sense approaches to uncovering value. At the same time, it provides a comprehensive overview of the quantitative metrics necessary to make well-informed investment decisions. Why does the REIT industry use funds from operations (FFO) and adjusted funds from operations (AFFO) in lieu of earnings per share? Why is "cap ex" so important? Why look beyond dividend yields? What is NAV? How is it calculated, and why does it matter? These and many other questions are adroitly handled.

The Intelligent REIT Investor Guide is a must-read, not only for investors in REITs, but for anyone hoping to gain perspective and understanding of the commercial real estate industry at large.

Mike Kirby – Co-founder and Director of Research, Green Street

About Green Street:
Green Street is the preeminent provider of actionable commercial real estate research, news, data, analytics, and advisory services in the U.S. and Europe. For more than 35 years, Green Street has delivered unparalleled intelligence and trusted data on the public and private real estate markets. Green Street is widely recognized as the unbiased authority on REITs, offering a time-tested approach to valuation with a strong track record for identifying the most attractively priced REITs and property sectors. The firm helps clients gain a thorough understanding of the entire REIT ecosystem at the macro, sector, REIT and property level to drive more informed investments. Learn more at www.greenstreet.com.

Introduction

In 1998, a very impressive man named Ralph Block published the first edition of a very big book titled *Investing in REITs*. He was so impressive and the book was so big that it's now seen four editions. Together, they have helped educate millions of investors around the globe, including me, about real estate investment trusts.

That's only a small portion of his legacy though. Ralph, who began investing in real estate investment trusts in the 1970s, led a career that spanned four full decades and established him as a significant voice for the industry and a well-respected institutional REIT investor. Like me, he had a passion for writing, which is why he formed Essential REIT Publishing Company, where he published hundreds of articles and books and inspired thousands in the process.

I know that Ralph was a great reader as well, though I admittedly can't tell you if he ever read *Repeatability: Build Enduring Businesses for a World of Constant Change* by Chris Zook and James Allen.

With that said, I think my old friend would have agreed with them that, "Differentiation is both the essence of strategy" and "the prime source of competitive advantage." The co-authors also wrote how, "You earn money not just by performing a valuable task but by being different from your competitors in a manner that lets you serve your core customers better and more profitably."

I can't help but think of that insight when I think about REITs and what they offer. A misunderstood asset class in too many ways, REITs perform a unique service to their customers and investors alike. By providing capital to those that need access to real estate, they also offer reliable cash flow, growth, and liquidity to investors. In that way, REITs truly can make an enormous difference in portfolio profitability, as I'll show in this book.

This brings to mind yet another great thinker: The father of value investing, Benjamin Graham. He once said that, "When I started, [investments] were almost entirely limited to bonds. Common stocks, with relatively few exceptions, were viewed primarily as vehicles for speculation."

Of course, that view would change during his career. In two of his books – *Security Analysis and The Intelligent Investor* – Graham detailed the importance of stocks and fixed income. And those who took his advice, like his protege Warren Buffet, went on to make millions and millions and millions of dollars as a result.

REITs weren't established until 1960 (as we'll discuss further in Chapter Three). So Graham, who passed away some 16 years later, would have been far less familiar with them. Even so, I believe he would have had a very good opinion of what they've evolved into: a force to be reckoned with, to be sure. They represent over $1.4 trillion in equity market capitalization, provided over $69 billion in dividend income distributions in 2019 alone, and have inspired similar structures in several dozen countries around the world since.

Put together, U.S. REITs own over $3.5 trillion in gross real estate assets. And those that are publicly traded own more than 520,000 properties, which is roughly 10%-15% of all institutional-quality commercial real estate in the country. So the potential for consolidation and further growth within this highly fragmented marketplace is powerful – as is the collective influence of the estimated 87 million Americans who now own REITs through their retirement savings and other investment funds.

Doesn't that sound like something you'd like a piece of too?

That's the purpose for this book: to teach you how to get exactly that. It unites Ralph's dedication, Graham's proven and profitable philosophy, and my passion for real estate securities to form something truly worth reading. A common tie between the three of us and a common theme of REITs is a solid appreciation of dividends, with Graham specifically including that investment perk in his time-tested principles:

1. A sufficiently strong financial condition
2. Stable and growing earnings
3. A strong dividend record
4. Shares that trade at a moderate price-to-earnings multiple that offers a margin of safety.

It's exceptionally hard to go wrong long-term when you follow those rules. Trust me. I know.

Why This Book?

Graham once explained that "the most durable education is self-education," and that's what I've done over the decades, including as a developer for over 20 years. That role taught me how to create value in real estate "from the ground up," giving me the building blocks I needed to eventually become an investment analyst with a deep understanding of real estate securities.

All told, I now have 30+ years' experience as a real estate investor, all of which I've put into this book – along with chapters' worth of insider information from the long list of expert contacts I've compiled along the way.

My main goal is to help educate readers by utilizing my experience in leasing, finance, development, and capital markets so they can better build their own wealth by owing shares in real estate investment trusts. As you may have already noticed, I titled *The Intelligent REIT Investor* after Graham's *The Intelligent Investor*. This was done on purpose to boldly highlight the link between valuation and real estate, which you now have access to.

I'm also proud to acknowledge the dream team of contributors who helped make this book happen – one more reason to make it the blockbuster of all works on the subject. Much of *The Intelligent REIT Investor* was, in fact, structured around Ralph's fourth edition (published in 2011).

While he passed away in 2016, I was fortunate to have considered him a friend in his later years. And so I'm extremely honored to carry his torch today. Knowing both his character and legacy, I dedicate *The Intelligent REIT Investor* to his memory in hopes that his knowledge, passion, humor, and love will be just as motivating and transformative now as they were during his lifetime.

A lot has, admittedly, changed since 2011. So I did add and revise quite a lot in the process of putting the following chapters together. There are new property sectors to expand on, important events and updates to note – including, of course, the 2020 pandemic's effects on the sector, parts of which may surprise you – and other key aspects to include.

I also decided to create a separate study guide to this book instead of including bulky appendices at the back. That way, there's less risk of overwhelming new REIT investors, while my more academic following will still have another resource they can turn to.

That additional information should be useful to anyone looking to dive deeper into current trends and statistics. And those who want even more up-to-date education can turn to my REIT Masterclass series, which will add even more day-to-day observations and analysis.

With that said, I truly hope that whether you're a novice in this area, an expert, or somewhere in-between, you find great insights into understanding the world of real estate investment trusts… and how to use them to achieve your unique financial goals.

Happy and successful investing,
Brad Thomas

REITs: What They Are and How They Work

"The true investor . . . will do better if he forgets about the stock market and pays attention to his dividend returns and to the operation results of his companies."

—Benjamin Graham

What's your idea of a perfect investment?

That's a trick question, for the record, since there is no such thing. Greater returns come with greater risk, while lesser risk comes with lower returns. You're just not going to find a stock that offers intense gains and intense safety at the same time.

Even so, those looking for above-average current returns, reasonably strong long-term price appreciation, and only modest risk should definitely consider commercial real estate that can generate reliable streams of rental income.

In the past, real estate investing was only available to wealthy entrepreneurs with deep pockets and the ability to acquire and actively manage portfolios of properties. Real estate investment trusts, or REITs (pronounced "reets"), were born out of that environment with the intent to allow small investors the same kinds of benefits.

Congress officially recognized REITs in 1960, patterning them after mutual fund laws. In the beginning, they were severely restricted, mostly meant to just provide investors with a non-taxed, passive flow-through form of income. The REIT vehicle received a dividend-paid deduction from corporate tax for every dollar distributed. And income was taxed only at the shareholder level instead of being double-taxed like most corporations.

They've since evolved into a highly attractive overall package that's very much worth considering: an uncomplicated way to buy and own real estate run by experienced professionals who give you some of the profits anyway. REITs offer access to reaping income from major office buildings, shopping malls, hotels, and apartment buildings. In fact, they work with just about any kind of commercial real property you can think of. Better yet, this all comes in an easily traded common stock like Apple or Amazon.

Perhaps best yet, they do all this while giving you the steady and predictable cash flows that come from owning and leasing real estate – and on a much larger scale than a mere individual can handle. Essentially, REITs put their corporate-strength access to public equity and debt capital into acquiring and building additional properties to grow their businesses. Combined, these features can add stability to their investors' portfolios.

Real estate as an asset class has long been perceived as an inflation hedge that, during most market periods, enjoys fairly low correlation with the performance of other categories.

As mentioned in the introduction, REITs have been around for 60 years now, though it's only been in the past 30 that they've become widely known. That's true because of several pivotal moments in their evolution, some of which were out-and-out crises at the time. We'll discuss those in more detail in Chapter 3, but suffice it to say for now that REITs evolved in very positive ways as a direct result of those experiences.

From the end of 1992 through the end of 2019, the size of the REIT industry has increased by more than 75 times, rising from a market cap just under $16 billion to almost $1.33 trillion. Since that's only about 10–15% of all institutionally owned commercial real estate, this extremely attractive sector is filled with vertically integrated operating companies that still have plenty of room to grow.

REITs Are Liquid Assets

I've already mentioned that REITs are easy to buy and sell. But you're excused if you'd like to point out how unwieldy commercial real estate can be.

A liquid asset or investment is one with a generally accepted value and accommodating market, where it can be sold easily and quickly at little or no discount to that value. In which case, direct investment in real estate – whether a shopping mall in California or a major office building in Manhattan – is far from liquid. People aren't exactly lining up outside of such buildings ready to buy them at the drop of a hat.

Most publicly traded stocks, however, are liquid, a rule that holds true for REITs. They're real estate – owning investments that enjoy the benefit of a common stock's public market trading and liquidity. So when you buy into them, you're not just buying properties; you're also buying the businesses they belong to. It's like when you buy stock in Exxon; you're buying more than oil reserves.

The vast majority of REITs are public real estate companies overseen by financially sophisticated, skilled management teams with the ability to grow their companies' cash flows (and dividends) at rates higher than inflation. It's not uncommon to get total annual returns of 8%. All you need is a 4% dividend yield and 4% capital appreciation resulting from 4% annual increases in operating cash flow and property values.

As we'll discuss in a later chapter, management and good corporate governance are critical to those kinds of results. Like other operating companies in the public market, REIT shares have a strong likelihood of increasing in value over time as their properties generate higher cash flows, the values of their properties increase, and they grow their portfolios – all of which management can, should and, in most cases, does add active value to.

Running a REIT isn't always a stress-free job (especially in the face of a global pandemic and subsequent shutdowns). But there are teams of men and women out there nonetheless who knock it out of the park. They operate their properties to generate steady income, only accepting risk where the odds of success are high. Because they recognize REITs' unique ins and outs, most of them are exceptionally careful when and where they invest retained earnings.

They search out ways to grow their property portfolios, values, and cash flows by taking advantage of new opportunities as they come along.

Types of REITs

There are two basic categories of real estate investment trusts to consider. An equity REIT, for one, is a publicly traded company that buys, manages, renovates, maintains, and sometimes sells real estate properties as its principal business. Many also develop new properties under favorable economic conditions. Meanwhile, mortgage REITs (mREITs) make and hold loans and other debt instruments that are secured by real estate collateral.

The focus of this book, it should be stated, is on the former. That's mainly because, while mREITs have higher dividend yields and can deliver spectacular investment returns at times, equity REITs are less vulnerable to changes in interest rates. And they've historically provided better long-term total returns, more stable price performance, lower risk, and greater liquidity.

In addition, equity REITs allow the investor to determine the type of property he or she invests in and often even the geographic location of the properties in question. Most equity REITs today are specialized, best-in-class operating companies that invest in only one or two property types. This makes them concentrated experts in their fields of business, which gives investors greater chances to reap significant benefits over time.

General Investment Characteristics

Performance and Returns

Although equity REITs' long-term performance varies depending on the exact timeline used, they typically relate very well with those of broader stock indices such as the S&P 500. Data provided by the National Association of Real Estate Investment Trusts (Nareit) shown in Figure 1.1 show that, during the 40-year period through June 2020, REITs delivered an average annual total return of 11.38%. This compares closely with other indices' returns during the same period.

FTSE Nareit All Equity REITs
Monthly Indexed Total Return

Figure 1.1
Source: Nareit website.

Admittedly, that makes them sound indistinguishable. So here's the difference: REITs enjoy largely unique benefits that include merely modest correlation with other asset classes, less market price volatility, more limited investment risk, and higher current returns – each of which we'll look at next.

Lower Correlations

Correlations measure how much predictive power the price behavior of one asset class has compared to another. So if we want to predict what effect a 1% rise (or fall) in the S&P 500 will have on an investment category – REITs, stocks, small caps, bonds, and so on – for any particular time period, we look at their relative correlations.

For example, if the correlation of an S&P 500 index mutual fund with the S&P 500 index is perfect (written out as 1.0), then a 2% move in the S&P 500 would predict a 2% move in the index fund as well. On the opposite end of the range, correlations can trend down to –1.0, in which case their movements are completely opposite. And in between is 0.0, which suggests no correlation at all.

This concept is important in the investment world, since it allows financial planners, investment advisers, and individual or institutional investors alike to structure broadly diversified investment portfolios with the objective of having the ups and downs of each asset class offset each other as much as possible. This ideally results in a smooth increase in portfolio values over time, with much less volatility from year to year or even quarter to quarter.

Cohen & Steers Senior Vice President and Global/U.S. Portfolio Manager Laurel Durkay – along with Senior Vice President and U.S. Senior Portfolio Manager Jason Yablon – gave some interesting insights on the subject in their September 2020 publication, "How REITs Benefit Asset Allocation."

They noted, "REITs have historically served as effective diversifiers, as they tend to react to market conditions differently than other asset classes and businesses, potentially helping to smooth portfolio returns."

They also wrote that "share aspects of both stocks and bonds – responding to economic growth like equities, but with yields and lease-based cash flows that give them certain bond-like qualities." In addition, they're "subject to real estate cycles based on supply and demand, with the added stability of commercial leases. And they tend to be more sensitive to credit conditions due to the capital-intensive nature of real estate."

The co-authors add that "these distinct performance drivers" have actually resulted in "low long-term correlations with stocks and bonds. Since 1991, U.S. REITs have had a 0.57 correlation with the S&P 500 and a 0.21 correlation with U.S. bonds (see Figure 1.2). Global REITs have also exhibited diversifying correlations, albeit to a more modest degree, due largely to higher correlations of Asia's real estate market with both [Asian] and U.S. equities." (See Figure 1.3.)

Accordingly, in markets where stocks are rising sharply, REITs may lag relative to the broad stock market indexes. This happened in 1995, when REIT stocks underperformed comparatively speaking while still providing investors with 15.3% total returns. And it happened again in 1998 and 1999, when their returns were actually negative. Conversely, during many equity bear markets – such as 2000–2001 – lower correlating stocks such as REITs tend to be more stable and may suffer less.

Differentiated Behavior
U.S. REITs

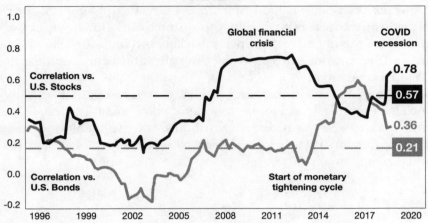

Figure 1.2

Source: Cohen & Steers.

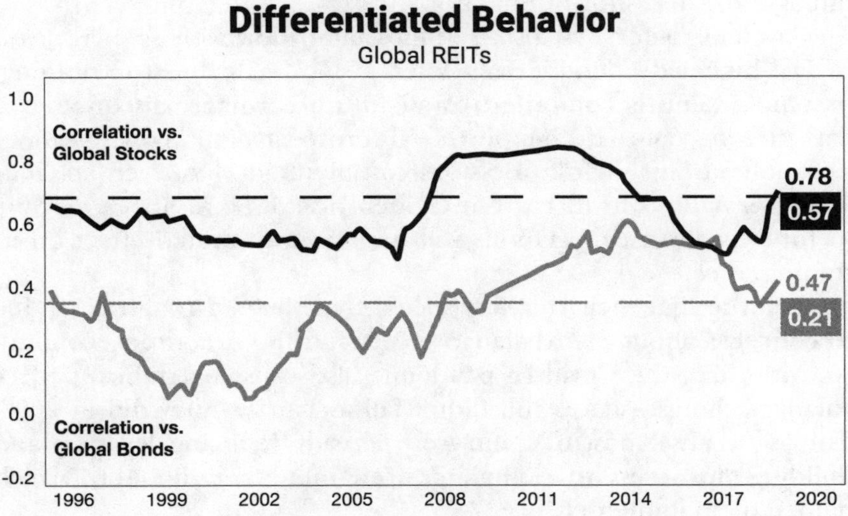

Differentiated Behavior
Global REITs

Figure 1.3

Source: Cohen & Steers.

Durkay and Yablon add that "sudden changes in bond yields can have a meaningful influence on short-term REIT performance. However, such periods tend to be temporary. In the long run, REIT returns are driven primarily by the distinct cash flows and growth profiles of the underlying property markets and the added stability of leases [that provide] the potential diversification benefits of an allocation to real estate."

Bottom line: Correlations will vary over time, particularly during short time frames. However, because commercial real estate is a distinct asset class with distinct attributes, it's reasonable to expect REITs to maintain fairly low relativity to other asset classes over reasonably long time periods.

Lower Volatility

A stock's volatility refers to how much its price tends to bounce around from day to day or even hour to hour. Over the past four decades or so, REITs have proved to be less volatile than other equities on a daily basis. This has even been despite their increasing size and popularity, which has brought in new investors with different agendas and shorter time horizons.

Another factor that usually helps tamp down on such issues is REITs' higher dividend yields. When a stock yields next to nothing, its entire value is comprised of all future earnings, discounted to the present date. If the perceived prospects for those earnings decline even just slightly, the stock can plummet. However, much of a REIT's value is in its current dividend yield. So a modest decline in future growth expectations will have a more muted effect on its trading price.

It's true that their volatility spiked from 2007 through 2009 due to concerns about their balance sheets and the American economy. And in 2020, the Covid-19 pandemic also caused significant REIT volatility, though shares still didn't fall as hard as they did in 2008. This is because most of them were already reducing leverage and building up access to capital to strengthen their liquidity, which helped them immensely.

On the larger issue of volatility, Cohen & Steers adds, "At its Core, real estate exists to support basic needs of individuals and businesses, providing shelter and facilitating commerce." And there will always be demand in that regard. It's only a matter of whether those needs are "housed in a different form or location," or reflect "current preferences, such as residents moving from multifamily apartments in dense cities to suburban single-family homes."

Investment trends can change quickly and unexpectedly. In some years, REIT stocks will be very popular; in others, they'll be all but ignored. Admittedly, some "trends may be more permanent: accelerated e-commerce adoption driving demand for industrial/logistics at the expense of retail." Some examples include "greater reliance on digital infrastructure benefiting data centers and cell towers" and "increasing acceptance of work from home affecting office utilization."

The rise of hedge funds – including those with very short time horizons – has added another wild card to the deck. REITs can sometimes become the sandbox in which these funds like to play, bringing more volatility with them than there otherwise would, or should, be.

The reason I bring this up is because it's important to know what can cause volatility in the stocks we purchase, REITs or otherwise. When our stocks go up, it's too easy to ignore risk in our pursuit of ever-greater profits. And when our stocks drop, we too often tend to panic, dumping otherwise sound investments because we're afraid of ever greater losses.

Consider missed market expectations, which can play havoc on otherwise stable stocks. Let's say you own shares in a "regular" company that reports a 15% year-over-year increase in earnings. Yet because analysts expected a 20% increase, the stock drops. That scenario has played out more than once.

Fortunately, REITs are superior to most common stocks in this regard. Analysts who follow these companies are normally able to accurately forecast quarterly results, within one or two cents, quarter after quarter. This is because of the sheer predictability of the operations at work, especially when it comes to any property type that uses long-term leases (which is most of them). That provides earnings stability that can't be found very easily elsewhere, further reducing both risk and volatility.

As a result, relatively few REITs have gotten themselves into serious financial difficulties over the years. Those that did were generally poorly managed and/or burdened by risky balance sheets.

Less Risk

Make no mistake: There are times to buy and sell. But prudent investors control their emotions, oftentimes by filling their portfolios with low-risk positions like REITs.

As we already established, there's no way to avoid risk completely. Even simple preservation of capital carries its own risk, with inflation taking its typical toll on almost everything. So it should come as no surprise that real estate ownership and management comes with potential problems too.

The previously referenced Cohen & Steers report already broached the subject. It's easy to see that retail REITs are subject to the changing spending habits of consumers and that rising online capabilities are affecting offices. But every other property type comes with its own set of potential pitfalls. For instance, apartment REITs have to deal with varying popularity of single-family dwellings and/or declining job growth. And the healthcare subsector constantly battles government decisions concerning healthcare reimbursement.

Again, there is no perfect investment. I can't stress that enough. The global pandemic and consequent government shutdowns certainly put significant stress on many REITs, especially already struggling malls, which we'll discuss in Chapter 5. Even so, the unique blocks these investments are built on do make them very worthwhile considerations.

The fact that they simultaneously provide a steady income of dividend payments even during the occasional bear market doesn't hurt either. They literally pay us to wait.

Higher Current Returns

Chapter 3 discusses the actual creation and evolution of REITs. For now, just understand that they pay out at least 90% of their pretax income to shareholders in the form of dividends. The result is typically higher dividends as a percentage of their free cash flows (FCF) and higher dividend yields to boot.

In addition, to stay compliant with the law, REITs usually have to increase their payouts as rents rise over time, historically resulting in steady dividend growth.

Some academics claim shareholders shouldn't care how much of a company's net income is paid out this way. But others argue that dividends really do matter with respect to shareholders' total returns.

In September 2010, *Barron's* quoted Ed Clissold, an equity strategist at Ned Davis Research. His research showed that the S&P 500 had delivered average annual price appreciation of 4.92% since the end of 1929. But its average annual total return had been 9.16%. In other words, dividends provided approximately 46% of those total returns, indicating that they do indeed count. A lot. And we haven't seen any evidence of that principle changing in the last decade.

Another related benefit is that REIT shareholders can partici-pate in income reinvestment plans, plowing their dividend income back into their holdings by buying additional shares. Or, should they so choose, they can invest it elsewhere or spend it on a vacation in Hawaii. Other shareholders don't have this advantage. They have to accept whatever decisions the board of directors puts in place in this regard.

Skeptics may point out that REITs' featured dividend yields are often below those of many corporate bonds. However, bond interest payments don't increase, whereas the REIT industry has a long-term track record of increasing dividends on a regular basis. The Great Recession and 2020–2021 Covid-19 pandemic both interrupted that run, it's true. But over time, their dividend action has still proven to outpace inflationary forces.

Back to Cohen & Steers again: "Real estate has inherent inflation-hedging qualities that we believe can help investors defend against erosion in buying power resulting from the rising cost of living." This includes how an inflationary environment can restrain new developments by pushing up the price of everything from land to materials and labor. As a result, landlords are in a better position to raise rents.

The article also mentions this: "Many commercial leases even have explicit inflation links, with rent escalators tied to a published inflation rate. As a result, REITs have historically benefited from inflation surprises, contrasting with the adverse reaction from broad stocks and bonds." Covid-19 did halt inflation for a time, but the long-term trend tells us that will change soon enough.

On a slightly separate note, there's also an intangible psychological benefit in seeing significant dividends roll in so consistently. Seeing a check come in for several hundred dollars every quarter – without the usual effort on your part – can provide substantial comfort . . . regardless of whether you intend to spend it or reinvest it.

High Current Returns Versus Slow Growth

Many people understandably wonder if those high dividends have a negative effect on REITs' growth prospects. After all, their 90% pretax-income payouts mean they can only keep so much money to build on.

Stock prices do indeed appreciate from rising earnings growth. Therefore, REIT shares do usually rise at a slower pace than non-dividend-paying companies. However, this is perfectly acceptable to their investors, who expect to make up much – or even all – of the difference through higher dividend payments over time.

Consider the study presented in the January/February 2003 issue of *Financial Analysts Journal.* Entitled "Surprise! Higher Dividends = Higher Earnings Growth," it was written by hedge fund manager Cliff Asness of AQR Capital Management and academic Robert Arnott of Research Affiliates. Together, they concluded that the earnings growth rates of companies with above-average dividend payments are actually higher than those with lower offerings.

These results tend to defy logic, I know. But the latter kind of company doesn't always do a good job of reinvesting its retained capital. Why should it? There's not the same incentive to be careful in this regard.

Regardless, REITs do have other means of obtaining growth (yet another to-be-discussed topic, this time in Chapter 10). They can make additional stock and debt offerings, exchange new shares or partnership units for properties, or get creative with buying and selling strategies.

With all that said, when dealing with most subsectors, it's often best to have relatively conservative expectations. In most cases, investors would be wise not to expect more than mid-single-digit growth over the long term. And when those conservative expectations are blown out of the sky, you'll want to do your due diligence.

It's not an automatic warning flag when a REIT's stock just keeps climbing. Some sectors perform better than others at varying times, which only makes sense. Real estate is a cyclical industry, so there will be down years. But rental rates do grow over time, meaning that healthy REITs' cash flows will grow as well.

These assets don't promise instant riches or even perpetual investment tranquility. But the sector does make for excellent long-term investments nonetheless. I've seen it happen too many times for myself and my readers to doubt that fact.

CHAPTER 2

REITs Versus Competitive Investments

"The investor should be aware that even though safety of its principal and interest may be unquestioned, a long-term bond could vary widely in market price in response to changes in interest rates."
—Benjamin Graham

When deciding if REITs are appropriate investments for you personally, it's often helpful to compare them with other assets. Admittedly, this isn't always easy considering how unique they truly are. But I still see it as a worthwhile endeavor, hence the purpose of this chapter.

To start off, REITs trade as stocks because, technically speaking, they are stocks. Yet they're markedly different from companies such as General Electric, Microsoft, or Disney because of their higher dividend yields and more modest capital appreciation prospects. Therefore, while it's useful to compare them to the broad equities markets, it might be more worthwhile to put them up against bonds, convertible bonds, preferred stocks, and higher-yielding common stocks, even master limited partnerships (MLPs).

These are the investments of choice for income seekers looking for lower volatility, zero to modest capital appreciation prospects, and reduced risk. So let's look at each of them.

Bonds

Bonds, particularly so-called junk bonds, usually provide higher yields than the average REIT. But the investor gets only the interest coupon and no growth potential. That's because they're so safe, promising repayment of principal at maturity. In the absence of bankruptcy or some other kind of default, bond investors always get their money back.

The same cannot be said about REITs.

With bonds, what you see is what you get: pure yield and very little else. Take a $10,000 investment in a bond that yields 5% and matures in 10 years. At the end of that decade, you'll have your $10,000 in cash, plus the cumulative amount of interest received ($10 \times 500) for a total of $15,000.

Now let's say you purchase 1,000 shares of a REIT trading at $10 that offers a 4% yield ($0.40 per share). It also increases its adjusted funds from operations (AFFO) – which, as we'll discuss in more detail later, is a rough approximation of FCF – by 4% annually and its dividend the same amount. The shares then rise in price 4% as well.

Ten years later, the REIT will be paying $0.593 in dividends, and the total investment will be worth $19,812: $4,992 in cumulative dividends received plus $14,820 in share value at that time. That's a difference of $4,812 between the two asset examples, as shown in Table 2.1.

Taxes, of course, will have to be paid on both, cutting into profits on either side. And conventional wisdom says that REITs should provide a higher total return in the end since they're riskier than bonds. However, that's not necessarily true if we consider the bond owner's exposure to inflation. REIT shares offer no specific maturity date, and there's no guarantee of the price you'll get when you sell them. However, bonds have no inflation protection. Their holders are at substantial risk of seeing their purchasing power decline with the dollar.

It's all a question of how one measures risk.

Also, when inflation rises, interest rates historically tend to do the same. This reduces bonds' market values while they're being held, to the further detriment of anyone who needs to sell them prior to

Table 2.1   REITs Should Produce Better Total Returns than Bonds

REITs: 4% annual dividend compounded at a 4% annual growth rate

End Year	Stock Price	Per-Share Dividend
1	$10.40	$0.400
2	$10.82	$0.443
3	$11.25	$0.450
4	$11.70	$0.468
5	$12.17	$0.487
6	$12.66	$0.506
7	$13.17	$0.527
8	$13.70	$0.548
9	$14.25	$0.570
10	$14.82	$0.593
		$4,992
1,000 shares	$14,820	$4,992
Total Investment value		**$19,812**

Source: Investing in REITs by Ralph Block.

maturity. On the flipside, if interest rates decline enough due to, say, lower inflation, many bonds may be called for redemption before their maturity dates. This deprives investors of what could have otherwise been very attractive yields and forces them to go out hunting again.

Admittedly, a REIT's stock price may decline in response to higher interest rates. But interest rates often climb alongside a growing economy, which helps to grow REIT cash flows over time.

For those who want to point out U.S. Treasury bonds as a solution, yes, those aren't callable prior to maturity. And, yes, they entail no repayment risk. But their yields are lower than those of corporate bonds, and they still fluctuate with interest rates regardless.

Bonds are certainly suitable investments for most investors. However, they shouldn't be regarded as good substitutes for REIT stocks in a broadly diversified portfolio. Nor should REIT stocks be seen as good substitutes for bonds.

Convertible Bonds

Comparatively speaking, convertible bonds may provide more competition for REITs. These securities offer comparable yields as well as appreciation potential if the common stock these bonds can be converted into rises substantially.

In general, these assets provide the security of fixed maturity dates in case their underlying common stocks fail to appreciate in value. So they can be relatively attractive investments.

The main problem here is that most companies just don't issue them. Some REITs have occasionally issued convertible securities, including convertible preferred stock. But investors should consider whether the extra safety they provide outweighs the often substantial conversion premium and their relative lack of liquidity.

Preferred Stocks

Many investors seeking higher yields have become interested in preferred stocks, including those issued by REITs. (That's one reason we included an entire segment on preferred shares later in the book.) Unlike bonds, these shares aren't guaranteed by the company in question to repay a specific amount at a specified date. And in the event of liquidation or bankruptcy, preferred shareholders' rights are subordinated to those of the corporation's creditors.

With that said, they do have seniority over common shareholders. Plus, most preferred stocks specify that common dividends cannot be paid unless preferred dividends are current.

Credit agencies treat preferred stocks as equity when everything is said and done. As for the companies themselves, they regard them as permanent capital that doesn't dilute common-stock-related interests, which sounds about right.

Most preferred dividend rates are set when they're first issued and remain that way for as long as the shares are outstanding. And since they have little if any appreciation potential on their own, their holders don't participate in the company's earnings growth. It's also important to know that the issuer can typically redeem them after a period of time – usually five years after issuance – at their original price. So if interest rates fall, the shareholder may be deprived of a good, high-yielding investment.

Then there's liquidity. It can be difficult to buy or sell large amounts of preferreds at a time. And there's often a significant spread between the bid and ask prices. Additionally, in admittedly abnormal cases where the issuer is acquired or goes private, preferred shareholders can be negatively affected by lack of disclosure concerning company information or by higher debt leverage at the newly private company.

These assets still appeal to many though because of their higher dividend yields compared to most common shares and corporate bonds (assuming comparable credit quality). This, alongside their payouts having priority over common stocks, makes them especially attractive during uncertain times, such as the 2020 pandemic.

Other High-Yielding Equities

Two better REIT comparisons to make include higher dividend-yielding publicly traded entities such as utilities and master limited partnerships (MLPs). Utility stocks, for one, have been a long-standing and reliable staple of the investment world. The industry's total market cap is in excess of $1 trillion, and the top 20 utility stocks have a combined value of $775 billion.

These businesses provide basic services such as electricity, natural gas, water, and wireline telephony to individuals and businesses. Competition isn't practical in most of these areas, allowing many of them to form what amounts to legal monopolies.

This is both good and bad for their shareholders. On the one hand, the utility doesn't have to compete with other providers, so its earnings and dividends are often quite stable. On the other, that stability can equate to very, very slow growth: perhaps 2–4% annually. Plus, these entities can only charge customers what the regulatory authorities permit, so they run the risk of fickle and sometimes politically motivated pricing.

In recent years, some utilities have been "unbundled," as it were. Those that generate or purchase power, and sell it to other service providers, for example, have become much less regulated. So their growth prospects are now better. Then again, their earnings are much less certain, and their dividend yields tend to be much lower.

Accordingly, utility stocks like those of Duke Energy and Southern Company may compete with REITs for investment dollars to some extent, especially because they've proved to be less volatile than REIT shares in recent years. As such, they can be good choices for people with very modest capital appreciation expectations and total return requirements.

MLPs, for their part, aren't limited so much by industry in a legal sense. Yet the vast majority of publicly traded ones are engaged in energy infrastructure such as gas pipelines and storage facilities, varying in how much exposure they have to natural resource prices.

According to MLP and energy analyst Alerian, the total market capitalization of the energy MLPs has grown rapidly to around $225 billion ($350 billion including Canada) as of September 30, 2020. The sector was almost $800 million in 2014, but MLPs have been consolidating since 2018.

Their dividend yields in November 2020 were close to 8%, which is generally higher than those of REITs. So they can provide investors with significant current income and diversification capabilities. And thanks to depreciation and other tax advantages applicable to the oil and gas industry, much of those cash distributions are not currently taxable as ordinary income.

MLPs are like other pass-through stock classes such as REITs, business development corporations (BDCs), and YieldCos because they're largely dependent on external capital markets and their unit counts generally rise over time.

They may trade like stocks, but they actually fall into a completely different category. Their legal structure means that investors receive a partnership K-1 form at the end of each year, which can make tax-return preparation challenging, to say the least. Also, if held in an individual retirement account (IRA) or other tax-deferred account, they can potentially give rise to "unrelated business taxable income." This would then open up their dividends to other forms of taxation under certain circumstances.

Rather like REITs, MLPs distribute most or all free cash flow to their partners. This means they'll need to raise outside capital from time to time if they want to grow, and such capital isn't always available.

All told, MLPs do compete with REITs for investment capital. However, they're different enough from each other that investors don't have to choose one over the other if they have enough capital to spread between the two categories.

Other Real Estate Investment Vehicles

As an asset class, real estate is usually a very good and stable investment as long as it isn't financed with large amounts of debt. A well-situated, well-maintained investment property should grow in value over the years, as should its rental revenue. While buildings may depreciate over time and neighborhoods may change, only a finite amount of land exists on which apartment communities, retail centers, and office buildings can be built. So if you own such a property in the right area, it can be – if not a gold mine – a continuing cash cow. New competitive buildings don't just pop up for no good reason, after all. They're only built if rents or property values are high enough to justify the cost of development.

In either such event, owners of existing properties will likely be better off.

This does once again bring up the issue of inflation. But the extent to which it affects commercial real estate owners isn't all that clear. There have been studies done on this issue, including that of David J. Hartzell, former professor of real estate at the University of North Carolina. He and R. Brian Webb concluded that property "returns tend to exhibit stronger relationships with inflation and its components" during periods of low vacancy rates. Therefore, inflation might not be a benefit to landlords when property markets are weak.

Direct Ownership

As we've mentioned before and will continue to explore, real estate has historically behaved differently from other assets. It therefore adds another dimension of diversity to stock, bond, cash, and even gold and art investments.

REITs are hardly the only way to take advantage of these factors though. Plenty of people choose direct ownership, for example, by being in the real estate business. In which case, they (hopefully) asked themselves questions like: Do I have the time to manage property? Do I know the best time to buy or sell? Do I have or can I obtain the insider information necessary to make it worth my while? Can I attract and retain the best tenants?

Depending on the market climate, buying real estate on the cheap to sell "on the expensive" is often more profitable than holding and managing it. That's why flipping houses holds such an appeal.

Then again, there's a reason why people can lose just as much as they can make on such ventures. Judging the markets appropriately, not to mention the costs and efforts involved, requires access to constantly evolving data. As for buying and holding to rent out to others, this necessitates effective and efficient property management. These cautions can't be overstated, especially since individuals often lack the time, money, and/or expertise to handle those tasks on their own.

It might seem intensely more profitable to keep all the profits from real estate instead of sharing it with fellow investors. But it's also riskier. Investment value is very often determined by the local economy. Therefore, at any given time, commercial properties may be doing well in one place and poorly in another. And most individuals simply don't have the financial resources to buy up a portfolio big enough to be safely diversified, either by property type or geography.

There's the problem of liquidity as well. Selling a single piece of real property can be very time-consuming and even costly. It's not a simple matter of determining to sell and pressing a button. Far from it. And maintenance and security make for even more headaches. Most people don't want to be the one taking calls about break-ins, clogged pipes, and stuck elevators. Yet using an outside management company can significantly reduce their profits.

Some investors claim they don't need to own either rental properties or REITs since they own their own homes. However, the dynamics of home values are often very different from those of commercial real estate – something we'll discuss again, albeit briefly, in Chapter 4. For starters, the same diversification and liquidity issues just described factor into owning just one home, as does emotional attachment. It's true that equity can be pulled out of one's home by refinancing, but that usually requires a tradeoff of substantially higher monthly mortgage payments.

So, simply stated, home ownership is no substitute for owning commercial real estate. That's why, for most individual investors, gaining access to real estate through professional rather than personal means is a far wiser course of action.

Private Partnerships

To solve those problems, some more entrepreneurial types trend toward private partnerships with 2, 10, or 20 partners: however many they see fit. They then delegate the tasks of property leasing and management, either to a general partner or an outside company. That comes at a price, of course. Plus, most private partnerships own only one or a few properties, once again rendering them something less than diversified.

Liquidity, meanwhile, may depend on the financial strength or solvency of the other investors involved. Although it's theoretically possible for one partner to sell his or her interest to another, that option comes with numerous potential problems. Conflicts of interest often abound between the general and limited partners with regard to such things as compensation, selling, and refinancing. And there's always the question of personal liability if the partnership experiences financial difficulties.

These private partnerships can be good investments at times under the right conditions with the right partners. But they still don't stand up to REITs more often than not.

Publicly Traded Limited Partnerships

Publicly traded real estate limited partnerships were once very popular, which was largely a shame. In the 1980s, these entities plucked billions of dollars from investors seeking the benefits of real estate ownership combined with tax breaks. The end result was their victims were lucky to recover 10 or 20 cents on the dollar.

There were several reasons for this failure, including the fees that were sometimes so high that they demolished all potential profits for the little guy. Often, there were conflicts of interest going on with the general partners. And in other cases, they bought into the real estate cycle too late. After grossly overpaying for properties, they hired mediocre managers, failing to recognize that real estate is a very management-intensive business.

As a result, publicly traded limited partnerships aren't popular today. Nor should they be.

The Private REIT Phenomenon

Beginning in 2000, another real estate alternative to public REITs burst onto the scene – non-publicly-traded, or private, REITs. Exactly as their names suggest, these entities comply with U.S. REIT laws but don't trade in public markets. Sponsored by various real estate organizations, they're usually sold to small investors by financial planners and investment advisers.

Like their public counterparts, private REITs will own a collection of commercial properties and distribute the resulting income to their shareholders as dividends. But they operate more as accumulators and aggregators of assets than vertically integrated operating companies. Their yields can be fairly high, though that doesn't make them automatically superior.

These investments actually come with a number of drawbacks. Perhaps most important is their lack of liquidity. And that's true even when they make offers to repurchase certain amounts of shares at certain times under certain conditions, as some of them do. Shares still can't be quickly sold by calling one's broker or pressing a button.

Furthermore, nonpublic REIT shares are usually sold with large commissions – often over 10% – that go to the selling agent. That means fewer investment dollars are available for real estate investment. Or for real estate investors. Too often, the corporate sponsor also earns significant additional revenue via property acquisitions and management fees. So there can easily be conflicts of interest and attempts to grow the REIT for exclusive gains instead of mutually shared benefits.

Investors should therefore carefully analyze these entities' organizational structures, balance sheets, acquisition criteria, operating costs and fee payments, prospective cash flows, and dividend coverage from recurring free cash flows.

Privately held REITs, privately held property, bonds, preferreds, utilities, MLPs, and the like can and do provide alternatives to REIT investing. But that doesn't make them replacements.

Publicly traded REITs focus entirely on commercial real estate, and their stocks have both liquidity and reasonable prospects for capital appreciation over time. Because of their structure, their management teams tend to hold closely aligned interest with share-holders. And their financial conditions and operating results are quite transparent via Securities and Exchange Commission (SEC) disclosure requirements and industry practices.

The key point is this: Publicly traded REIT shares are unique and distinguishable from other higher-yielding investments, including other forms of commercial real estate ownership. As such, it doesn't need to be an either/or choice. A wise investment strategy is to own both REITs *and* other higher-yielding stocks along with other invest-ments. You should always strive for the right investment mix for your personal financial situation, tolerance, and goals . . . all of which we'll discuss going forward.

CHAPTER

3

REITs over the Decades

"Investing isn't about beating others at their game. It's about controlling yourself at your own game."

—Benjamin Graham

As we discussed briefly in Chapter 2, few assets are more illiquid than commercial real estate such as office buildings, shopping centers, apartments, and the like. They're also very expensive to own and operate, which made them a "boom and bust" business in the past. Fueled by unreliable information (or at least a serious lack of good information), fortunes could be lost on these purchases.

Then again, fortunes could also be made – provided one already had a small fortune to begin with. Commercial real estate was the quintessential "you've got to have money to make money" example before the mid-twentieth century. It was a wealthy man's game until REITs came along.

The concept was really spawned by a real estate management company in Boston, Massachusetts, that used a business trust vehicle to avoid paying double taxes on its holdings. It was ultimately taken to court over this, with the court's decision basically boiling down to "if it walks like a duck and acts like a duck, it's probably a duck." And so ended the earliest REIT ancestor.

Yet that defeat prompted a new battle as the same company hired a law firm – Goodwin Proctor – to design a vehicle that would be legally acceptable. This time, it met with success. Congress accepted the accurate argument that small investors were unable to benefit from commercial real estate investing. As such, it agreed to allow a new business classification using mutual fund rules as a model.

(Interestingly, that's why REITs originally had to involve outside property managers: because the company that created them was precisely that. Self-interest, right? It's a beautiful thing.)

REITs were officially defined and authorized by Congress in the Real Estate Investment Trust Act of 1960, and the first actual examples were organized that same year under the following understanding:

1. A REIT must distribute at least 90% of its annual taxable income, except for capital gains, as dividends to its share-holders (most pay out 100%).
2. A REIT must have at least 75% of its assets invested in real estate, mortgage loans, shares in other REITs, cash, or government securities.
3. A REIT must derive at least 75% of its gross income from rents, mortgage interest, or gains from the sale of real property. And at least 95% must come from these sources, together with dividends, interest, and gains from secu-rities sales.
4. A REIT must have at least 100 shareholders with less than 50% percent of the outstanding shares concentrated in the hands of five or less shareholders.

The concept was pretty popular right out of the gate. Some of the earliest to go public were Washington, Pennsylvania, and Bradley REITs (the latter of which was not named after me) – small companies for small investors who only wanted to buy up 10, 100, or 1,000 shares. A large number of other equity REITs queued up for their IPO (initial public offering) spotlights as well. But the assassination of President John F. Kennedy in 1963 threw the mar-kets into turmoil, permanently pushing most of those debuts back.

It was a major setback to the sector's early evolution.

According to *The REIT Investment Summary*, a 1996 report published by Goldman Sachs, there were really only 10 of these businesses worth noting in that first decade. The companies in question ran portfolios worth $11 million to $44 million, and many of them were attached to management companies that were affiliated with members of their boards. It goes without saying that this could and did too easily create issues.

Even so, they did manage to perform well enough, thanks in part to the real estate market at the time. Cash flow (the original stand-in for the to-be-explained funds from operations, or FFO) grew an annual average of 5.8%, with 6.1% average dividend yields. All told, they easily returned more than the S&P 500 between 1963 and 1970 (11.5% versus 6.7%).

The Tax Reform Act of 1986

In 1968, big banks began to realize they could use the REIT structure to lend money to companies building commercial real estate. And so they created construction and development mortgage REITs – far too many of them and all of which acted far too aggressively. All told, these bank-backed entities lent more than $20 billion to such companies and contractors, which helped fuel overbuilding. Which led to a subsector disaster.

As developers walked away from projects that no longer made sense to continue, the financial forces behind them failed as well. Their shares fell and fell hard – 21.8% in 1973 and 29.3% in 1974. Only a few actually went bankrupt after that, but the rest were liquidated for pennies on the dollar. The debacle gave REITs in general a bad name all the way into the early nineties.

This was a shame considering how equity REITs continued to perform well in the 1970s, all things considered. When Goldman Sachs studied 10 representative entities during this period, it found they offered an annual average 6.1% compounded cash flow growth rate. This was fairly consistent too, with only one year ending with that calculation going negative. They also enjoyed 4.2% average annual price appreciation and dividend-yield-enhanced total returns of 12.9% per year.

Still, it was clear that more could be done to enhance their abilities and reputation. For one thing, because REITs were pass-through entities that relied on yields for most of their returns, many saw them as proxies for Treasury bills and public utilities. This led them to fall in and out of favor depending on how they held up comparatively speaking.

REITs were also hampered by their structure as passive flow-through investments and the fact that they couldn't manage their own properties. Frankly, they remained too illiquid, too disorganized (in that they weren't focusing their efforts on certain property types and/or areas), and too difficult for the average investor to calculate. The way most publicly traded companies reported generally accepted accounting principles (GAAP) net income simply did not line up well with the intricacies of owning real estate.

This came to further light in the 1980s, when mortgage loans were coming complete with 12.5–14.8% interest rates, depressing their ability to grow. According to the Goldman Sachs January 1996 *REIT Investment Summary*, its equity REITs' per-share FFO growth fell from 26.1% at the turn of the decade to 4.4% in 1983. Higher rents and a continuing undersupply of new real estate did help balance things out though to produce an 8.7% average for overall FFO. And shareholder average annual total returns from 1980 through 1985 were a whopping 28.6%.

That's not to say they didn't have competition. Because they did, and lots of it, thanks to the Economic Recovery Act of 1981. That legislation allowed real estate owners to cite property depreciation as a tax write-off. Just like that, both public and private investors wanted to get involved in real estate, putting a dollar in and deducting four off their tax liabilities. It was a win-win for developers – who got money to develop – and investors, who got outsized returns. And so what if buildings were going up that might or might not be economically viable?

This is when groups like major brokerage firms first formed real estate limited partnerships, adding to the growing bubble. Unlike REITs, they (and private investors) didn't have to show positive cash flow. Therefore, they could outbid for properties without facing any negative short-term side effects. This naturally led to an even more unhealthy real estate market with ever-rising prices, prompting developers to get involved even more heavily for their piece of the pie. And banks were more than happy to finance them – even up to 90% of costs.

Real estate was obviously overbuilt – and suffering for it – by the time the Tax Reform Act of 1986 repealed the tax shelter, leaving investors doubly stranded. Yet this was a significant milestone in the REIT industry, since it relaxed some of the restrictions they bore. For instance, they no longer had to hire outside companies to provide property leasing and management services. This gave them the chance to save both money and efforts should they so choose.

Over the years, most of them have done exactly that. The vast majority of today's REITs are fully integrated operating companies that can handle their business internally, including:

- Property acquisitions and sales
- Property management and leasing
- Property rehabilitation, re-tenanting, and repositioning
- New property development.

As should be expected, that efficiency easily translates into more stable profits for shareholders over time.

The 1990s: The Modern REIT Era Begins

In the second half of the 1980s, REITs' dividends had been rising faster than their earnings. Their stocks didn't suffer for it at the time, outperforming the S&P 500 in 1986 and 1987, and only slightly underperforming in 1985 and1988–89. But that changed the very next year as REIT share prices fell and fell hard.

That was quite the shock for their investors, who had only experienced one year of negative total returns between 1975 and 1990. That was in 1987, and they only dropped 3.6%. This time around though, they simply couldn't fight fate. The past overbuilding craze in office buildings and apartment communities finally caught up to them, no matter if they themselves hadn't participated in it. At the same time, the rise of Walmart and other discounters was beginning to encroach on traditional retailers and their landlords. Add to that their high payout ratios, which they themselves had encouraged and could no longer sustain, and a resulting round of dividend cuts. Combined, it was enough for investors to ditch greed as a motivator and let fear drive them instead.

REIT shares fell to unreasonable levels on that sentiment. Fortunately, they weren't a fledgling category anymore, and so the sector was able to bounce back by 1991. In fact, between 1991 and 1993, Nareit notes that their total annual returns averaged 23.3%. This was partially because they'd been so ridiculously undervalued and partially because they began aggressively taking advantage of the rest of the real estate world, which was still trying to emerge from its own bubble bursting back in 1986. That meant REITs were able to obtain properties at very good prices.

Speaking of that, the Federal Reserve was busy gradually lowering its interest rates to ease the shallow yet long recession the country had been stuck in. REITs benefited from that too, since their substantial dividend yields and ramped-up earnings growth once again looked good to investors, who bought right in. The combined environment inspired a range of subsector-specific IPOs, almost all of which were inspired by Nareit workshops. The trade association was spreading the word about its representatives to businesses, wealth managers, and legislators alike, and not only in the U.S. It went global too, holding more meetings in Paris, Frankfort, London, Edinburgh, Zurich, Amsterdam, Tokyo, and Singapore, sowing the seeds for REIT legislation around the world.

This is when U.S. REITs really came into their own in investor opinion. At the end of 1990, their market cap was estimated at $5.6 billion. By the close of 1994, it had risen to $38.8 billion. A year later, it was up to $60 billion – still a micro industry but a growing one nonetheless, with new subsectors such as malls, outlet centers, industrial properties, manufactured home communities, self-storage properties, and hotels.

Plus, there were two new designations for REITs to take advantage of.

UPREITs and DownREITs

In studying different REITs, you might come across the term "umbrella partnership real estate investment trust," or UPREIT. It's a corporate structure that allows management to offer operating property units (OPUs) in exchange for purchases instead of cold, hard cash. This gives the seller the opportunity to still benefit from the property without the associated hassle, and the REIT the opportunity to better maintain its expenses.

The UPREIT concept, which was first implemented in 1992 by creative investment bankers, means that the REIT itself might not own any properties directly. What it does own is a controlling interest in a limited partnership that, in turn, owns the real estate. Its fellow partners could easily include management and private investors who had indirectly owned the properties in question before they became part of a REIT portfolio.

Owners of the limited partnership units have the right to convert them into shares, to vote as if they already own shares, and to receive the same dividends too. In short, they enjoy virtually the same attributes of ownership as public shareholders.

DownREITs, meanwhile, are actually structured similarly but are usually formed after the REIT becomes a public company. And members of management aren't usually going to be limited partners in the controlled partnership.

Both corporate structures can exchange OPUs for interests in other real estate partnerships that own properties the REIT wants to acquire. That enables sellers to defer capital gains taxes and have a more diversified form of investment. And that, in turn, can give UPREITs and DownREITs a competitive edge over a regular REIT when it comes to making deals with tax-sensitive sellers.

One negative aspect about them, though, is how they open the door to potential conflicts of interest. After all, management can own units in the partnership, which usually have a low-cost basis. The sale of a property could therefore trigger taxable income to them – but not to the actual REIT's shareholders. This can make management reluctant to sell a property – or even the REIT itself – despite its not performing well or receiving a generous offer.

REIT Modernization Act, RIDEA, and Capital Recycling

REITs' average total returns fluctuated significantly in the 1990s after that initial bear market, going from low single-digits to 35.3% right up until 1998 and 1999. That was when they experienced their first consecutive down years since 1973 and 1974, at 17.5%

and 4.6%, respectively. Part of those falls related to overenthusiasm in 1996 and 1997, including from speculators who cashed out and moved on to the dot-com craze.

There were also too many REITs entering the market and/or raising money all at the same time. In fact, the total raised between 1997 and mostly early 1998 was $54.2 billion. That amounted to 69% of the equity market cap of all equity REITs as of the end of 1996. Not to mention that the entire industry's value in this regard was less than that of Microsoft.

In addition, many REITs pursued aggressive acquisition strategies from 1995 to 1997, often relying heavily on short-term debt and what Ralph Block called "exotic hedging techniques." As should have been expected, they overextended themselves, helping lead to what became known as the Great REIT Pie-Eating Contest. That wasn't a compliment.

Still, the decade didn't end on a bad note, thanks to the REIT Modernization Act (RMA) signed by President Clinton in December 1999. This enables every REIT organization to form and own a taxable REIT subsidiary, or TRS. By owning up to 100% of one, a REIT can develop and quickly sell properties while providing substantial services to its property tenants without jeopardizing its legal standing – a major issue in the past.

This law also greatly expanded what and how much a REIT can engage in, such as offering concierge services to apartment tenants, investing in "merchant" property development, and engaging in other real estate–related businesses. The TRS can also form joint ventures (JVs) with other parties to provide additional services.

However, certain limitations do apply. For example, no more than 25% of a REIT's gross assets can consist of TRS securities. Originally, it was 20%, though that changed with the REIT Investment Diversification and Empowerment Act of 2007 (RIDEA). Loan and rental transactions between a REIT and its TRS are also limited. And any transactions that aren't conducted on an arm's-length basis incur substantial excise taxes. Plus, income from the TRS is subject to taxes at regular corporate income rates.

Another area the RMA affected was restrictions on hotel and lodging REITs concerning the leasing of properties to a "captive" or controlled subsidiary. They're now allowed to do so, provided that each TRS-held property is operated by an outside manager or independent contractor. This way, they can capture more of the economic benefits of ownership for their shareholders. And Nareit suggests there are several other benefits involved in the legislation. These include better quality control over the services offered, since they can now be delivered directly by the REIT's controlled subsidiary. Plus, the sector now has an opening to earn substantial nonrental revenues as well.

As for RIDEA, almost all of its provisions were incorporated into the Housing and Economic Recovery Act of 2008 signed by President Bush. It provides REITs with more certainty and flexibility relating to the purchase and sale of assets . . . the size of the TRS relative to a REIT's total assets . . . and overseas investments and foreign currencies. It also expands the flexibility that hotel and lodging REITs enjoy in leasing properties to a TRS to their healthcare associates as well.

These laws have opened up a new range of tools for the sector to utilize. However, any tool can be used wisely or carelessly toward a positive outcome or a pointless one. So far, the value of the TRS asset in particular is still subject to debate. Many early ventures – especially with respect to technology and internet investments in the late 1990s – have been failures.

Prior to the Great Recession, TRS activities performed well such as developing new properties, leasing them up, and selling them. However, complexity risks did evolve when REITs with "conglomerate-like" platforms invested in areas outside of their areas of expertise.

Another important change that came out of the 1998–1999 bear market was capital recycling. Since REITs had less of an ability to raise equity capital to fuel purchases and acquisitions, they turned to making that kind of money through sales instead. In so doing, they changed an entire mindset. In the past, selling properties was seen as a sign of failure: of something going very, very wrong. Yet it's become much more commonplace in the last two decades, and that's a very big deal. This allows management teams to create value for themselves and shareholders in a whole new way, giving REITs much more control over their ups and downs (see Figure 3.1).

Timeline of REIT Listings by Property Type

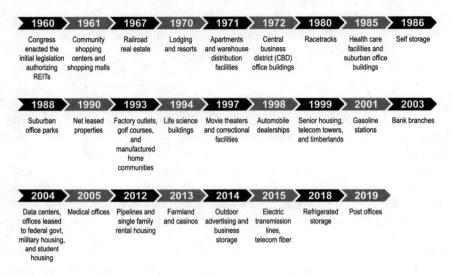

Figure 3.1
Source: Nareit.

The 21st Century (So Far)

Every bear market leads to a bull market eventually, and every bull market leads to a bear market. Moreover, one sector suffering will often lead to another's rise and vice versa. So it's not surprising that the highly speculative dot-com bubble bursting would send despondent investors back into safer stocks like REITs. That renewed interest in value investing brought REITs to levels they had never experienced before . . . right up until the next bubble burst. And that one was directly tied to housing.

The MSCI U.S. REIT Index reached a closing high of 1233.66 on February 7, 2007. Yet 25 months later, it bottomed out at 287.87. It took REITs the next two years to recover most of what they'd lost.

Sometimes stocks and sectors suffer from their own foolishness. Other times, they're the victims of outside sources beyond their control. And, in this case, it was much more the latter. A volatile cocktail of government policies, a lack of banking integrity (or intelligence), and public enthusiasm – among other factors – sent property prices skyrocketing. And when the housing market proved to be less than perfect, those bank bets came crashing down, leading to the collapse of Bear Stearns and Lehman Brothers, Merrill Lynch selling itself to Bank of America, Wachovia selling itself to Wells Fargo, and AIG almost collapsing under its own weight.

While national leaders and legislators decided to bail big banks and car companies out, REITs weren't anywhere as lucky. They were left to deal with the fallout on their own, including vacancy rates as high as 17.5% in certain subsectors. They also had to handle overall debt leverage levels that shouldn't have been unmanageable but were anyway due to the circumstances.

Like most property owners, REITs have always used debt to finance their purchases. Heading into the 2007 downturn, leverage ratios of about 45% were consistent with recent norms. With that said, ratios of debt to earnings before interest, taxes, depreciation, and amortization (EBITDA) had risen. Combine that with the perfect storm that erupted, and you have intense problems indeed.

Fortunately, most REITs rose to the occasion. While most did have to cut their dividends – 35 in 2008, 56 in 2009, and another seven in 2010 – they worked hard to reduce their debt leverage by raising equity, selling some properties, forming joint ventures for others (a trend that developed specifically to handle the depressed conditions), and preserving cash however else they reasonably could. As a result, they were able to rebound sharply in 2009 and 2010. In fact, by the end of that second year, they were much healthier than their private real estate counterparts.

The sector went on to grow for much of the next decade, including by adding new subsectors such as prisons, farms, and gaming – all of which we'll discuss in greater depth in subsequent chapters. New REITs went public, some of which through C-corp spinoffs where already publicly traded companies turned their real estate into separate businesses altogether.

On that last note, President Obama did sign an omnibus appropriations bill on December 18, 2015, which contains significant changes to U.S. taxation of REITs. It limits the use of the spinoff transaction in two ways according to the Proskauer Law Firm:

"First, the Act disallows tax-free treatment in a spinoff if either the distributing corporation or controlled corporation is a REIT. Second, the Act prohibits a taxable corporation that is a party to a tax-free spinoff from making a REIT election for a ten-year period beginning on the date of the distribution."

The Act does not, however, impact the ability of a REIT to spin off another REIT, such as the spinoff of DDR Corporation into Retail Value Trust or Spirit Realty into Spirit MTA REIT.

There was also merger and acquisition (M&A) activity during this time, such as Prologis Inc. taking over DCT Industrial for $8.5 billion in 2018, Omega Healthcare purchasing MedEquities Realty for $600 million in 2019, Healthcare Trust of America acquiring Duke Realty's medical office building portfolio for $2.75 billion in 2017, and Mid-America Apartment buying up Post Properties for $3.9 billion. Then there was the "mega-mall" marriage between Simon Properties and Taubman Centers that was first agreed on in February 2020. Due to the shutdowns that soon followed, the deal was later closed at $2.6 billion and involved Simon acquiring an 80% stake in Taubman Realty Group, the operating partnership through which Taubman Centers conducts its operations.

2016 in particular was a big year considering how the S&P, Dow Jones, and MSCI gave equity REITs and similar companies their own separate and distinct designation on the Global Industry Classification Standard (GICS). Before that, they were listed under the financials sector. To understand the importance of this decision, you have to know what Nareit does: that "GICS is the industry classification methodology that both companies rely on for their proprietary stock market indexes. And it serves as one of the primary classification systems for equities for investors around the world."

Another enormous year was 2020, though on the downside in many ways. As Covid-19 spread from China out into the West, governments around the world began shutting down group gatherings, including those held in office buildings, hotels, malls, shopping centers, and so many other REIT-held properties. Some of them literally couldn't open for months on end, forcing dozens and dozens of dividend cuts and other measures taken to prevent total collapse.

Through October 2020, 65 equity REITs either cut or suspended their dividends because of this, with most of the volatility seen in the lodging, retail, office, and healthcare spaces. We'll explore how that global pandemic impacted REITs on a subsector level over the course of the next several chapters.

Lending REITs Versus Ownership REITs

If you recall, REITs don't have to own real properties. They're also allowed to originate, acquire, hold, and even securitize real estate mortgages – such as those backed by residential or commercial properties – and related loans. As of July 31, 2020, there were 35 mortgage REITs, with 21 focusing on the residential side and 14 on the commercial. Hybrid REITs, which both own properties and hold mortgages on others, were popular some years ago. But they're not widely prevalent today.

In the late 1960s and early 1970s, lending REITs were exceptionally popular since many large regional and "money-center" banks and mortgage brokers formed their own real estate–specific institutions. Almost 60 came to life back then, most of them lending funds to property developers. That worked well enough until interest rates rose substantially in 1973, causing a crash in demand for new developments. Nonperforming loans then spiked to fearsome levels, and most of these entities crashed and burned, leaving investors in the lurch.

A decade later, a new round sprang up to invest in collateralized mortgage obligations (CMOs), only to suffer a similar end.

A number of mREITs – particularly the residential kind – also performed very poorly in the Great Recession, though that didn't stop many new ones from forming. As hundreds of traditional bank failures ballooned, big private equity companies seized the opportunity to lend to property owners. And several other players with more specialized lending platforms also emerged in the wake.

Today, I'm happy to say that the quality of mREITs has improved substantially. However, they still present several challenges, starting with their tendency to be more highly leveraged with debt than their equity counterparts. This increased leverage can make earning streams and dividend payments much more volatile. Plus, they tend to be more sensitive to interest rates. A general increase or even a significant change in the spread between short-term and long-term levels can impact earnings substantially. And, because they don't own easily valued real estate, valuing their shares can be equally tricky.

They also lack the transparency you get with traditional equity REITs. So you rarely see them providing street addresses in their investor presentations. In short, mREITs are perhaps best viewed as trading vehicles whose business strategies, balance sheets, and ties to interest rates must be constantly and carefully monitored. They can be good investments, particularly if well managed. But they're a specialty niche in the REIT world nonetheless.

Accordingly, most conservative long-term investors prefer their counterparts instead. That's why, going forward in *The Intelligent REIT Investor*, the term REIT will refer exclusively to the equity kind.

CHAPTER 4

Residential REITs

"The true investor . . . will do better if he forgets about the stock market and pays attention to his dividend returns and to the operation results of his companies."

—Benjamin Graham

Certain things are true of *all* commercial properties. For instance, their value and profitability depend on property-specific issues such as location, lease revenues, property expenses, occupancy rates, prevailing market rental rates, tenant quality, and replacement costs. There's also market capitalization (cap) rates, supply/demand conditions, and local competition to consider, as well as "macro" forces like the economy, employment growth, consumer and business spending, interest rates, and inflation.

Yet that doesn't make every property type equal. The owner of a large, luxury apartment complex, for example, has very different financial concerns than a neighborhood strip mall landlord or someone who runs a large office building. That's why it's important to understand the ins and outs of each before you begin investing in any of them.

The four principal commercial property types are residential, industrial, office, and retail. Some of those have subtypes with their own unique characteristics, including manufactured home communities and student housing for residential; lab, research space, and warehouses for industrial; and malls, outlets, and shopping centers for retail.

There are still other important areas of focus from there, such as hotels and lodging, self-storage, and several kinds of health- and senior-related properties. There are even timberland and a movie theater REIT, the latter of which has been beaten down hard by the shutdown and social distancing mandates. Figure 4.1 provides a glimpse of the diversity within this universe, with the size of each "planet" consistent with its relative market capitalization.

Figure 4.1
Source: Wide Moat Research.

Ups and Downs

Real estate prices and profits in general move in cycles. They're often predictable in type, though not in length or intensity. In addition, there are two kinds of cycles to know about: the "space market" cycle, which describes the supply of and demand for real estate space, and the "capital markets" cycle, which relates to levels of investor demand for commercial real estate assets and the prices and valuations at which they trade.

If you're a long-term, conservative REIT investor like I am, you might choose to buy and hold most of your REIT stocks even as these phases play out. That can be a very healthy way to operate – as long as you're aware of how they affect cash flows, dividend growth, and stock prices.

For those who consider themselves more short-term market timers, they can try to structure their portfolios in accordance with real estate, property sector, or capital market cycles. Though, despite the levels of predictability we'll soon show, this is easier said than done well.

The Real Estate Cycles

Consider the following phases of a space market cycle:

- **Phase 1: The Recession/Depression** – Vacancies are high and rents are low, making it common for landlords to offer concessions in the form of free rent and improvement allowances. Many properties, particularly those financed with excessive debt, may be in foreclosure. And there's little to no new construction being done, for obvious reasons.
- **Phase 2: The Gradual Recovery** – Leasing activity accelerates, and occupancy rates stabilize. Rents first firm up and then gradually increase, better balancing the bargaining power between owners and tenants. Meanwhile, developers begin to seek out new entitlements from planning commissions and try to line up financing for new projects.
- **Phase 3: The Boom** – The most desirable vacant spaces are absorbed, allowing property owners to boost rents more aggressively and get better returns. In fact, properties may start trading at prices above replacement cost, while

profit-promising new construction allows developers to flex their muscles. Both investors and lenders alike are confident, ready, and willing to provide ample financing. Some will even argue that "it's different this time."

- **Phase 4: Overbuilding and Downturn** – Too much enthusiasm spawns rapidly rising rents and overbuilding, which then spawns higher vacancy rates. Rental rates flatten or decline, and economic recession may follow, perhaps due to high interest rates or an unexpected shock to the U.S. economy. Regardless, the returns on real estate fail to meet excessively rosy expectations and new developments are canceled, leading right back into Phase 1.

As Cohen & Steers explained in a February 2019 article called "A REIT Defense for the Late Cycle": "U.S. REITs have outperformed the S&P 500 by more than 7% annually in late-cycle periods since 1991 and have offered meaningful downside protection in recessions, underscoring the potential value of defensive, lease-based revenues, and high dividend yields in an environment of heightened uncertainty." (See Figure 4.2.)

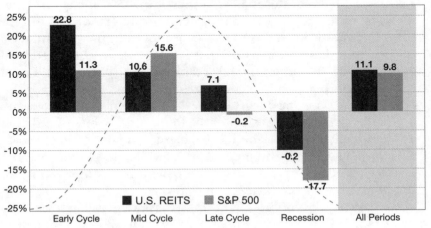

REITs Have Been Resilient in Late Cycle and Recessions

Annualize Total Return by Cycle Phase, 1991-2018

Figure 4.2

Source: Cohen & Steers.

One of the first to research these business cycles was land economist, appraiser, and consultant Homer Hoyt. His 1933 book, *One Hundred Years of Land Values in Chicago,* proved the cyclical nature of Chicago land values. In addition, he developed the economic base and sector theories for urban growth models elsewhere while serving as principal housing economist for the Federal Housing Administration.

As he showed so vividly, real estate cycles are very important to understand. Most stock prices follow known business cycles, tracing changes in general economic activity as measured by GDP, income, employment, industrial production, sales, and so forth. But real estate business cycles are over three times longer, primarily because of the difficulties involved in building up new properties.

It typically takes four years for a real estate project to be completed from site plan to rent check, whereas other businesses can adjust their production schedules in a matter of weeks or months.

On the plus side, this can mean that the brick-and-mortar asset class has a high degree of predictability, as shown by Hoyt's 18-year real estate business cycle illustrated below. With just a few exceptions – one because of WWII and another due to the Fed doubling rates in 1979 – it's maintained the same basic level of predictability that Hoyt observed.

Table 4.1   18-Year Real Estate Business Cycle

Peaks in Land Value Cycle	Interval (Years)	Peaks in Construction Cycle	Interval (Years)	Peaks in Business Cycle	Interval (Years)
1818	**	**	**	1819	**
1836	18	1836	**	1837	18
1854	18	1856	20	1857	20
1872	18	1871	15	1873	16
1890	18	1892	21	1893	20
1907	17	1909	17	1918	25
1925	18	1925	16	1929	11
1973	48	1972	47	1973	44
1979	6	1978	6	1980	7
1989	10	1986	8	1990	10
2006	17	2006	20	2008	18

Source: Fred E. Foldvary, "The Depression of 2008."

Sometimes the capital and space markets are in sync, with property prices and owners' cash flows rising and falling together or with a mere modest lag. Other times, as in 2000–2004, they appear much more disconnected. But ultimately, they do tend to converge, making existing and prospective "conditions on the ground" an important but not exclusive component of commercial real estate pricing.

As already alluded to, commercial real estate is also tied closely to both national and local economies. Some of the more vivid past proofs of this include when the steel mills in Pittsburgh or the rubber companies in Akron laid off workers.

From retail to real estate, these communities quickly became depressed, losing their label of "Smokestack America" for the far less flattering "Rust Belt." Some families doubled up, with young adults moving back in with their parents. Or people gave up on their communities altogether, leaving for greener pastures elsewhere. And as the number of households declined, apartment, office, and industrial vacancy rates rose significantly.

Conversely, when the Olympic Committee decided to hold the 1996 summer games in Atlanta, the entire local economy picked up. Business improved for residents across the board, from dentists to dry cleaners, and job growth expanded. I saw something similar firsthand in my hometown of Spartanburg, South Carolina, when BMW decided to build a plant there. As a direct result, I was able to help negotiate a site for one of its primary suppliers, Lemforder, and many other residents benefited as well.

In short, commercial real estate markets are always sensitive to economic conditions.

Now, there are times when prices become either truly manic or depressive on their own. For instance, in 2020, U.S. residential real estate and associated commercial real estate went "through the roof" despite the generally unhealthy state of the economy. On the flip side, our nation's space markets were healthy in 2006–2007. Yet property values rose to ridiculous levels anyway.

I know we touched on this in Chapter 3 already, but it bears mentioning again in this new context. Many buyers accepted historically low initial investment returns of 4% or less, thinking they could more than make up for it in future rent and operating income growth. The situation was worsened still by existing laws and government guidelines, and lenders who loosened their underwriting standards at exactly the wrong time.

Anyone reading the news at the time knows there was the issue of commercial mortgage-backed securities (CMBS) as well. Those allowed lenders and investment bankers to package real estate mortgage loans and sell them to naïve investors. No doubt, they wouldn't have ended well regardless. But combined with everything else, it was an especially potent recipe for disaster.

Essentially, when commercial real estate is doing well, everyone wants in on the action: developers, syndicators, private equity managers, lenders, and even legislators, with both positive and negative consequences. So, one way or the other, REIT investors should expect their investment returns to go through ups and downs, back and forth. As we endure the painful portions of these cycles – including those that come just once in a lifetime through, say, worldwide shutdowns – investors should repeat to themselves, "This too shall pass."

While strong markets can lead to overbuilding and eventual depressed operating income, weak and troubled markets can offer unusually good growth opportunities. Financially solid REITs frequently have far better access to capital during weak markets, allowing them to buy properties with good long-term prospects at bargain-basement prices. They may even be able to earn even higher returns on these new investments by upgrading them and bringing in new and more attractive tenants.

It really depends on the exact economic details, geographical areas, and a whole host of other factors – including the subsector in question.

Apartments

When considering apartment REITs, we do need to quickly consider how they differ from residential real estate – and not just because private homes are primarily bought for shelter and possibly lifestyle instead of income. Even when rented out, traditional living space usually results in very modest cash flow thanks to mortgage payments, taxes, insurance, and maintenance expenses. To be blunt, commercial real estate has much greater capacity to generate much greater income.

This includes apartment REITs, a blend of the two that own and manage apartment communities, particularly in the United States. As of July 32, 2020, there were 15 apartment REITs, not including one student housing, three manufactured housing, and three single-family rental REITs. Of the pure-play apartment variety, AvalonBay was the largest, with an equity market cap of $21.8 billion.

Today, most of their capitalization rates range from 4% to 5.5% depending on location, property quality, age, condition, and supply/demand factors. According to NCREIF, "The market had little price discovery with so few transactions in the [second] quarter [of 2020], so investors will have to wait to see what impact the COVID-19 pandemic will have on apartment cap rates."

Apartment owners do particularly well when the economy is expanding because of the new jobs created that then bring in new workers. Because apartments compete with the single-family home market for customers, their profitability also hinges on home prices, affordability, the cost and availability of home financing, and even the perceived attraction of houses and condominiums as an investment.

Another perhaps obvious but still extremely important factor for apartment owners is the rate of construction of new units in the area or areas it operates in. Competing properties present the risk of lowering other owners' occupancy rates and forcing them to offer additional perks such as reduced rents, thereby reducing income all around.

Then there's the complicated question of inflation. It can cause higher operating expenses for everything from maintenance to insurance to interest on debt, which can't normally be passed along to the tenant. Then again, it can be a boon, prompting everyone involved to raise their rates, which cuts back on competition in the form of new construction.

Amazingly, national rents – as measured by the CPI: Primary Rent Index – haven't seen negative full-year growth since the Great Depression. Over the last two decades especially, apartment REITs have been among the strongest-performing property sectors thanks to the tailwinds of an unyielding urban revival. And over the last decade especially, rent growth has been relentless. There are exceptions to this strong showing, of course, some of which we'll discuss. But the larger trend is obviously there nonetheless.

Moreover, the $4–5 trillion U.S. multifamily apartment market is highly fragmented, leaving lots of room for expansion. REITs own roughly 500,000, or 2%, of the nation's estimated 25 million rental units in a combined $40 trillion housing market.

With that said, they have accounted for a greater share of new residences being built since 2010. Following a decade of historically low levels of home construction, as mentioned before, today's housing markets remain historically tight. Q2-20 data from the U.S. Census Bureau indicates that vacancy rates for both rental and owner-occupied units remain at or near 40-year lows. That's at the same time homeowner vacancy ticked down to its lowest level ever of 0.9%. As such, there's much more room for apartment REITs to expand from here.

None of this is to say these investments are risk-free though, especially when it comes to location. As I said before and will no doubt say again, even if the national economy is doing fine, individual areas can suffer downturns. This is clearly more of an issue for REITs with narrow geographical focuses, but overbuilding can occur just as easily on a national level. Poor property management can also cut into their profitability, and so can general cluelessness concerning rising or falling industry trends.

Fortunately, these adverse developments rarely occur overnight, giving apartment REIT owners ample room to spot them and act accordingly. The real trick is to distinguish a temporary blip from a long secular decline.

Speaking of long secular declines, apartment ownership profits do go through their own specific cycles just as much as any other REIT subsector. This takes us back to overbuilding. Remember how we mentioned before how financial institutions were handing out loans left and right in the late 1980s and early 1990s? That directly impacted apartment owners, who found it increasingly difficult to earn reasonable returns. Blinded by the economic light, investors put large amounts of capital into new construction, only to find those buildings worthless in short order. And this then led to the inevitable next phase of recession/depression.

The supply-demand imbalance began to right itself in 1993 as the economy strengthened, and rents followed suit by 1995. Before 1996 was through, occupancy levels had risen to over 90%, destined to remain firm up until the next national recession in 2001. Then, weak job growth, low mortgage rates, and competition from single-family housing competition brought apartment REIT profitability right back down again until the cycle bottomed in 2004.

Prices for apartment communities rose rapidly up through late 2007, when the Great Recession began, sending rental revenue and operating income into another decline. This time, it lasted until mid-2010, when home ownership fell out of favor, promoting the leasing system once again.

Moving forward to 2020, pandemic-related lockdown policies in urban gateway markets like New York City, Los Angeles, San Francisco, Chicago, and Portland have plunged them into uncontrolled tailspins. The result has been intense surges of unemployment and violent crime that make them far less attractive places to be. Further incentivized by continuing work-from-home policies, residents have been fleeing to lower-cost and safer semi-urban and suburban markets, including more business-friendly Sunbelt metros (in the Southwest and Southeast).

Outside of these troubled markets, however, national apartment markets stayed remarkably resilient during the pandemic (as of September 10, 2020). Aided by fiscal stimulus measures, rent collection remained essentially on par with 2019. On the flip side, apartment REIT earnings were negatively impacted by generous pandemic-related concessions, and new lease rates did dip. Fortunately, these companies typically operate within higher-income bracket areas, which helped cushion that impact.

Mark Decker Jr., CEO of Investors Real Estate, explained to me that "As management, I love the operational aspect of the apartment business. It's interesting and dynamic – there's always something to improve, and you can see the results over a leasing cycle. As an investor, what's appealing to me is that we provide a basic need – homes. We can't live in the internet; however, we can use technology to compete well. The public apartment companies are sophisticated and disciplined capital allocators, and that's a great opportunity for shareholders. Compared to other sectors, I think the shorter nature of our one-year leases are also attractive when you think about capturing the benefit of an economy on the rise."

Assuming a reasonably stable economy, moderate job growth, and properly managed assets, apartment ownership looks as though it will continue to be a rewarding investment for REIT investors

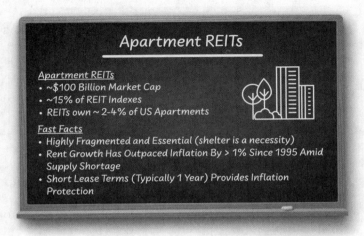

Figure 4.3
Source: Wide Moat Research.

despite occasional blips in local markets and recurring real estate cycles. My expectation is for average annual rent increases of close to 3% in most areas, with expenses rising alongside inflation.

This would add up to some pretty decent total returns with less risk than that found in many other property sectors. (See Figure 4.3.)

Manufactured Housing REITs

Apartment communities comprise the largest space within the "residential" property category. But they're hardly alone. Over five decades ago, an enterprising individual incentivized a number of mobile home owners to relocate to a remote parcel of land he owned. He then semi-affixed the movable dwellings to foundations and called the resulting collection a "mobile home park."

So-called trailer homes help satisfy America's need for affordable housing. The Manufactured Housing Institute (MHI) says these cheaper options have an average construction cost per square foot of 10–35% less than a site-built home, excluding land costs. And the average rental price for a 1,250 square foot home is $1,018 per month, while it's $1,723 for a traditional 1,000 square foot rental. And so a business was born.

Sun Communities specifically, one of the three REITs that work in this space, says manufactured homes provide 25% more space at about 50% less cost per square foot.

Most manufactured home residents own their own homes and lease the underlying land at varying monthly rates (generally $200 to $500+) from the community's owner. Some of these neighborhoods cater only to seniors, while others are open to all ages. And while there are certainly rundown, worn-out developments of this nature, many of today's REIT-owned manufactured-home communities bear little resemblance to the typical picture that comes to most people's mind. The residences there generally have the quality and appearance of site-built houses.

In addition, homeowners enjoy amenities such as clubhouses, pools, tennis courts, putting greens, exercise rooms, and laundry facilities. According to Equity Lifestyle Properties, another such REIT, there were approximately 50,000 manufactured home communities in North America at last check. And according to data from MHI, approximately 19 million people, or 6% of the U.S. population, live in them.

None of the three publicly traded REITs that are solely devoted to this category are very large. The third manufactured housing REIT is UMH Properties with enterprise value of around $1.1 billion. Together, they own just 2.5% of available supply with a combined market cap of just $27.7 billion as of July 31, 2020.

There's been a trend in declining occupancy rates at the all-age communities. Plus, the industry has grappled with a substantial multiyear decline in new home shipments. However, turnover rates have been low, leaving the larger businesses stable to the point of even being recession-resistant. The average tenant stays for about 14 years, whether economic boom or economic bust.

If anything, demand may increase during recessions. While these homes don't appreciate like traditional houses do, they're cheap and convenient like an apartment. Yet they feel more permanent – more owned – mainly because they are. Hence, the longer timespan that people stay in them once they settle in.

Also attractive for investors is how community owners face few capital expenditures. They have to worry about keeping up the grounds and common facilities, as well as property taxes. But actual home maintenance falls squarely on their tenants' financial shoulders. Better yet, overbuilding has rarely been an issue thanks to how difficult it is to get properties zoned and entitled, not to mention the long lead times involved in filling these communities.

When it comes to risks, there are the occasional flare-ups concerning rent control that landlords have to deal with. But a more menacing risk is the potential for negative publicity. For instance, in 2019, late-night TV show host John Oliver highlighted his understanding of corporately owned manufactured home parks. What he said was inaccurate but effective anyway in prompting considerable unflattering media attention in the short term.

Headline risk matters intensely in today's world of social media outrage, which flows far too easily into congressional speeches and subsequent policy. If manufactured housing parks become a longer-lasting hot topic, the risk of rent controls, mandatory property enhancements, sector-specific taxes, and other regulatory risks are very real.

Nevertheless, this property type will appeal to investors who appreciate stable cash flows, predictable rent increases, and very modest capital expense requirements. (See Figure 4.4.)

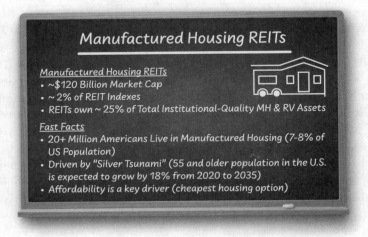

Figure 4.4
Source: Wide Moat Research.

Student Housing

Another property type that's recently become available to REIT investors is student housing. American Campus Communities – the one and only pure-play company left in this field – went public in August 2004. By mid-2020, it owned, managed, or had developed 206 properties across 96 university campuses. Of that, it actively owned a total of 111,900 beds at 68 universities, the majority of which were in high-value, on-campus, or near-campus facilities at major flagship four-year schools.

As its name describes, this type of property asset is uniquely designed to hold temporary residences for college students. Typically, a single community can accommodate several hundred to over 1,000 of these tenants at a time. And students lease the space on an annual basis over a college year at monthly lease rates from about $300 to $700 per bed. It's a model that may have started out on some shaky ground, but it's notably matured over the last decade.

This subsector (including non-pure-play participants) is among the most active REIT developers, utilizing several different models to create value. The most attractive of these might very well be the public-private partnership (P3). This happens when a university or business is in need of new housing but doesn't want to expend the necessary capital. So it leases land to a REIT – which then builds, owns, and manages the facility, paying rent for the land beneath it and getting a substantial amount more for the rooms in it.

Purpose-built student housing facilities make for unique investments with distinctive operational attributes. For one thing, they're generally cheaper. For another, they're equipped with more applicable amenities for their residents than the average offering young adults pursuing a higher education can expect. So they're attractive assets for both colleges and college students alike.

One downside is how they generally have much shorter leasing windows, with unclaimed beds at the start of the school year likely remaining that way until the following one. Student housing is also exposed to changes in university policies, including health plans and procedures, as we learned in 2020. These can sometimes result in significant vacancy losses and long-term asset impairment.

Additionally, student housing businesses typically operate at lower margins than their conventional multifamily peers. This makes sense considering the increased costs associated with more frequent turnover. And oversupply concerns can plague the market too.

It's also true that Americans' attitudes regarding college curriculum and costs have soured. Yes, a large-enough population still sees higher education as a necessary evil at this point because of the much higher return on investment it offers. Georgetown University's Center on Education indicates that workers with bachelor's degrees earn 31% more than those with associate's degrees and 84% more than those with high school diplomas alone. But online education – particularly under the influence of the 2020 shutdowns – does present an obvious money-saving appeal.

With that said, the supply-demand equation for college housing appears favorable in the short- and mid-terms at least. Due to their experience and relationships with college administrators, REITs offer strong competition in this property type. Plus, they have the added potential of benefitting from external growth opportunities such as new developments, joint ventures with colleges and universities, and property acquisitions. (See Figure 4.5.)

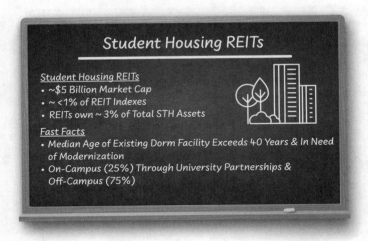

Figure 4.5
Source: Wide Moat Research.

CHAPTER

5

Retail REITs

*"We have a long list of retailers that have struggled. . . . And 80%
to 90% of that list have been over-levered so they couldn't turn left
or right."*
—David Simon, CEO of Simon Property Group

For the entire first half of the twentieth century, shoppers bought everything locally at small stores on Main Street or in downtown shopping areas. It wasn't until 1956 that retail-related real estate possibilities changed enormously. That was when the first enclosed shopping mall was built in Edina, Minnesota, an immigrant-inspired, Europe-reminiscent model that quickly became an American institution.

Since Southdale Center's debut, the number of shopping alternatives and retail venues has exploded in ways previous eras never could have imagined. Today's consumers can shop at enclosed malls; neighborhood shopping centers; big-box megastores such as Walmart, Costco, Target, or Ross; and sprawled-out outlet centers.

It's quite the variety, to say the least. And, for the first two decades of the twenty-first century, most of these places – even newer concepts such as "lifestyle" centers that look like something between an outlet center and a strip mall – were taken for granted. Even while shoppers were slowly but surely turning toward online options, many did so under the assumption that physical retail would remain as-is.

But the game changed drastically thanks to the Covid-19 pandemic and subsequent shutdowns. As CNBC reported on August 30, 2020, retailers were "reporting some of the biggest online sales gains in their history thanks to the coronavirus pandemic, which temporarily closed stores, holed consumers up at home, and pushed more people to the internet to browse and buy groceries, clothes, and workout gear."

The same article reported that "Best Buy online sales were up 242% during its fiscal second quarter, with people stocking up on electronics and equipment for their home offices." And Dick's Sporting Goods, Home Depot, Lowe's, Target, Tiffany, and Home Depot all reported triple-digit growth as well. (See Figure 5.1.)

Other retailers with large physical presences, however, struggled to stay afloat. According to S&P Global Market Intelligence, 44 companies – including Stein Mart, Pier 1 Imports, J.C. Penney, Sur la Table, and Neiman Marcus – filed for bankruptcy in 2020. And Coresight Research added that more than 6,000 permanent store closures were announced by mid-September.

Year-Over-Year Online Sales Growth
Q2 2020

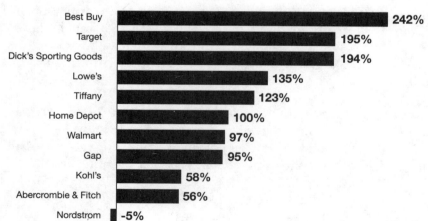

Best Buy	242%
Target	195%
Dick's Sporting Goods	194%
Lowe's	135%
Tiffany	123%
Home Depot	100%
Walmart	97%
Gap	95%
Kohl's	58%
Abercrombie & Fitch	56%
Nordstrom	-5%

Figure 5.1
Source: CNBC.

If the shutdowns seemed like a retail game changer, they were. Yet not nearly so much as many people assume.

Truth be told, the U.S. was already vastly overstored, with 50 square feet per person in early 2020. Canada, meanwhile, had one third of that; and the E.U. featured single-digits in this regard. In short, there was no way the United States could sustain such an excessive amount for too long. The virus simply accelerated the inevitable, possibly disposing of a third of existing brick-and-mortar retail in the end.

Those that survive will have to rely on omnichannel strategies, where they improve user experiences and drive sales across multiple platforms that work together:

- Social media
- Mobile applications
- Video/cable
- Physical locations in malls, strip centers, pop-up stores, free-standing facilities, outlets, etc.

As Tim Mason and Miya Knights, co-authors of *Omnichannel Retail: How to Build Winning Stores in a Digital World*, explain:

> "The internet is undeniably the biggest and most relevant recent change in retail because of its impact on the way businesses engage with and serve customers. Where the average business traditionally operated a single, physical sales channel – the store – many now support multiple digital and physical sales and marketing channels through the store and e-commerce websites and marketplaces to social media networks and traditional advertising media, including print, television, and radio."

In this powerful new paradigm, some retail REITs are, admittedly, better equipped than others.

The Mall Sector

Whereas neighborhood shopping centers were built to provide the basics, regional malls provide greater consumer choice, luxury items, and opportunities to interact with friends and family.

However they were originally conceptualized, they grew into entities that had far less to do with what people needed and far more to do with accessorizing.

Naturally then, mall economics are very different from neighborhood shopping center economics. Traditionally, rent payable by the tenant was higher. But so were sales per square foot, allowing individual and corporate store operators to do very well. And that's still true today – if intelligence and luck are both on their side. Accordingly, it's crucial that mall owners operate in favorable locations and sign leases with the most successful retailers.

Working within those boundaries, some mall REITs own prestigious supermalls that consist of one million square feet or more. Rents can easily exceed $40 per square foot in such places, while sales per square foot can reach over $500. Since that kind of pricing or profitability doesn't work everywhere though, other owners specialize in smaller malls. Usually located in less densely populated cities, their rental rates are more in the mid-$20s range per square foot and matching sales don't get much above $300.

Over the short term, mall owners' profitability depends on the national, regional, and local retail economies, as well as trends in consumer spending, household net worth, and income growth. Over the long term, they depend on how well they can work within our increasingly digitized world.

Before the 1990s, most malls were solely owned by large, private real estate organizations and institutional investors. That's a shame considering how the 1980s launched a golden era for the regional mall. Women, who were starting careers in record numbers, had to buy business clothes. And so they flocked to malls. At the same time, Baby Boomers were spending their double incomes on all types of consumer goods. And so they flocked to malls.

Stated succinctly, mall-based stores sales were rising so briskly that major national and regional retailers alike felt compelled to get their slice of the pie. This allowed their landlords to increase rental rates without fear.

By the early 1990s, this great era of consumerism stalled, creating waves of corporate restructuring. Wage gains were hard to come by, fears of layoffs were rampant, and consumer confidence declined. "Deep discounts!" became the American consumer's rallying cry around the same time as many Baby Boomers were wising up to their upcoming retirements. All of a sudden, they decided that investing in mutual funds might take precedence over owning Armani suits.

And that was when large shopping mall developers and owners such as Martin and Matthew Bucksbaum, Herbert and Melvin Simon, and the Taubman family "REITized" their empires by going public.

It wasn't until the mid-1990s that sales really rebounded though, driven by full employment, strong wage gains, and a buoyant stock market. That lasted up through 2001, when another recession hit, though this one was padded out by low interest rates and some well-timed tax cuts. So consumer confidence rose in shorter order, and mall sales and occupancy rates again began to trend higher.

It goes without saying that the Great Recession in 2008 pushed the cycle around another time. As the stock market fell, household net worth declined, and unemployment spiked, leading people to spend less and save more (or just spend less). According to a September 15, 2010, Green Street report, sales for the average in-line mall tenant – those with exterior storefronts and patron entrances – fell 4.5% in 2008 and 6.9% in 2009. And mall occupancy in general fell from 92.8% at the end of 2007 to 90.8% at the end of 2009.

Fortunately, thanks in part to good balance sheet management and inventory control by the large retailers, tenant bankruptcies were modest. So occupancy rates were able to begin stabilizing in 2010, even seeing an uptick.

Then came the rise of online retail. It started out slow enough, but it became more of a threat every year nonetheless until 2017, when store closures seemed to really pick up. Everyone was talking about the retail apocalypse by 2019, where even solid economic growth and relatively strong retail sales couldn't save malls from suffering a fourth consecutive year of underperformance.

As already stated, 2020's national and global-wide shutdowns exacerbated the situation all the more. Since most retailers fell squarely into the dreaded "non-essential" category, the pace of retail bankruptcies rose exponentially, perhaps hitting malls the hardest. Unable to open at all, it came as no surprise that they collected less than 50% of rents in the second quarter – the worst of all the property subsectors. By comparison, housing, industrial, technology, self-storage, and office examples collected an average 95% or more.

This prompted every mall REIT – besides Brookfield Property REIT (BPYU), which is actually a diversified player – to eliminate or reduce its common stock dividend. This didn't eliminate their problems though. Many of them had sky-high leverage levels thanks to their past, continuing, and increasing woes. At the end of July 2020, Nareit showed four of them operating at debt ratios above 80% and three over 94%.

None of this is to say that all mall REITs are destined to delist, leaving their assets to become hollowed-out shells. Some of them likely will fall apart, but select analysts see potential in others as they finally move away from their old-school "business-as-usual" strategies. Take Simon Property Group, which went on a shopping spree in 2020, buying up portions of distressed tenants such as Brooks Brothers, Lucky Brand, Forever 21, and J.C. Penney.

If that seems strange, consider how it's a strange environment to work within. Besides, the REIT did successfully pull off this stunt before by acquiring Aeropostale in 2016.

As mentioned in Chapter 3, Simon also used its "scale advantage" to acquire Taubman Centers in a deal that was initially agreed to on February 10, 2020 at $52.50 per share. On June 10, however, Simon terminated that merger agreement, claiming Taubman Centers had breached certain operating covenants and suffered materially adverse effects. Taubman then counter-sued, claiming breach of the agreement.

After much uncertainty and many legal fees (Simon spent $21 million on litigation expenses in Q3-20 alone) and court proceedings, the two companies reached a new agreement at $2.6 billion, or $43 per share, which was 18% below the original agreement. All other terms remained intact though, primarily Simon acquiring an 80% stake in Taubman Realty Group, TCO's operating partnership.

Ultimately, I see well-located, well-managed, high-productivity suburban malls as standing a good chance of surviving the decade ahead – qualifiers that cannot be stressed enough. CoStar, the world leader in commercial real estate information, says there were approximately 1,400 malls in the U.S. in 2010. By the end of 2025, that figure could be cut in half.

Several weaker mall REITs did file for bankruptcy in 2020, namely CBL Properties and Pennsylvania REIT. And it appears that the "survivors" in the mall wars will be the REITs that have the necessary capital to redevelop a growing pipeline of redevelopment projects as department stores fade and are replaced with other mixed-use possibilities.

Those that don't adapt appropriately will find themselves on the losing side of the retail aisle, and that seems to capture the state of affairs the best. As Charles Darwin would have said, "survival of the fittest."

Factory Outlet Centers

For their part, factory outlet centers have enjoyed increasing popularity with consumers since the early 1990s. Their primary tenants are major manufacturers – such as American Eagle, Coach, Nike, and Ralph Lauren – that want places to offload oversupply, irregular goods, odd fashion choices that didn't work out at regular price, and the like. So, as a general rule, they sell everything at 25–35% off those regular prices at specifically advertised discount shops.

Outlet centers are normally located away from densely populated areas since retail product manufacturers don't want to compete with their regularly priced stores elsewhere. With that said, outlets can also be found in or around major tourist destinations, such as Myrtle Beach, South Carolina; Lancaster, Pennsylvania; and Branson, Missouri.

Almost all the early outlet REITs have long-since disappeared by now. Some were acquired and others suffered from poor management, leaving Tanger Factory Outlet Centers as the only pure-play participant in this category. But overall, this type of property has performed quite well in recent memory, particularly during tough economic times.

Speaking of such, in the era of Covid-19, outlets maintain two saving graces: They're not enclosed, and they have no department stores. There are roughly 400 U.S. outlet centers, according to the *Wall Street Journal*, which means that outlet centers aren't struggling against the same oversupply that's plagued traditional malls. They are struggling, mind you, as multiple tenants go bankrupt; but they're in a comparatively better place to build off of nonetheless.

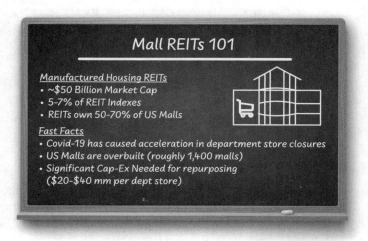

Figure 5.2
Source: Wide Moat Research.

While not entirely the same, most analysts include them in the mall REIT subsector because of the large collection of stores they feature per location. (See Figure 5.2.)

Shopping Centers

Another more cushioned retail REIT is the kind that invests in neighborhood shopping centers. Sometimes the convenience of going online to order just can't be beat by the "immediate" gratification of getting what you need 5 or 10 minutes away. There's also the fact that these strip malls often feature necessities such as grocery and drug stores, quick-fix eating options, and specialists such as dry cleaning or nail salons.

At last count, there were 17 REITs focused on such ownership, amounting to roughly $35 billion in market value.

The property owner charges a minimum rent amount for each space, typically for 5–15 years at signing. Most contracts include CPI-based or fixed annual "rent bumps" to account for assumed inflation and rising operating costs. Leases might also include "overage" rental provisions, which obligate tenants to pay increased rent if their annual sales exceed certain minimum levels. And they're often "triple-net" in nature, placing the burden of real estate taxes and assessments, repairs, maintenance, and insurance on tenants instead of the landlord.

There's also plenty of room for expansion considering how REITs own a mere 5–10% of existing shopping center properties. The private sector owns the rest. With that said, owners face their own set of perpetual challenges. For one thing, their margin profiles involve roughly 20% of annual net operating income (NOI), which is well above the REIT sector's average. For another, the retail apocalypse, 2020 shutdowns, and social distancing mandates have hurt some of their lessees.

When it comes to the ongoing push toward digitized everything, it might not matter that nearly 90% of total retail sales still happen in person rather than online. Online sales still account for around a fifth of certain categories, such as clothing, sporting goods, books, and electronics, all items that strip malls have historically offered. For that matter, so do major discounters such as Walmart – which also often offer everything grocery stores do and so much more.

Convenient location is therefore extremely important (as it always is) in determining which REITs are worth investing in. Carefully cultivated neighborhood shopping centers located close to one or more major residential areas and leased to stable tenants offering recession-resistant products and services should continue to thrive. That way, there will be tenants waiting to fill any vacated spaces fairly quickly.

The best of the best shopping centers are usually anchored by at least one supermarket or drugstore, with additional shops that offer other basic services and necessities. Those staples tend to enable properties to be pretty resilient, which is why about half of REIT-held existing shopping centers today include a full-service grocer.

That's why it's helpful to further categorize shopping center properties, as real estate research platform Wide Moat Research does, into grocery-anchored, power center, and street retail entities. These lines can get admittedly blurry if a Walmart, Costco, Target, or some such thing is involved, considering how they offer such a wide variety of products, including foods. Then again, many REITs have been working hard to better allocate their tenants between experiential offerings and grocery-related services in order to provide the most sustainable mix.

Shopping center REITs reported rent collection averaging around 70% in Q2-20 and 80% by that August, according to company reports and the latest Nareit survey. This fairly admirable amount (considering the unprecedented conditions) still resulted in 13 of them having to reduce or eliminate their dividends. All told, they were the third-worst performing REIT subsector for the year as of the third quarter's close.

To their credit, 2019 was their second-best year of the 2010s. That was because of how hard they worked to recover from the wave of big-box store closings between 2015 and 2018. This included "deboxing" those empty spaces into smaller shops for a wider variety of vendors. That kind of creative initiative offers significant hope that shopping center REITs will be able to recover in 2021 and beyond. If they did it before, they can do it again.

Other positive trends worth noticing include the suburban revival we referenced in Chapter 4, which should give these landlords further room to run as the decade continues. It's also encouraging to see the growing use of in-person shopping alternatives such as in-store pickup, curbside pickup, and delivery-from-store capabilities, which should aid them as well. (See Figure 5.3.)

Figure 5.3

Source: Wide Moat Research.

Nothing but Net Lease

When I began my career as a real estate investor, one of my first clients was a company called Advance Auto Parts. I vividly remember contacting the chain in order to pitch a location for a new store in Union, South Carolina. At the time, I was just 23 years old. So I had no clue I was going to build a sizable net worth by developing dozens of similar freestanding stores over the next several years.

My earliest property contract with Advance Auto was a "gross lease," which means I paid most of the operating expenses, such as taxes and insurance. However, I quickly realized the obvious: that there was more value in requiring the tenant to bear the burdens of what I call "the three T's": toilets, trash, and taxes. This takes us back to net leases, a term referenced earlier in the chapter. But this time, the concept defines an entire subsector.

The common way of looking at net leases is through the triple-net lease structure, whereby tenants pay all expenses related to property management: property taxes, insurance, and maintenance. While nearly every property sector uses it to some degree, the term "net lease REITs" refers to companies that operate freestanding buildings with this kind of payment structure.

There's no denying that net lease REITs are beautiful things. Boring, but beautiful. They court high credit-quality corporate lessees that are willing and able to sign 10- to 25-year contracts, usually with contractual rent bumps. So they tend to offer very reliable income streams.

Boiled down to their basics, "cost of capital" (i.e., equity and debt) is the name of the game. And share price performance and acquisitions are exceptionally critical components in how these businesses are able to operate. They typically operate with higher stock prices and lower interest rates, a powerful combination that helps them grow even more. It's also important to recognize how they tend to work best when their share valuations are a little higher compared to their net asset value (NAV).

Because of their exact structure, net lease REITs work more like financing companies than other subsectors. With greater access to public equity markets, they have a noteworthy competitive advantage.

According to Randy Blankenstein, owner of the Boulder Group, the subsector is highly fragmented and represents around $3 trillion worth of properties across the U.S. – and that does not include office and industrial properties. Given the enormous fragmentation within the net lease subsector, I wouldn't be surprised to see these REITs become the most dominant players over the next decade.

While I'm clearly including them in the retail chapter (and Nareit classifies them that way as well), some net lease REITs do buy up industrial and office assets as well. Combined, I estimate the entire universe of net lease buildings in the U.S. could be around $10 trillion.

Thanks somewhat to a growing demand for stable income, investors have gravitated toward the larger category over the last 10 years. And with that rising demand has come a number of new REITs. Far too many see them as "bond proxies" due to their defensive characteristics and high sensitivity to interest rates. Yet stocks – even the safest stocks – are never bonds. Never, ever, ever.

At the outset of the 2020 shutdowns, investors got a harsh reminder of this lesson since the net lease subsector has such heavy exposure to "non-essential" industries. Several of these REITs focus almost exclusively on a single industry, while other REITs own diversified portfolios that may or may not include experience-based categories like movie theaters and fitness centers.

Under normal circumstances or even the average recession, net lease REITs operate with significantly higher gross margins and have lower capital expenditure requirements. But their steady-stream perks do still depend on tenants actually paying rent. Sumit Roy, president and CEO of Realty Income, explains:

> Investing in net lease real estate, as evidenced by historical performance, provides investors an attractive risk-return profile. The ability to surgically invest based on a curated set of industries and operators allows net-leased companies to create a stable, well-diversified real estate portfolio of freestanding single-tenant properties under long-term net lease agreements that continue to perform well relative to other sectors. Further, the growth outlook for the sector, which is largely predicated on external acquisitions, has remained strong through a variety of economic environments.

This subsector truly does have an excellent long-term track record. Since 1994, net lease REITs have outperformed their larger index by an average 200 basis points (bps) per year. Their dividend yields also tend to be higher, and they're very operationally efficient.

On the bearish side, the Covid-19 era could cause more pain and even bankruptcy for retailers and restaurants alike in ways that hit net lease REITs especially hard. A full two-thirds of their tenants fall into these two categories, which have had to operate under especially restrictive rules since early 2020.

Beyond that, many of them are also at greater risk of inflationary pressures since they operate on fixed-rate escalators. And they're among the most interest-rate sensitive subsector due to their dependency on cheap capital, long-term leases, and limited same-store growth capabilities.

Despite both current and previous difficulties, three net lease REITs – Realty Income, National Retail Properties, and W. P. Carey – managed to increase their dividends anyway (Figure 5.4). Overall, investors continue to appreciate them and their peers for their historically very predictable income and strong returns. I know, for my part, when I think of net lease REITs, I'm reminded that boring is better and helps me sleep much better at night!

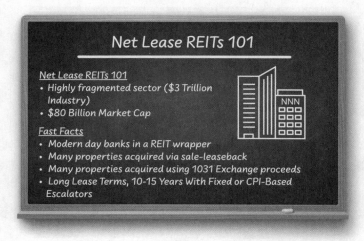

Figure 5.4
Source: Wide Moat Research.

CHAPTER

6

Office, Healthcare, Self-Storage, and Lodging REITs

"Successful investing professionals are disciplined and consistent, and they think a great deal about what they do and how they do it."
—Benjamin Graham

REIT investors tend to group office buildings and industrial properties together often enough. To some degree, this makes sense since they're the primary types of properties leased directly to businesses that don't rely on consumer traffic. In this respect, they're quite unique. But in so many others, they're exceptionally different, hence the reason why industrial properties are included in the technology chapter instead.

This chapter's resulting list of the office, healthcare, self-storage, and hotel/lodging subsectors might seem random. And it's true that they have little direct connections other than that they're publicly traded landlords and commonly recognized members of "REIT-dom."

Let's not waste time on further reflection about the macro REIT universe just yet though. There will be plenty of time for that in future chapters. Instead, let's delve into the "micro" business of leasing offices and the like.

Office Buildings

Accounting for roughly $75 billion in market value, there are 26 office buildings REITs that can be further broken down into two categories: gateway and non-gateway REITs. Gateway REITs hold portfolios concentrated in six of the largest U.S. cities: New York City, Chicago, Boston, Los Angeles, San Francisco, and Washington, D.C. Non-gateway REITs own assets elsewhere, generally in so-called Sunbelt regions and/or secondary U.S. office markets.

Office REITs as a whole almost always operate under longer-term leases, often of 5 to 20 years. They might include small annual rent increases tied to the CPI or some other inflation index, but they're almost always fixed. Landlords will often add in expectations for tenants to help shoulder any increased tax or building-related operating expenses that come along. But they do involve higher degrees of fixed costs (regardless of whether they're occupied or not), leading to higher degrees of operating leverage.

Office buildings have historically been a stable property type, which makes sense. After all, millions of employees who provide service to customers and clients have to have someplace somewhere from which to serve them. And keeping those employees together for collaborative and supervisory purposes was a no-brainer in the past. Since that was a given, most businesses had no problem signing longer-term leases. That created relatively stable cash flows for their landlords, especially when compared to the oh-so fickle (or at least very cyclical) job market.

This isn't to say they never experienced downturns, because they did. Overbuilding can happen, for one thing, making mid-term and long-term growth more difficult. While their longer leases can protect them against loss of income, attracting new leases obviously becomes more time-consuming and perk-intensive, leading to more expenditures. So net operating income can decline during intense booms or, of course, recessions, where they also have to cater to existing and incoming clients.

Back to overbuilding specifically, it takes time to obtain the building permits necessary to construct a new office building, much less to actually construct one. A boom can turn into a bust within that frame. As such, many landlords (across property sectors, in fact) will sign a certain number of tenants before they break ground. It's the smart move to make and a relatively easy fix to a potential major problem during normal times.

A much more complicated threat office REITs have seen is this century's technological advancements. As CNBC wrote on October 10, 2019, "Technology has radically transformed how – and where – Americans work. Working remotely is more popular than ever before. One Gallup survey found that 43% of Americans work from home occasionally. That's up from 39% of those who did in 2012. And, according to Quartz, U.S. Census data indicates that 5.2% of U.S. workers completely worked at home in 2017 – that's about 8 million people."

Now, much of that no doubt could be attributed to the rise of entrepreneurs and freelancers who wouldn't need an office anyway. So it was nothing that might make a sizable dent in the average office REITs' revenue. But then the 2020 shutdowns happened. Just like that, vast numbers of workers were parked on their couches – either because they'd been laid off or were told to handle their employment responsibilities remotely.

As of January 2021, that situation was still playing out, leaving plenty of room to speculate about how the work from home (WFH) paradigm will affect office REITs long-term.

Early on in the shutdowns, survey data and additional commentary from corporations indicated that WFH would last much longer than the pandemic, especially with continuing social distancing fears. Technology suites – including those produced by Zoom, Slack, Google, and Microsoft – have long-since emerged as competitive threats to the old-school way of doing business. And, in 2020, with so many people forced to rely on them day in and day out, it only makes sense that a large number would start seeing them as a "new norm." Even a welcome one.

CBRE Global Research did a study in June 2020 of 126 senior-level global real estate executives. The results showed that over half of them (54%) were predicting an office space reduction after the pandemic was over. Only 16% said the opposite – that they would probably add on.

Also worth noting is how almost three-quarters (74%) reported achieving a better work-life-balance through their WFH programs. Only 17%, however, wanted to eliminate office time altogether, a saving grace for office REITs. That means white-collar employment, though probably changed for good, isn't permanently going away.

Other surveys done indicated that most employers expected to cut back on their office footprint. And sizable majorities agreed that

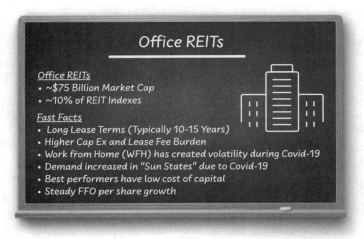

Figure 6.1
Source: Wide Moat Research.

they would allow select individuals – up to 10% of their workforce – to sign in remotely altogether. On the positive side, those surveys were taken relatively early on in the shutdowns. On the negative side, a more recent study done by Partnership for New York City showed that, by mid-August, a mere 8% of NYC office employees were back at their out-of-home desks. And only half of them expected to return by the end of summer 2021.

Yet another angle to consider is the housing trend (mentioned in Chapter 4), which has people moving away from big coastal cities into Sunbelt and suburban regions instead. Office REITs are often a much more location-bound subsector instead of spreading out their portfolios geographically speaking. As such, even with WFH in place, those companies in the country's new hotspots will undoubtedly experience some favorable tailwinds. Big-city-bound landlords, however, continue to be seen as struggling for the time being.

Overall, office REITs tend to benefit later in the economic cycle. So investors and potential investors in this subsector do need to keep that in mind. After the Great Recession, they only saw so much success – a trend that looked like it was beginning to break in 2018 and 2019 (Figure 6.1). Ultimately, only time will tell how they pan out from here. But I remain cautiously optimistic about key players in the meantime.

Healthcare

On the surface, healthcare REITs seem self-explanatory. They're REITs that offer space for healthcare-related properties: senior housing (primarily assisted- and independent-living facilities), skilled nursing, medical office buildings (MOBs), hospitals, life-science offices, and labs. The landlords themselves don't practice medicine; they only lease to those who do. This is through triple-net leases that provide historically stable income, including some protection from cyclical downturns and modest upside when business is good.

The vast majority of healthcare REITs' revenues come from independent lessees that sign long-term contracts with renewal options. Quite often, leases also contain provisions for additional rent due at specified times or based on inflation. In addition, individual property leases with a single medical institution are often bundled together under a master lease. This makes it much more difficult for the lessee to cherry pick the best properties for renewal or default on some but not others.

Then there's the RIDEA legislation first mentioned in Chapter 3, which allows – but does not require – healthcare REITs to lease properties to taxable REIT subsidiaries. The main requirement here is that the properties are managed by outside sources, while the main perk is that REITs can then participate more fully in the properties' upside. Admittedly, they suffer more from their downsides that way too, which is why not every healthcare landlord takes advantage of this clause.

These property owners usually prefer the slow-but-steady approach, which helps make them so recession-resistant. Under most circumstances, healthcare services are a necessity, not a luxury service people can survive without during hard times. So it makes sense that corresponding REITs' shares have a fairly strong track record of performing much better than their peers during periods of economic weakness.

Overall then, healthcare REITs tend to enjoy only modest internal cash flow growth, which they try to balance out through acquisitions and, to a lesser extent, new development. This isn't an immediate issue considering how the 18 entries together amount to just $110 billion in market value – a mere one-tenth of the $2 trillion in U.S.-bound healthcare-related real estate assets. So there are plenty of buildings to buy.

Taking advantage of that availability naturally requires sizable access to reasonably priced capital, but that's only occasionally an issue. Healthcare REITs tend to feature some of the most well-capitalized balance sheets available. So it typically takes the investment community by surprise when these companies do take a significant downturn.

That did happen in the late 1990s, when skilled nursing and assisted living facilities experienced individualized mini-crises thanks to government-mandated reductions in Medicare coverage for the former (always a concern to keep an eye out for) and over-development for the latter. Excessive debt leverage from those same tenants exacerbated the problems, sending their landlords' shares tumbling too.

Fast-forward to 2020 then, and you have a much more wide-spread crisis. It's not entirely inaccurate to say that the entire range of healthcare REITs have felt the most direct impact of the pandemic. Moreover, there will be both near-term and long-term consequences to varying degrees across the subsectors.

Consider senior housing, where independent and assisted living facilities alike are facing record-low occupancy rates. The nursing home deaths in states such as New York, New Jersey, Pennsylvania, and Michigan led to much more widespread fears. As a direct result, residents began leaving at much higher rates than normal, with far fewer people moving in to fill that financial void. On top of that, nobody is certain how long this obvious uptick in mistrust will last.

Skilled nursing REITs are also having significant issues with their once-again troubled operators. Hospitals are battling the continuing fallout of suspending so many elective surgeries. This stretched their already immensely tight budgets and prompted them to lay off literal tens of thousands of doctors and nurses. And medical office buildings might not need nearly so much square footage if telemedicine continues much longer.

One silver lining – and perhaps an intense one – is the dawning of the "silver tsunami." Baby boomers, those born between 1945 and 1965, are a large generation that's more and more stepping into retirement age. For that matter, the 80+ population will just about double over the next three decades, growing at an estimated annual 4% through 2040. While baby boomers tend to be healthier than their predecessors, they're also much more focused on staying that way. Between that and their greater wealth levels, experts have long-since predicted they'll be consistent healthcare customers.

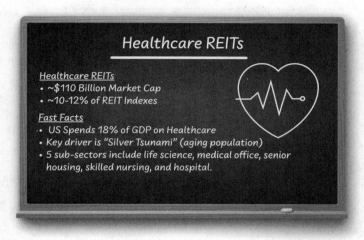

Figure 6.2
Source: Wide Moat Research.

More shutdown drama could still play out from here. Only time will tell. Just like only time will tell if the subsector goes on to use the 2020 recession like a shopping spree, as it has with much more "garden-variety" recessions of the past. Healthcare REITs have been known to take advantage of economically damaged properties to a total tune of tens of billions of dollars. So, considering their strong share price performance and net asset value premium they boasted in 2018 and 2019, there is that chance of more bargain-hunting and easy pickings in 2021. (See Figure 6.2.)

Self-Storage

It wouldn't be surprising to learn that Neanderthals kept a lot of "valuable" items on the back shelves of their caves. It seems like simply human nature to save stuff. Even if we live in a small apartment or when our collection of old lawnmowers exceeds our garage space, we have a solution to maintain our piles of stuff: self-storage centers.

Originally, these facilities were built in the 1960s on the edges of towns or near industrial parks on an experimental basis. But as they slowly but steadily increased in popularity, new construction started happening in more convenient locations with nicer landscapes. In fact, today, convenient proximity is the most important factor in customers choosing which facility they'll use.

Individual storage units normally range from 5 to 20 square feet. Rented by the month, they allow people to store everything from personal files to furniture, and even recreational vehicles and boats. Sometimes businesses will use them too to store irregularly used items, with the clientele breakdown consisting of 70% residential and 30% companies, students, or members of the military.

There are reportedly some 50,000 self-storage facilities in the U.S., and about 1 in 10 households use them for extra room. The five largest self-storage REITs combined own only around 20% of their industry and have a combined market value of roughly $60 billion.

There is a profits-denting oversupply thanks to how easy these buildings are to construct. Yet that just means there's a lot of room for REITs to acquire already existent smaller businesses. And experts foresee that kind of activity to be a key driver of outperformance over the next decade. As it is, they have major advantages over their private market competitors, with superior access to equity capital, scalability, revenue management systems, and call-in centers. Obviously, they also have brand value on their side, since they run bigger, more widespread operations.

Self-storage REITs also operate with some of the most well-capitalized balance sheets across the real estate sector, thanks in part to a very low cost of doing business. The five largest have debt ratios below the 43% REIT sector average. In short, they're efficient machines with NOI margins of 70%, some of the highest available in real estate.

Key factors for further growth include housing developments going up around self-storage facilities, moving rates, and baby boomers downsizing (when it comes to home size, not the amount of possessions). As such, companies with well-located properties can make a sizable profit, even in a recession. Potential customers with well-paying jobs have the luxury of renting extra space, whereas people who are struggling financially often move into more affordable spaces, shoving their extras where they can.

As for risks, once again, overbuilding has taken its toll on the big five in the past. They have no real moat to work with, so there's always the threat of competition. Any long-term decreases in consumer spending would also hurt them. And while we haven't seen it yet, the short-term nature of their leases and therefore high levels of turnover could have significant detrimental effects on them depending on what the future may bring. (See Figure 6.3.)

Figure 6.3
Source: Wide Moat Research.

Hotels/Lodging

It's not easy being a hotel operator. Even in the best of (realistic) economic conditions, it's a capital-intensive line of work that relies on two extremely finicky sets of customers: tourists and business travelers. Yet the leisure and hospitality industry nonetheless is an enormously important segment that typically employs 16.8 million Americans. Meanwhile, there are about 50,000 hotel properties with a total of five million hotel rooms across the U.S.

That's not to say lodging REITs own the majority of that, however. This is an even more fragmented subsector than self-storage. The 18 biggest members own less than 5% of all hotel properties in the U.S, with a combined market cap of roughly $25 billion. Nor are they the major names you recognize in the industry. Marriott, Hilton, and Hyatt are hotel operators, not hotel owners.

For the record, it's also not easy being a hotel owner. They run with an asset-heavy model and adjusted NOI margins of only 10–20% in a regular year. That's the lowest of all REIT subsectors. This means they have a lot of operating leverage and are – like the hotel operators who pay them – very sensitive even to small changes in supply and demand. They're not the most agile investments in taking advantage of opportunities or avoiding danger, and they have slower growth rates than their clientele.

This can, however, pay off nicely for investors under the right circumstances, since lodging REITs offer bigger dividends as a perk for taking a chance on them – with "can" being the keyword. It doesn't always work out.

Case in point: The national hotel industry was performing nicely in 2019, enjoying record-high occupancy and revenue. It wasn't doing as well as other subsectors due to longstanding oversupply issues, but it was still doing well – until the 2020 shutdowns hit.

With most lodging facilities having to close for weeks or even months on end, and travelers putting off their jet-setting arrangements for fear of catching Covid-19, lodging REITs suffered the most out of every other property sector. Worse yet, they will likely continue suffering the most going forward. Final 2020 revenue will probably be down 50% when all the numbers are in. And nobody expects a full recovery until 2023. At least.

These stocks were much beloved for investors looking for high yields from the mid-2010s through 2019. But by the second-quarter 2020, all 18 had suspended their dividends. That only makes sense. After all, it's tough to pay out extras when you're barely able to support the basics. (See Figure 6.4.)

Figure 6.4
Source: Wide Moat Research.

Summed up, this subsector isn't for the risk-adverse. It wasn't in the past, it isn't in the present, and it doubtlessly won't be in the future. Not when there's always the chance of recessions, depressions, and national or global disasters. There are too many fixed and variable costs of operation involved that can't be easily removed or otherwise changed should the need arise.

So investors are always spending money without the promise of always making it back.

CHAPTER 7

Technology REITs

(*Contributed by* Jennifer Fritzsche)

"A stock is not just a ticker symbol or an electronic blip; it is an ownership interest in an actual business with an underlying value that does not depend on its share price."

—Benjamin Graham

While technology has become a critical element for almost every real estate subsector, much of the recent focus has been on how e-commerce is challenging retail landlords (as detailed in Chapter 5). Now it's time to discuss the segments doing that damage: cell towers, data centers, and industrial properties. These three are at the heart of the digital ecosystem, providing critical infrastructure for the e-commerce value chain.

As Cohen & Steers explains, "Every time you make a purchase on your smartphone or computer, it sets a sequence in motion that travels through a network of communications, data, and logistics facilities."

Since many of those properties are owned by REITs, it's more than safe to say that they "play an integral role in getting your package from

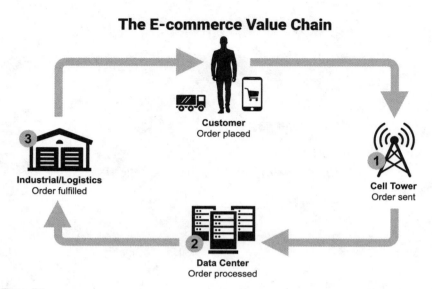

The E-commerce Value Chain

Customer
Order placed

Cell Tower
Order sent

Industrial/Logistics
Order fulfilled

Data Center
Order processed

Figure 7.1
Source: Cohen & Steers.

the warehouse to your doorstep, giving investors a way to participate in the potential growth of e-commerce." (See Figure 7.1.)

Obviously, there are other avenues to do this. But Cohen & Steers adds that the REIT way offers "some of the more attractive opportunities we see today. With consumers spending more online and organizations modernizing their operations, there seems little doubt that the e-commerce marketplace should continue to grow in size and sophistication, progressing in ways that have not even surfaced yet." That's why it's very interested in understanding the REITs behind that scene. The average investor would do well to do the same.

Tower REITs

Unlike many other REIT structures, the wireless tower model is simple and straightforward. Wireless devices (i.e., basic phones, smartphones, tablets, connected cars, etc.) transmit data over the air via wireless spectrum, from radios inside the devices to those mounted at the top of towers, or cell sites. That data is transferred back to the core network over fiber or copper lines – or spectrum, in some situations – then directed toward the appropriate end user's location via the nearest tower. (See Figures 7.2 and 7.3.)

Wireless Towers Are Critical Infrastructure in the Wireless Ecosystem

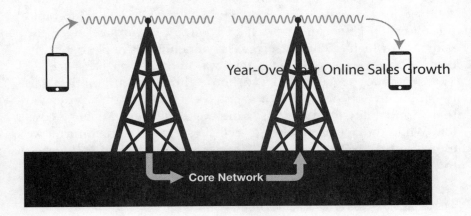

Year-Over-Year Online Sales Growth

Core Network

Figure 7.2

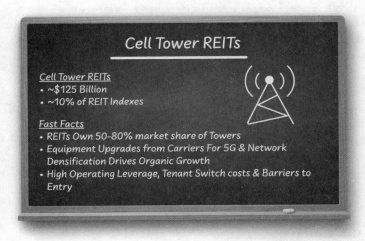

Figure 7.3
Source: Wide Moat Research.

As such, tower REITs can be compared to apartment owners, with wireless carriers as their renters. The big difference is that they don't need to spend capital to attract big customers or to keep them. All they need is a good zoning staff and $200,000–$300,000 to build the tower. Or they can work off of rooftops. Regardless, once the structure – which essentially serves as an antenna – is in place, tenants come to them, even going out of their way to claim available space.

Each tower has the ability to house three to four wireless carriers, and tower companies own just the structures themselves. So their profitability possibilities are high and their maintenance costs low. While the actual number of cell sites isn't easy to confirm, we estimate there were about 150,000 towers in the U.S. in 2020, each with an average four to five tenants.

A Quick History Lesson of the Tower Industry

The start of the tower industry can really be traced back to the vision of one man, the late and great Steve Dodge, who founded American Radio Systems. In 1998, that company merged with CBS Corporation, which then completed the corporate spin-off of American Tower Corp. And so the foundation of a new REIT subsector was born, though it would take a few more years before American Tower adopted the actual legal name and structure.

Its REIT competition comes in the form of Crown Castle and SBA Communications, all three of which were aggressive in their M&A efforts in the beginning. Unfortunately, their consolidation efforts resulted in more leverage than they could respectably handle, leading to stock price declines across the sector. It was a necessary wake-up call for the industry, which took the hint and employed a variety of creative balance sheet measures. As a result, tower REITs were able to shore up their costs of capital and overall debt levels to get back to growing again.

Now, before the mid-2000s, most wireless carriers actually owned their own tower assets. But they began to realize their forward-looking strategies could work better if they sold those holdings and redeployed the capital elsewhere. Moreover, they were willing to make attractive offers to their to-be landlords. From the tower companies' standpoint, this was an important avenue to build scale. And so they've been doing precisely that ever since.

The same major players remain today, with a few derivative land-lords like Landmark Infrastructure Partners owning some of the land beneath the towers. As for the "pure players," they probably account for a share of U.S. tower companies, since several private players exist as well.

While none of them have abandoned their roots, American Tower and SBA have been seeking more growth opportunities through international moves INTO places like Latin America, India, and Africa. And Crown Castle, for its part, has been aggressive in acquiring fiber assets to play up the small-cell market, where low-powered nodes provide cellular radio access to much smaller areas, covering ranges from several yards to a few miles at most.

Naturally, each has its pros and cons.

The Economics of the Tower Model

As already implied, the tower model is an extremely passive infrastructure investment. Wireless carriers maintain their own cell site positions, and with good reason. The equipment there protects the integrity of their entire networks, after all. Poor network quality is the number one reason customers switch to competitors, and nobody is going to care about limiting that churn more than the providers themselves.

For that same reason, providers are also in charge of installing their own equipment at their own cost. So, as stated before, the only real expenses the tower companies have to worry about after building their structures are real estate taxes if they own the land they've built off of or rent if they lease it. One of the industry's jokes is even that the main cost involved is sending someone to mow the lawn! Naturally then, the contribution margins (i.e., margin on every added dollar of revenue) are extremely high.

Tower companies charge varying rents based on site location, square footage being leased, and the amount of weight being placed on a structure (known as wind loading). So a tower with three tenants and a monthly base rent of $1,650 per tenant will have gross contribution margins in the high 90% range. And return on invested capital (ROIC) would approach 25%.

It's difficult to find any other REIT model – or business model period – with similar margin performance. Yet this doesn't make it an automatically easy space to operate in. The sector has faced increasing zoning pressure that limits where they can build new structures. Put simply, the "not in my backyard," or NIMBY, mantra is alive and well here. Though, funny enough, much of that is inspired by tower companies themselves.

Say a new tower is proposed in a specific town or city. You'd better believe the first entity to fight it will be the incumbent tower company, ready to rally residents with demands to keep property value pretty: "Do you really want a big ugly tower in here ruining your property value?!" It's a line that usually works well in zoning meetings, hence the reason why the typical U.S. wireless tower will stand alone for a good mile. And since suitable proximity matters quite a lot in this business, players with scale – namely the three REITs – are very well positioned, while newcomers are not.

Opportunities and Drivers

The tower sector has tremendous tailwinds behind it. These include but are not limited to: additional spectrum coming to market, greater smartphone penetration, traffic growth expanding by double-digits in each of the past few years, the emergence of new wireless competitors, and the rollout of 5G – which we'll talk more about shortly. Basically though, exponential growth in data usage is driving carriers to fortify their networks or add capacity by layering on incremental spectrum and building new sites.

Right now, the FCC is putting more and more spectrum out to carriers. And the importance of this cannot be overemphasized. Radio spectrum (RF for radio frequency) is the portion of the electromagnetic frequency range reserved for communications. Their signals decay naturally though, limiting the length each band can transmit RF, known as propagation.

As a general rule, spectrum bands in lower frequencies tend to propagate further than mid- or high-band spectrums. Today, wireless carriers are exploring incremental supply in ultra-high frequencies (millimeter waves) to layer network capacity and possibly handle backhaul where fiber might be either unavailable or less economic. Yet the higher the spectrum band, the shorter the propagation. And the shorter the propagation, the more cell sites are needed. The more cell sites needed, the more growth tower companies should see.

As for their yearly operations, the tower model is known for its recurring revenue nature. These companies typically know how 90% of their annual revenue will look as of day one of the fiscal year. That's because tower contracts are long-term in nature (usually 10 years), typically non-cancellable, and structured with multiple renewal options. Plus, tower companies have embraced signing master lease agreements (MLAs) with carrier customers to help expedite network builds. This allows them to have tremendous visibility in terms of their long-term revenue growth.

Speaking of revenue, typical towers have three ways of bringing in additional money: 1) adding on new tenants, 2) amendment revenue, which is when a current tenant adds more equipment to their current cell site, and 3) annual escalators, which are usually about 2–3% in the U.S. and tied to the CPI of each respective country internationally.

Going back to 5G now (with G standing for generation), this is so much more than just a buzzword. It offers a sea of change to wireless operations with the potential to open up many new industries in the process. For instance, 4G allowed for the creation of companies like Uber and Lyft. And 5G will no doubt be even more of a game-changer.

If 1G moved communication capabilities from a walking "speed" to that of a skateboard, 2G progressed us to a bicycle, 3G to a car's pace, and 4G to a plane's . . . then 5G is a rocket all the way. (See Figure 7.4.)

To fully utilize this new stage, however, densification is key. Adding cell sites, whether macro or small cells, will both help better manage the increase in wireless data traffic and reduce lag time between communications. In fact, adding cell sites is downright crucial.

If you've ever heard of IoT before, you probably know of it as an abbreviation for "internet of things." But a much more accurate way of putting it might be "infrastructure of things." And towers are the core of that infrastructure. Without them, 5G can't do anything at all.

This is why experts estimate that the three big tower REITs will spend billions in total capital expenditures in 2020 and even more in 2021. Some of that will be for other segments, of course – including DISH's emerging goals as it enters the wireless arena. But you'd better believe tower companies are taking 5G seriously. They have to.

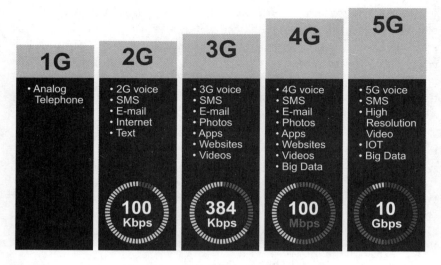

Figure 7.4
Source: Dense Networks.

Risks

The more customers a business has, the less chance it has of falling prey to a single client's bad news or bad behavior. In which case, it needs to be said that tower REITs are intensely undiversified, especially after the recent consolidation in the wireless industry. Some 95% of their U.S. revenue comes from just three customers: AT&T, T-Mobile USA, and Verizon. While DISH could help diversify this revenue mix, it won't be by a lot.

In recent years, these carriers have been challenging the business model – particularly amendment fees – as they try to build networks more efficiently. Historically, tower REITs produce strong free cash flow characteristics. However, times are changing. Both revenue pressures (driven by T-Mobile's disruptive pricing approach of the past few years) and expense pressures are taking their toll.

Plus, there are now many demands on their capital these days, from spectrum purchases to backhaul and fronthaul fiber needs, de-leveraging, and dividends. Many are even facing hard questions about where to best put the capital they're generating, sending them into "pause mode" in buying up "properties." This could put network decisions on hold, which could pressure tower companies' organic growth rates in turn.

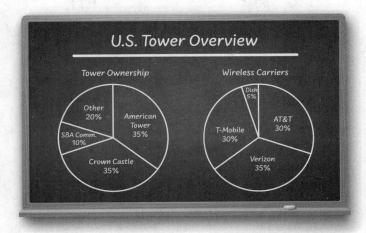

Figure 7.5
Source: Wide Moat Research.

With that said, these landlords are fairly protected due to the longer-term contracts they operate under and their absolute importance in carriers' business models. (See Figure 7.5.)

Another issue is how there are many different types of wireless infrastructure aside from macro towers, such as small cells, fiber, and edge data centers. While towers are the point of centralization right now, small cells could take priority as higher band spectrum is deployed, since the one serves the other more naturally. This could cause short-term pressure on tower companies' same-store organic growth outlooks.

These REITs are also highly levered in order to fund much of their growth and scale. So they're very interest-rate sensitive. If and when we enter a period of rising rates, it will become more difficult to expand thanks to higher costs of capital. And, last but not least in terms of risk reviews, cell tower REITs own only about a third of the land their structures rest on. So the cost of their leases could easily go up in a few years when it's time to renew.

Speaking of cost, relentless outperformance over the past five years has pushed cell tower REIT valuations to the most "expensive" end of the real estate sector, especially in terms of AFFO per share. Plus, they're among the lowest-yielding REIT sectors, offering an average 1.9% dividend yield.

Then again, the typical REIT doesn't necessarily see the same accelerated customer spending trends, high contribution margins, and investment-grade customers. And it's not as if towers go out and squander the money they don't pay out in dividends. The roughly half of free cash flow they retain leaves ample funds for external growth and eventual dividend hikes. American Tower has increased its dividend by around 20% every year since 2015, and Crown Castle has grown its dividend by an annual average of 8%.

Data Centers

Data centers are very specialized real estate facilities that house computer servers and network equipment within a highly secure environment. They come complete with redundant mechanical cooling, electrical power systems, and network connections. You can think of them almost as microwaves to "cook" all the data that's generated. (See Figure 7.6.)

Typically, these landlords own the building, the power and cooling infrastructures, and exchanges and cross-connections. Customers, meanwhile, provide their own servers, storage, and networking equipment. Digital Realty was the first data center REIT to complete an IPO in 2004. But it wasn't until the larger real estate sector received its own Global Industry Classification Standard that

Components of a Typical Data Center

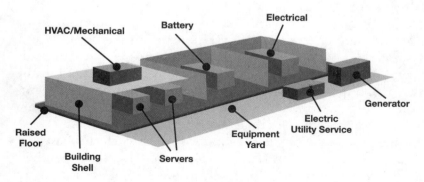

Figure 7.6

the subsector began to stand out to investors. Today, there are five pure-play public data center REITs – CoreSite Realty, CyrusOne, Digital Realty, Equinix, and QTS Realty Trust. And though document storage still accounts for the majority of its revenue, Iron Mountain is making strides in this area as well.

There are several types of data centers, with the two main ones being wholesale/hyperscale and colocation facilities. The former offer more space and power potential to their clients by taking on fewer customers per facility, usually with 5- to 10-year contracts. Demand for these arrangements tend to be "lumpier" since they're more exclusive, driven by large cloud players like Azure, Amazon Web Services, Google, Apple, Facebook, and the like. These companies purchase multiple megawatts (MW) of space – more than they immediately need so they can grow into them. As a result, it's not unusual to see hyperscale centers have one strong year followed by a weaker one.

The key hyperscaler markets in the U.S. are Virginia, Dallas, Silicon Valley, Chicago, New York, the tri-state area, and Atlanta. In Europe, Frankfort, London, Amsterdam, and Paris have been key regions of focus. And Brazil, Mexico, and Asia also represent important areas of growth. Players in the hyperscale arena include CyrusOne and Digital Realty.

Colocation players, meanwhile, tend to have more customers per facility and shorter contract lengths. Yet they also have higher margins thanks to co-location revenue, which is driven by the interconnects (or cross connects) that link clients within these facilities. Confused? That's understandable. But try thinking of interconnects as a USB cord that stretches from one specific center customer to another, creating faster connections. "Colo" players can charge an additional fee for this feature on top of normal rent, making their revenue margins well above 80%.

Players in this arena include Equinix, Coresite, and Digital Realty through its Interxion acquisition. These businesses have wide moats that help ward off competition more so than wholesale companies. The simple reason for this is because cross-connects act as a "magnet" to bring in more business. Typically, these facilities see very low turnover, and when someone does move out, there's already a wait-list to draw from. Therefore, it would be difficult – almost impossible – to break into this client base.

A third and probably growing segment of the data center space is comprised of hybrid properties that serve businesses wanting to adopt both a public and private cloud strategy. This often applies to large, highly regulated companies such as financial institutions. The way it's looking now, connectivity and access to cloud on-ramps will be a major focus for certain companies, especially in the wake of Covid-19.

But this is not a game for laggards. So make sure to look for data center REITs that are staying on top of the industry's ever-changing realm.

Even now, it's entering a new chapter: "the edge," which brings computing power closer to the point of use. This can accommodate the continuing rise of artificial intelligence (AI), the internet of things, and perhaps most importantly, 5G. It's also opening the need for smaller data centers in non-primary markets, which some companies are already acting on. This theme should only build as demand for a more holistic solution climbs.

Drivers and Opportunities

There are several considerations to take into account when picking and choosing which of these stocks are best for your portfolio. For instance, the 2020 Uptime Institute Data Center Survey found that about 58% of enterprise IT workloads are still located within enterprise-owned data centers. Approximately 16% are housed in third-party colocation properties, and about 12% sit in the public cloud.

Now, a significant 21% of respondents said they had plans to at least somewhat shift to the latter. But over 50% were extremely wary of that option. They understandably don't want to give up control over their mission-critical data to something that seems so hackable. And that aversion supports the already bullish signs for hybrid data center models as an alternative.

Here's another thing to consider: There's a fairly good balance between supply and demand right now. Most wholesale data centers are waiting for pre-leasing orders before they build new facilities. Naturally, that helps de-risk development returns, something too many of these tech-hosting companies didn't consider nearly as much as they should have in previous years. Their pre-lease rates of 0–20% in 2011 and 2012 led to oversupply in 2012 and 2013.

Today, though, industry pre-leasing rates are typically in the 40–50% range. And demand has picked up, with wholesale providers working hard to provide matching supplies, especially in the top markets.

In the midst of all this, REITs in this space are taking advantage of sale-leaseback tactics with existing data center providers to boost revenue further. This gives owners-turned-tenants quick cash and more experienced industry insiders to handle their data. Meanwhile, the new owners get immediate access to particular markets and additional cash flow as well.

This trend is probably still in its early stages, so expect more of it in the years ahead.

As the subsector stands now, these REITs are already looking good when it comes to rewarding their investors. Between (2015 and 2019, they grew dividends per share at an average of 13%, with smaller-cap examples accelerating even faster. Data centers can continue to raise that rate above and beyond their AFFO growth thanks to the lower interest rates they're working with and continued margin expansion. Those with investment-grade ratings are even better positioned with lower costs of capital.

Risks

That's the upside, but a downside does exist too. For one thing, increased demand leads to bigger companies. And bigger companies lead to lower pricing and compressed yields, especially for hyperscale players. A few years ago, they were safely offering 12–14% yields. Today, they're down to 6–8%.

We also have to go back to scale here since it's a key element in the data center industry. Equinix and Digital Realty are the two biggest players in this field, and they both have global reach, with operations in the U.S., Latin America, Europe, and the Asia-Pacific region. An international appeal is difficult to build thanks to the influx of capital being put into such spaces. So their dominance makes it difficult for smaller competitors like CyrusOne and QTS to branch out in turn.

Then there's regulatory costs in the form of renewable energy, energy efficiency, and waste reduction, all of which are increasing. That trend is almost undoubtedly here to stay.

Next, let's consider capital expenditures (capex). The typical data center REIT's capex is between 2% and 5% of annual revenue, and that works for now. But it might not soon enough. Remember that these companies operate both power and cooling systems, both of which cost money to purchase, much less maintain. And the bigger they build them, the more money they will have to shell out.

Speaking of such, the Uptime Institute recently surveyed a number of data center owners. It found that most of them were already working to be ready "for the next pandemic." Again, that costs money, which will in turn affect short-term profits.

Last but not least, don't forget that big-name potential tenants like Microsoft are aggressively gobbling up acres and acres of land in key markets to facilitate their own properties. And even if that activity does slow down, the threat of big tech trying to take over could cause hyperscalers to offer less profitable contracts in order to secure customers.

With that said, the data center model still offers more tailwinds than headwinds, with tremendous runway ahead of it. As the cloud's outsourcing appeal grows – whether through full public access or hybrid solutions – this space should continue to see accelerating growth trends.

Industrial

It might seem strange to include industrial REITs in the technological loop, but bear with us all the same.

For starters, this subsector is made up of distribution centers, regular and bulk warehouses, light-manufacturing facilities, research and development facilities, and "flex" space for sales, administrative, and related operations. Together, this makes for an enormous field.

As Justin Smith explains in *The Logistics of Leasing*, "If the total amount of industrial space were all consolidated into one gigantic warehouse, it would cover the entire sprawling city of Los Angeles under one roof, and all of its [4 million] residents."

Demand for industrial properties is driven by GDP growth, trade, U.S. manufacturing activity, growth in inventories, and retail sales trends. And this is why I've included it in the technology trio: because retail sales are taking place online more and more these days. They're electronic transactions submitted via cell towers, collected by data centers, and fulfilled through warehouses to form an ever-growing triangle of profits.

As we've addressed before, the stay-at-home economy significantly accelerated e-commerce adoption and penetration. It jumped from less than 15% at the end of 2019 to nearly 25% percent in May 2020. And nearly half of retail sales were completed through such channels during the following spring and summer months.

E-commerce is actually far less efficient than traditional brick-and-mortar from an industrial space-usage perspective. Brick and mortar shelf space is effectively "replaced" by back-end logistics space. With e-commerce though, each dollar spent requires roughly three times more logistics area. That's according to estimates from subsector player Prologis Inc., and retailers have invested heavily in supply chain densification as a result.

When I say "retailers," I don't just mean Amazon. As first mentioned in Chapter 5, traditional brick-and-mortar powerhouses such as Walmart, Home Depot, Target, and Costco have honed the omnichannel approach with significant success. They've been among the biggest investors in e-commerce distribution over the last several years, and industrial property owners have reaped the obvious and immediate benefits.

That movement comes on top of growth in outsourcing and rising U.S. imports, which are making global industrial production increasingly important for this sector. As such, large distribution hubs located at airports and seaports often perform particularly well.

We've seen consolidation in the industry, with larger users and logistics companies looking to upgrade and make their supply chains more efficient. With that said, ownership in this economic area is highly fragmented. There are 14 industrial REITs in all, accounting for roughly $100 billion in market value – a figure that keeps growing as they continue to deliver seemingly relentless outperformance. Once viewed as a chronically underperforming subsector with limited barriers to entry, industrial REITs have been on fire for the last half-decade.

They outperformed the broader REIT index for four consecutive years through 2019, and they're on pace to outperform yet again in 2020. That's in large part due to their enormous trend away from manufacturing and toward industrial usage for consumer-oriented tenants.

Industrial REITs own roughly 5–10% of total industrial real estate assets in the U.S., but a higher percentage of higher-value distribution-focused assets in that category. Their building sizes average around 200,000 square feet – facilities that have seen significant rent growth and more favorable supply/demand conditions due to tangible constraints on land availability. It's therefore not hard to categorize them as growth REITs that see the majority of their total returns from FFO increases.

In addition to robust organic growth, industrial REITs continue to benefit from the added tailwind of external growth. After years of relying on ground-up development, 2019 allowed them to go on a buying spree and get back to doing what REITs do best: use their equity to fund likely acquisitions.

Of course, strong fundamentals come at a price. So industrial REITs haven't come "cheap" for the better part of a decade. They continue to trade at sizable free cash flow premiums as measured by AFFO, funds available for distribution (FAD), and cash available for distribution (CAD) to REIT averages. Noting that, the sector can still be pretty attractively valued when we factor in medium-term growth expectations.

Principal risks do exist in this sector, such as the potential decline of domestic and/or global economic and business conditions. Periods of weak retail sales and imports could also take it down a notch or two. And possible overbuilding is another factor to watch out for, since it isn't prohibitively expensive to build a new industrial property, Many are built on the presumption that a buyer will come along, so active developers should be watched more closely.

On the one hand, development pipelines can be shut down relatively quickly. But if a REIT stock is priced on the basis of very profitable future plans that don't come to fruition, shareholders are likely to suffer.

Figure 7.7
Source: Wide Moat Research.

With that said, the economic and societal directions are once again very bullish for this last member of our tech trifecta. It's worth paying attention to as a result. (See Figure 7.7.)

CHAPTER

8

Specialized REITs

"Unusually rapid growth cannot keep up forever; when a company has already registered a brilliant expansion, its very increase in size makes a repetition of its achievement more difficult."

—Benjamin Graham

The U.S. REIT market has expanded significantly over the past decade, as we've already somewhat discussed. What we haven't discussed yet are the many new, specialized REITs that now provide investors with unique diversification benefits. These subsectors include billboards, farms, prisons, and timber. And while there are no publicly traded parking garage, amusement park, stadium, or airport REITs at this time, they might not be that far off.

Two interesting (already existent) new REIT classes we discuss in this chapter are gaming and cannabis. Both of these subsectors have recently entered REIT-dom and have performed extraordinarily well so far, with good reason to expect more positive results from here.

Gaming

The last 40 years have seen lots of legalizations when it comes to commercial casinos. Recognizing the tax gold mines they'd been previously prohibiting, states are now increasingly open to businesses that had originally been sequestered in Las Vegas, Atlantic City, and Native American reservations.

Just one example is Pennsylvania, where gaming now represents close to a quarter of its state tax revenue. And New York, Nevada, and New Jersey, among others, have similar stories. Twenty-five states have "gone to the dark side" at last check to allow commercial casinos. And this has led to the formation of several REITs that were more than happy to go all-in.

Believe it or not, casino REITs aren't that big of a gamble (outside of economic shutdowns, anyway). They use ultra-long-term, triple-net contracts of 15–25 years each to sign on tenants. So most of the risk – both financial and operational – lies squarely on their tenants' shoulders, such as Las Vegas Sands, MGM Resorts, Wynn Resorts, Caesars Entertainment, Churchill Downs, Eldorado, and other fairly famous names.

Admittedly, any additional upside also goes to those tenants. But that's okay considering how, as I've already mentioned, the triple-net structure offers landlords high-margin and pretty predictable income streams. These bond-like qualities do mean they're more sensitive to interest rates and less so to larger market movements, for better or worse. However, as I've also already mentioned, there is no such thing as a perfect investment. Not even here.

Amounting to roughly $21 billion in market value, the three gaming REITs – VICI Properties, Gaming and Leisure Properties, and MGM Growth Properties –own over a third of U.S. commercial casino and gaming properties altogether.

Incidentally, MGM Growth Properties only leases to MGM Resorts, whereas VICI caters especially to Caesars, Penn National, and Century; and Gaming and Leisure offers space to Penn National, Boyd Gaming, and Eldorado. So it shouldn't come as much of a surprise to hear that they began as spin-offs meant to more clearly delineate between capital-intensive real estate ownership and operationally intensive traditional business ownership:

- Gaming and Leisure spun off from Penn National in 2013.
- MGM Growth spun off from MGM Resorts in 2016.
- VICI was formed out of Caesars' 2018 bankruptcy procedures.

Figure 8.1
Source: Wide Moat Research.

As the VICI genesis indicates, these REITs' tenants aren't always stellar. Many casinos go back and forth, up and down, in making a profit. And their track records include a few too many bankruptcies and reorganizations for many investors' liking.

In addition, gaming REITs' supply growth is limited on two counts: 1) They can only cater to a relatively small amount of clients; 2) There are significant barriers to entry, with most states enacting significant regulatory and economic policies on the subject. Essentially, these governors and legislators want to have their cake and eat it too. (See Figure 8.1.)

Billboards

Billboard REITs operate in the out of home (OHH) advertising market, a circle that centers around static and digital signage strategically placed to nab commuters' attention. This mostly involves billboards but does include transit displays as well. Limited to Outfront Media and Lamar Advertising for the time being, these companies get around 75% of their combined revenue from owning about 44% of those oh-so-familiar 300,000+ markers up and down the highway.

In the last several years, they've been moving toward providing more affordable services for clients while also taking in better profits. This would be through digital billboards over the traditional, printed plastic, and very static ones. Instead of images being physically lifted up and secured high above the ground, they can now be projected and programmed onto displays, flipping between two, three, or four of them every minute. As a result, they can bring in two to four times in revenue.

As a general rule, OHH advertising is extremely cheap on a cost-per-impression (CPM) basis. In fact, it's the cheapest, bar none. Yet businesses tend to give less thought to getting their message out this way. Fortunately for billboard REITs, that thinking is changing – perhaps as much as an annual 3% through mid-2023.

As it stands now, customers typically include tech companies, TV producers, retailers, professional services such as law firms, and restaurants. They pay for 1- to 12-month spots, the exact cost of which depends on the size and placement of their selected signs.

The legislation surrounding billboards is both a positive and a negative, creating an almost impenetrable moat for would-be competitors and a very damaging block for current owners. Since 1965, this has been an intensely regulated industry, with the majority of existing signage found along federal highways grandfathered in. Any new construction permits are very difficult to come by.

Even upgrading or improving existing ones can be difficult. Some cities demand that landlords remove two or three existing billboards for every digital switchover. Again, this doesn't necessarily make it a worthless endeavor, but it is a frustrating restriction nonetheless.

Like their cell tower cousins to a certain extent (discussed in Chapter 7), billboard REITs own the structures themselves but rent the land beneath, often from thousands of individual property owners, for 5 to 15 years at a time. Unlike cell tower REITs, however, they work with relatively low margins. In addition, they have to employ a stable staff of salespeople, plus professionals to update their static displays based on customer contracts and turnover. This means that, while the rest of the real estate investment trust sector manages average operating margins of 65% to 70%, billboard REITs work with 30%.

Much more reasonably, their capital expenditure costs are much closer to 5% of revenue. Yet even there, you'll need to factor in the trend toward going digital. Though making that switch is a smart

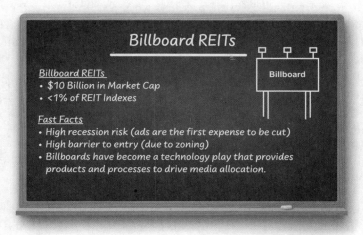

Figure 8.2
Source: Wide Moat Research.

long-term move, it obviously elevates capex spending in the short term. And even after the displays are up, running, and making money, upgrades will no doubt have to be made as new capabilities come out.

Billboard REITs are one of the least interest-rate-sensitive subsectors but one of the most economically so. As such, they make good counterbalance portfolio positions that don't sacrifice dividend yields. Investors should just keep in mind that advertising has a bad habit of getting cut first during tough economic times – like during shutdown-inspired mini-depressions. (See Figure 8.2.)

Prisons

On a global scale, the U.S. comes first for prison incarceration rates and population size. Since the 1970s, that number has quadrupled to over 2 million (though it's decreased 10% since 2009 thanks to criminal justice reform legislation), meaning that it accounts for almost a quarter of the world's prisoners. Perhaps not surprisingly, that's very much been driven by the war on drugs.

Due to rising numbers that neither state nor federal facilities could completely handle, business began to pop up to "house" the overflow in the 1980s. As of 2019, roughly 5% of inmates were incarcerated in these private prisons, with two in particular domi-nating the space through a total of 125 correctional buildings. Those would be CoreCivic, which used to be Corrections Corporation of America, and The GEO Group.

Combined, the two have a $4 billion market value, which includes the facilities they operate for state and local governments, and those they triple-net lease to states.

CoreCivic was founded in 1983 and the GEO Group in 1984, with both becoming REITs in 2013. While CoreCivic renounced its REITship in 2020, electing to become a regular C-corp again, we're including it in our evaluation here in case it changes its status again sometime in the future.

Contrary to certain criticisms, prison REITs are worthwhile entities that operate with the same – or better – standards as government-operated facilities do. Yet they cost taxpayers 5–15% less per inmate according to some estimates. Even so, it's not uncommon for them to come under attack by non-profit organi-zations, politicians, and even financial institutions. Neither private prison entity can get further financing from Bank of America, JPMorgan, or Wells Fargo, for instance.

It's a rough business to be in all around. (See Figure 8.3.)

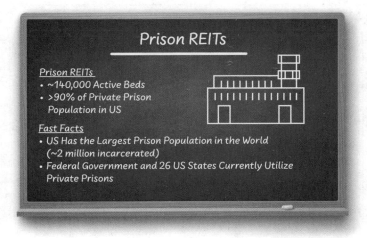

Figure 8.3
Source: Wide Moat Research.

Timber

There are about 200 million acres worth of commercially forested timberlands in the U.S., most of which can be found in the Pacific Northwest and the South. Even with the last few years being filled with forest fires, there are still more trees in the country than existed a century ago. That's in part because of timberland companies that are very invested in maintaining and even growing the existing amount.

The past four decades has seen a lot of consolidation in the timberland industry, but it remains very fragmented, with thousands of individual and corporate owners dotting the landscape. This includes four timber REITs, a subsector that first appeared in 1999. Each one has earned either Sustainable Forestry Initiative (SFI) or Forest Stewardship Council (FSC) approval. In part, this is because they usually plant many more trees than they harvest in any given year.

Together, CatchMark Timber, Rayonier, Weyerhaeuser, and PotlatchDeltic own almost 30 million acres and account for roughly $30 billion in market value. The first two are more pure-play companies that focus very heavily on supplying timber. Therefore, their shares are very commodities-related. The second two, however, have greater hands in timber-related production processes, making them more like "normal" stocks.

The larger lumber industry is crucial to the economic landscape, since traditional single-family homes in the U.S. are built mostly from wood – 150 to 300 trees per house. (The material is even being used more often in multifamily and commercial buildings.) You could easily make the argument that timber REITs are therefore a play on the housing market. And since the pandemic sent homebuilding "through the roof," we're looking at greater demand going forward, possibly for the rest of the decade. In which case, it would be a bright change over the previous one.

After the Great Recession, the need for new homes fell significantly as few people wanted to take the risk of building up to another bubble – and another crash. The love of homeownership decreased as well, with many opting to rent instead. Therefore, even as economic confidence began to increase, new home construction lagged, leaving existing examples aging. Admittedly, that sort of

Figure 8.4
Source: Wide Moat Research.

environment provides an opportunity for timber REITs too, this time in the home repair and remodeling arena.

It also needs to be stated that these specialty real estate investment trusts don't just grow and harvest trees. They also offer value through the real estate they own, which they can and do lease out to miners, energy companies, and recreational groups. Some of them also operate mills to turn raw product into more immediately useful offerings such as engineered wood or paper. (See Figure 8.4.)

Farmland (*Contributed by* David Gladstone)

Farmland is an extremely stable asset, an extremely diverse one, and an extremely evolving one, with advances being made every year in plant genetics, machinery, irrigation, and so much more. It's also an extremely regulated industry, both by the USDA and state agencies. That latter factor is how we know that the U.S. holds around $2.7 trillion of farmland, with 80% of it owned privately.

Contrary to popular opinion, not all of that farmland consists of corn or grains, such as wheat. Though it is true that U.S. grain fields – mainly found in the Midwest – produce enormous amounts of produce every year. Then again, so do many former Soviet countries, as well as Brazil and Argentina. The result is that the commodity doesn't cost much at all, making it difficult for farmers in the U.S. to make a living that way.

But there are also farms that supply fruit, vegetables, and nuts; dairy farms; and those that raise livestock for food supply. And again, most of these are run by individuals or families. Either way, it's extremely fragmented and therefore difficult for investors to get involved in – outside of the opportunities provided by farmland REITs Gladstone Land and Farmland Partners.

In February 2020, The Motley Fool's Millionacres publication accurately listed these three reasons to invest in farmland as a real estate play: low volatility, low correlation, and as an inflationary hedge. In other words, this asset doesn't tend to be as subject to market irrationality as so many other sectors are, "including the 10-year U.S. Treasury bond, S&P 500, gold, and Dow Jones REIT Index," which makes it impressive right from the start.

As for low correlation, farmland does experience its cycles just like every other investment. Yet it's not likely to lose favor at the same time as other classes, thereby helping to balance portfolios out during otherwise tough times. Just as worth noting is how it's practically inflation-proof. As inflation goes up, so should the real-asset value of both acreage value and crop income. Obviously, that's a major perk of investing in these kinds of companies. (See Figure 8.5.)

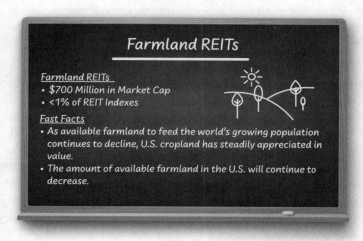

Figure 8.5
Source: Wide Moat Research.

Cannabis (*Contributed by* Paul Smithers)

Cannabis REITs – those that rent out land and buildings to marijuana producers – operate within a very complicated field. As of November 2020, 35 U.S. states and Washington, D.C., have legalized cannabis for medical use, recreational use, or both. Therefore, a large majority of the U.S. population now has some government-approved access to marijuana. And most if not all the places that have decriminalized it are implementing robust regulated programs to ensure product quality and safety, proper distribution, and responsible consumption.

As for states that still don't allow it, ArcView Market Research and BDSA both forecast that all 50 will have authorized at least medical cannabis by 2025, and nearly half will be permitting more than that. That represents enormous growth potential, to say the least. The regulated market already expanded to an estimated $12.4 billion in 2019, a 37% increase over 2018. And for 2020, experts believe it employed roughly 245,000 to 295,000 full-time workers. Looking forward, it's expected to approach $34 billion by 2025 (again, according to ArcView and BDSA).

Polling of U.S. citizens also continually shows 90%+ support for medical-use cannabis and strong support for regulated recreational programs too. While the federal classification of cannabis has significantly hampered formal research into its alleged therapeutic properties, state-run studies show a variety of potential treatments for HIV/AIDs, pain, nausea, seizures, muscle spasms, multiple sclerosis, PTSD, migraines, arthritis, Parkinson's disease, Alzheimer's, lupus, and terminal illness, to name a few.

With that said, cannabis continues to be classified as a Schedule I controlled substance under the Controlled Substances Act of 1970. That means, under federal law, possessing, cultivating, producing, and distributing remains illegal. Several bills have been introduced in Congress to change financial regulations concerning cannabis and allow states to develop their own programs without interference from the federal government. But none have passed as of this publication, so there continues to be extreme inconsistency between federal and state laws on the subject.

Given their requirements to strictly adhere to federal law, traditional financial institutions have been reluctant to participate in the industry. This includes state-chartered banks and other local entities that maintain federal deposit insurance. Cannabis operators and those working with them must therefore turn to a much smaller pool made up of private equity and debt investors for funding. Without that and other creative measures, the larger-scale industry doesn't stand a chance.

Producing marijuana legally is capital-intensive. And, naturally, the bigger the production, the more capital intensive it becomes. Large-scale facilities require highly specialized buildouts with exacting environmental controls in order to generate consistent, high-quality products and meet the specifications of robust state rules. So, to better handle those expenses, many operators have turned to alternative capital solutions such as sale-leaseback trans-actions and tenant improvement funding under long-term leases. These can offer key sources of capital, both for them and the institu-tions that own the land they work off of.

The cannabis real estate market is generally highly fragmented. And the only pure-play REIT that has staked its claim here is Innovative Industrial Properties. Founded in 2016 by REIT veteran Alan Gold, it's since created a portfolio of over five million rent-able square feet spanning 16 states. However, Power REIT and AFC Gamma are also making big plays in the subsector.

Innovative Industrial boasts some of the top names in the industry as its tenants, a roster it works hard to cultivate. With access to the public markets, IIP is also uniquely positioned to provide growth capital to its existing tenants over time. It's teamed up with a large percentage of its tenant base in follow-on transactions in other states and continued enhancements of capacity at existing properties to meet rapidly growing demand.

The company focuses on long-term, triple-net leases, with double-digit initial yields and annual escalations. This appeals to oper-ators, who get to maintain full control over their mission-critical facilities. Yet it works just as well for Innovative Industrial, giving it a weighted-average lease term of over 16 years as of the date of this writing. Any REITs to follow in this field will no doubt be taking some significant notes from this frontrunner.

Don't overlook, however, that the regulated cannabis industry is still very, very young. It only faced its first recession in 2020, so we only have so much to go off of in analyzing it. Yet, so far, it's shown a rather unique resiliency in maintaining its healthy growth thanks

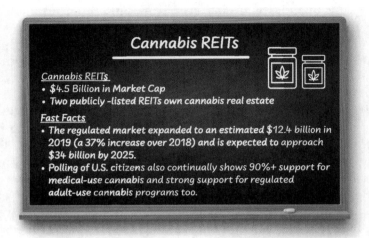

Figure 8.6
Source: Wide Moat Research.

to the large majority of state and local jurisdictions deeming it "essential" to continue working as usual. So it only stands to reason that post-pandemic numbers can increase even more. In short, the window of opportunity continues to be open for cannabis real estate companies to continue advancing in their role as long-term partners to best-in-class regulated cannabis operators. (See Figure 8.6.)

CHAPTER

REITs: Mysteries and Myths

"The essence of investment management is the management of risks, not the management of returns."

—Benjamin Graham

The more time that progresses, the more REITs have a chance to settle into investors' minds as investing norms. That's especially been true this century, as one REIT after another was ushered onto the S&P 500 index. It began with Equity Office Properties – the largest REIT at the time – in October 2001 and progressed from there. By the end of 2019, there were 31 such listings, representing $773 billion in market value, according to Nareit.

This isn't to say that everyone knows about them. They're still somewhat "niche-ish" and too often viewed as an alternative to Treasury Bills and utilities on a yield-comparison analysis. Even so, there are a growing number of people becoming very familiar with them as the long-term wealth-builders they are. And that's an intense improvement from the hard feelings and misunderstandings of the past.

Some investors have walked away from REITs because of the unique combination they offer, being both real estate and stock plays at the same time. That's hardly a traditional mix. Traditionally, you were either a landlord or a business big enough to be publicly listed. The two didn't combine. And though REITs trade as stocks by another name, that other name can make investors tense, automatically conjuring up the potential for complicated buying, selling, and tax operations.

Today, we know that REITs tend to trade like equities in the short term, while medium- and long-term holders will see the returns of the underlying business. But that understanding requires a somewhat intimate investing relationship with the sector, something not everyone has. People too often have their preconceived notions instead.

Let's face it: Traditionally, most real estate investors have chosen to put their money directly into property by buying up apartment complexes, shopping centers, malls, office buildings, or industrial properties, either individually or with partners. And since real estate values have climbed since the Great Depression, that can work out well with the right amount of planning and a little bit of luck, as we touched on in Chapter 3.

Ten percent appreciation on a building bought with 25% cash down generates 40% investment returns – not to mention a tax shelter via depreciation expenses for property-operating income. So it's understandable that some real estate investors don't want to throw away their financial independence and expertise to faceless fund managers who could squander their money over months, or speculators and day traders who could do the same over a much shorter span.

The perception is that REIT shares aren't tangible assets. Traditional real estate purchases are. And REIT prices could fluctuate too easily. Traditional real estate purchases couldn't and wouldn't.

On that last complaint, I'll bring up two points, the first being that REITs are typically less volatile than other stocks. Besides, every asset value fluctuates. It's only a matter of how easily those fluctuations are recognized. Some are hard to see on a day-to-day basis. There's also the factor we've previously discussed, which is that "volatility" is tied in with freedom, as in the freedom to sell one's assets easily should the need or desire arise. Though that deserves a clarification in and of itself.

Let's remember that the REIT vehicle was an invention of real estate developers and managers who used the business trust vehicle to invest and own real estate. The evolution since has been slow but steady, with more and more qualified businesses choosing to adopt this title as it was gradually modernized to fit with the reality of owning and operating commercial real estate.

While REITs have been around for 60 years now, this market was very thinly traded before 1994. As previously hinted at, it's only been in the last quarter-century that institutional investors have considered them worth buying into. Even a decade ago, pension funds were showing reluctance to get involved due to liquidity issues. That's not a problem anymore, but the tradeoff is more volatility, all made possible by the sector's increasing size and liquidity.

Here's the bottom line, though: According to a 2020 CEM Benchmarking analysis sponsored by Nareit analysis that covered over 200 public- and private-sector pensions with combined assets under management (AUM) of \$3.9 trillion, REITs placed second for average annual returns out of the 12 asset classes between 1998 and 2018. Moreover, listed equity REITs returned an annual 10.2%, whereas private real estate came in at about 7.5% – some 270 basis points less than their corporate counterparts.

Here's another bias that needs to be addressed: For the longest time, common stock investors were conditioned to think in terms of products and services. That's where the money was. It didn't help that so many of the more intrepid members of their community who invested in construction-lending REITs and real estate limited partnerships in the 1970s and 1980s got badly burned. So they pegged all publicly traded real estate entities into the same category marked "Do Not Touch."

Furthermore, they saw REITs as the equivalent of real estate mutual funds. It wasn't until the Tax Reform Act of 1986 allowed REITs to manage their own properties that perceptions began to change – slowly. More progress was made in 2001 when the IRS ruled them to be active businesses, and again with the allowance of UPREITs.

Throughout this – and even today – there's also still that crowd that believes high dividends equal low growth. Wrong though that notion is, these people understandably assume that a company faithfully paying out a high percentage of its earnings won't have much left to invest in itself. As for income investors, many remain content to stick with bonds, electric utilities, and the like.

Brokers haven't exactly helped any of these misconceptions either over the years. Until about 30 years ago, most major firms didn't bother to employ REIT analysts. Ipso facto, most of their clients never even thought about the option. Again, many of these issues have been cleared up this far into the twenty-first century. But some myths should still be addressed.

Myth #1: REITs Are Packages of Real Estate Properties

Most of the earliest REITs were, in many respects, only collections of properties, or "real estate mutual funds." This isn't surprising since they were modeled after mutual fund rules and regulations. But, as I've said and will continue to say, they've come a long way since then.

Any kind of asset that simply owns properties while relying on outside companies to manage them does present undesirable possibilities for investors. For one thing, they might very well be paying dues and fees to people who don't actually care about providing superior performance in return: people who are paid regardless of how the portfolio does. So there's too often no long-term vision or strategy to create a safe and steadily growing asset for "the little people" backing it. And even if they do care, they might not have the financial ability to take advantage of promising opportunities that come their way.

In stark contrast, most REITs today are first and foremost vibrant, dynamic real estate business organizations. The "investment trust" part of their designation comes second. Therefore, they're extremely motivated to grow in all the right ways that benefit not just them but also their tenants and backers. And they plan intelligently as a general rule with the capital to act on those plans.

Better yet, because they're public entities, they operate under the scrutiny of buy- and sell-side analysts, pension fund analysts, and a host of requirements the SEC imposes on them. Included in the rigors of being public are having a diverse board of directors, transparent corporate governance that's accountable to investors and analysts, and REIT ownership via a liquid security that can be bought and sold in an open market daily.

People who shun them as mere property collections do themselves a disfavor much more than they hurt the REITs they're avoiding.

Myth #2: Real Estate Is a High-Risk Investment

For many years, the real estate industry was boom and bust, with high risks and high rewards. But REITs provide a means to "get rich slow" for small investors who want to avoid the swashbuckling days of private real estate machinations. Far too many people believe that real estate is a high-risk investment that can decimate their net worth by way of difficult tenants and property-value declines. (In which case, the 2008 crash didn't help.) Ipso facto, REIT investing must also be risky.

Part of their suspicions comes down to the debt leverage used in real estate for both individual properties and wider portfolios. But every business relies on that kind of book balancing to some degree or another. For that matter, every investor who buys stocks on margin does the same. The more debt a person or company uses, the greater the potential gain or loss, since a small decline in the asset's value will cause a much larger decline in one's investment in it – or vice versa.

Besides, many REITs have earned the trust of the capital markets and investors alike in this regard. And the larger concept is a credible and trusted means for investors to co-invest with large public companies managed by knowledgeable real estate and public market leaders.

For now, we'll leave it at that. But Chapter 12 will cover leverage in further depth. Until then, let's once again acknowledge that REITs do have their risks. That's why you diversify, holding a portfolio that's properly balanced between appropriate investment categories, real estate included.

Appropriate diversification should be the mantra of every investor, even within each asset class one owns. In which case, REITs do the trick with their collective tenants spread across multiple sectors – from technology to retail to the medical community and beyond – and their individual businesses investing in multiple properties.

Finally, we have to go back to management, which makes an enormous difference. That might seem like an obvious statement, and perhaps it should be. But it's also very easily taken for granted. As we'll discuss in further detail in Chapter 10 (as previously promised), good management teams acquire the best properties and attract the best tenants. Plus, they really can create value in addition to the cash flow from their tenants.

Real estate, like any other business investment, can't simply be bought and ignored. Maintaining it, much less growing it, requires active, capable, hands-on oversight. Solid executive teams choose lucrative properties to purchase and avoid those that won't appreciate appropriately. And, as alluded to earlier, public REIT CEOs operate in the open with analysts and regulators watching their every move. Between that and their legal structure, there's a lot of pressure on their executives – and a lot of very impressive results.

Myth #3: Real Estate Is Merely an Inflation Hedge

Because real estate consists of a building or buildings situated on a plot or plots of land, it's a tangible asset like copper, gold, oil, or scrap metal. So its value will ebb and flow, including via inflation. The key word there, however, is "including." There are plenty of other factors that influence its worth, from supply of and demand for space, to economic conditions, interest rates, consumer spending, government policies, global conflicts, commodity prices, and investment trends.

Investors in the 1970s may be somewhat excused for seeing it more simply. Real estate did indeed do well during that inflationary period, while stock ownership didn't, comparatively speaking. This was probably a coincidence, however. Or perhaps it was driven by market psychology.

Regardless, there have been studies done that show how the equity market and real estate markets can each serve as long-term inflation hedges. And over time, neither is substantially better or worse in this regard since different factors are constantly at play or waiting to come into play.

On the positive side for real estate, this can lead to boosted rental rates under properly balanced conditions. On the negative side, inflation can increase operating expenses such as property maintenance, management costs, insurance, and taxes. In some markets, these higher costs of operating can be passed through to the tenants.

Higher inflation can also negatively affect real estate in regard to the Federal Reserve, which acts as a watchdog for inflation. When there's a perceived inflationary threat, the Fed will raise short-term interest rates to slow the economy – which can then prompt a recession, which can then make it difficult for property owners to maintain their rental rates and occupancy levels.

Inflation can affect the price of real estate as well. Property value is often at least partially determined by applying a multiple to its existing or forward-looking annual net operating income or, alternatively, its cap rate. But those figures fluctuate. Admittedly, some buyers will pay more or accept a lower cap rate during inflationary periods. Since investors view real estate as a hard asset, they may be willing to put more money down for the promise of inflation-based higher rents.

But there's also the opposite position, which says that higher inflation can drive up interest rates, which then increases the "hurdle rate of return" demanded by investors in a property. This then bumps up cap rates and decreases perceived values. Conversely, property values may rise even when there's no inflation, such as in 2003–2005 when inflation was at a modest level. It happened again in 2010, when inflation was almost nonexistent.

Consider it this way: If demand for apartment units in a given city exceeds supply, rents will increase, as will the owner's NOI. However, if that's all due to an overheated economy that prompts higher interest rates to cool things down, the cap rate applied to the net operating income might also rise, which could then decrease the property's price.

Then again, if supply exceeds demand, rents and net operating income may weaken while value still rises. This can occur if a lower cap rate is applied to that NOI because a buyer is willing to accept a more modest return on his or her investment – all of which has little to do with inflation.

Real estate replacement costs usually rise during inflationary periods. But that doesn't automatically increase a property's market value if its profitability falls short of a buyer's requirements. It only means that new models probably won't go up until market values approach replacement cost again. So don't think that properties can't trade at prices well below replacement cost for substantial periods of time.

In short, there's always a market clearing price for real estate that benefits the buyer or seller depending on whether or not the bulls are running real estate perception or the bears are.

Myth #4: REIT Performance Is Anchored to REIT Property Performance

Because REITs own and operate commercial real estate, their performance and investment returns are closely related to commercial real estate markets over time. But there are other factors involved.

Rapid global industrialization, for one, is a major and long-lasting phenomenon that pits U.S. companies against foreign competitors virtually everywhere. This has led them to cut costs via downsizings, restructurings, and outsourcing. In and of itself, that could lead to moderate returns for commercial real estate investors. Add in Covid-19 then, and you had a definite drain on corporate cash flow, though only a temporary one. Most property sectors believe they'll grow earnings and total returns in the next few years. And some REITs, especially those tied to technology, even outperformed in 2020.

That's obvious good news for their investors. If a moderately expanding economy can spur average free cash flow growth of 2–3% . . . and if REITs can increase that to, say, 4% through modest amounts of debt leverage, then 8% average annual total returns could easily happen. (Yields were averaging 3.7% for all REITs and 3.97% for equity REITs at the end of 2019, per Nareit data.) That should then make them very competitive with other investments bearing similar risks.

With that said, history has shown their performance and profitability can beat the vast commercial real estate markets a number of ways. For instance, smart management teams view difficult conditions – even tenant bankruptcies – as growth- and value-creation opportunities. As mentioned in Chapter 3, this occurred most dramatically in the early 1990s. With real estate markets in disarray, many REITs were able to buy quality assets at unusually cheap prices. One healthcare REIT was actually able to acquire loans secured by nursing homes at 16–18% yields.

Many expected a similar event to unfold in 2010 due to the commercial mortgage-backed securities (CMBS) debacle. However, very low interest rates, lenders' not-entirely-altruistic willingness to work with troubled borrowers, and ample saved capital prevented this from happening. Nevertheless, when space markets are favorable, gifted property developers can create substantial value one way or another. The reverse can obviously be true as well, but that kind of mismanagement isn't nearly as common.

Also keep in mind that REIT shares are priced as stocks first and real estate second. Therefore, they look forward, estimating future worth rather than current value. This isn't completely inaccurate either considering how, unlike with direct real estate owners, REITs enjoy external growth prospects in most environments.

That's what made the 2020 pandemic sell-off so irrational for them (and so many other stocks). Shares in many high-quality companies fell 40–50%, while the private real estate market saw no significant price changes whatsoever. As a result, uninitiated REIT investors either lost out or missed out on substantial gains, whereas their savvier counterparts were able to purchase shares at huge discounts.

Myth #5: REIT Stocks Are Trading Vehicles

Just because REITs are tied to commodity prices doesn't mean they should be traded that way. Although speculators could theoretically dance in and out of positions at times, these stocks are best when owned, not traded. And thinking otherwise can lead to dangerous losses and missed opportunities.

As a category, REITs are the ultimate buy-and-hold investment. Their 10-year compound annual total return as of December 31, 2019, was 12.59%, according to Nareit, which is very competitive with the broader equities markets.

And over all meaningful time periods, REITs' total returns have averaged in the double digits. Close to 50% of the returns they offer investors can come from dividend yields, depending on the period. So shareholders literally get paid to wait for their holdings to appreciate in price. REITs aren't typically growth stocks, but they still make the journey very worth the while.

In fact, most market wealth happens when investors buy and hold excellent companies in their portfolios. There's very little evidence that stock traders and market timers make consistent amounts of money in general.

For REITs specifically, in order to successfully time a purchase and sale, one must be able to accurately forecast 1) the short-term and long-term direction of interest rates, inflation, and unemployment; 2) real estate markets throughout the U.S.; 3) capital flows of both institutions and individuals; and 4) every other factor that determines real estate and stock prices. Since this can't be done consistently, 99% of investors, if not more, are advised against even bothering.

CHAPTER

10

REITs: Growth and Value Creation

"If past history were all there was to the game, the richest people would be librarians."

—Warren Buffett

W arren Buffett has famously said, "In the short run, the market is a voting machine, but in the long run it is a weighing machine." I think what he meant by this is that share prices are moved, in the short term, by transient investor psychology and insubstantial news. But over the long term, a stock's price is determined by its intrinsic value.

Therefore, if a stock is to rise in price over time, the company's fundamental value must increase on a per-share basis. There are a number of ways to measure increases in company value, but measuring and valuing streams of income and cash flows is perhaps the most commonly used metric in the world of equities.

There are, of course, other metrics. Although not very popular today, book value has been used by some investors to determine the worth of a stock. But book value is based on historical cost minus depreciation. So it doesn't reflect the current market values of company assets, many of which are worth much more – or less – today. And how can it help determine the fair values of intangible assets such as brand names, superior management teams, and customer goodwill?

A number of countries outside the United States have adopted fair value accounting, which measures real-time estimates of the market value of certain types of assets. Accordingly, most U.S. investors generally value stocks – even those of companies owning commercial real estate – on the basis of net income and EBITDA. As such, they make earnings a key determinant of share price. Sure enough, steadily rising earnings normally indicate that a REIT is generating higher income from its properties and perhaps making favorable acquisitions or completing profitable developments as well. Higher income is also usually a precursor of dividend growth.

That's why most REIT investors assume that a growing stream of cash flow means higher share prices, increased dividends, and higher asset values over time. This assumption isn't always valid, however, since growth in income and cash flows can be "bought" through increases in debt leverage. That means it's sometimes fleeting. Conversely, a REIT can create value for its shareholders through investment activities that aren't immediately reflected in current income or cash flows. However, as income metrics are most easily quantifiable and are used by most equity investors – and remain important – let's consider them first.

The Significance of FFO

Investors in common stock generally use net income as a key measure of profitability, with the term clearly defined under GAAP. Since most REITs are publicly traded companies, they will always list net income and net income per share on their annual audited financial statements. And unaudited net income is reported quarterly.

Yet these net income figures are less meaningful for REITs than they are for other types of companies. The reason for this is that, in accounting, real estate depreciation is always treated as an expense. But in the real world, not only have most competitive properties retained their value over the years, but many have appreciated substantially. This is generally due to a combination of rising land prices due to inflation and increasing construction costs, steadily rising rental and operating income, and property upgrades. That's why REITs tend to report FFO as well, which adds real estate depreciation under GAAP back into net income.

When calculating FFO, there are other adjustments that should be made as well, such as subtracting from net income any capital gain income recorded from the sale of properties. The reason for this is that REITs can't have it both ways. They can't ignore depreciation, which reduces a property's carrying costs on the balance sheet, and then include the capital gain from selling that property above the price at which it's been carried. Furthermore, GAAP net income is normally determined after "straight-lining," or smoothing out, contractual rental income over the term of a lease. But in real life, rental income on a multiyear property lease will often rise from year to year.

For this reason, some investors, when examining FFO, adjust reported rent revenues to reflect the actual contractual rental revenues received during the reporting period.

Funds from Operations (FFO)

Historically, FFO was defined in different ways by different REITs, which caused investor confusion. To address this problem, Nareit stepped in. In 1999, it refined its definition of FFO to mean "net income computed in accordance with GAAP, excluding gains (or losses) from sales of property, plus depreciation and amortization, and after adjustments for unconsolidated partnerships and joint ventures. Adjustments for unconsolidated partnerships and joint ventures should be calculated to reflect funds from operations on the same basis."

Even so, there are a number of problems with FFO. For one thing, commercial properties can, in fact, slowly decline in value year after year, due to wear and obsolescence. Owners have to invest in occasional improvements and structural replacements if a property's value is to be retained (e.g., new roofs or better lighting). Merely adding back depreciation to net income then when determining FFO can provide a distorted and overly rosy picture of operating results and cash flows. It fails to account for these major but recurring capital expenditures.

Also, items that investors should consider part of ordinary property maintenance (e.g., an apartment building's carpeting, curtains, and dishwashers) are usually capitalized and depreciated rather than expensed for accounting purposes. But since FFO ignores those depreciation expenses, it's artificially inflated, giving a misleading picture of a REIT's real cash flow. Practically speaking, carpeting and related items really do depreciate over time, and the costs to replace them are real and recurring.

Additionally, commissions paid to leasing agents when renting offices or other properties are usually capitalized, then amortized and written off over the term of the lease. But paying leasing commissions can perhaps stabilize or improve occupancy; however, it doesn't add anything to the property's value. It's a real expense that, when ignored in calculating FFO, will overstate profits and cash flows. The same can be said about tenant improvement allowances, such as those provided to office and retail tenants. These are out-of-pocket costs that are often so specific to particular tenants' needs that they don't increase the property's long-term value.

Finally, not all REITs capitalize and expense similar items in similar ways when reporting their FFO. Some ignore noncash investment write-offs, for example, while others do not. Some even include certain property sale gains. Simply put, there's a lack of consistency here.

But all is not lost. The concept of adjusted funds from operations (AFFO), which was coined many years ago by Green Street, a leading REIT research firm, can help remedy some of those deficiencies. (See Figure 10.1.)

What Is FFO?

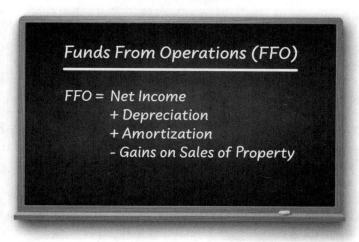

Figure 10.1
Source: Wide Moat Research.

Adjusted Funds from Operations (AFFO)

AFFO begins with a REIT's FFO and adjusts for expenditures that, though capitalized, don't enhance property value. It also eliminates rent straight-lining. This makes it a reasonable, albeit imprecise, measure of operating performance and a fairly effective tool to measure free cash generation and dividend health.

Unfortunately, REITs don't regularly report AFFO since there's no single accepted definition for the term. Investors and analysts usually have to calculate it on their own by reviewing financial statements and related footnotes and schedules. Knowing that, the following is an oversimplified, but perhaps useful, way of looking at this methodology:

1. All revenues (including capital gains), less operating expenses, write-offs, depreciation, amortization, interest expense, and general and administrative expenses = **Net Income**.
2. Net income, less capital gains from real estate sales, plus real estate depreciation expenses = **FFO**.
3. FFO, less normal and recurring capital expenditures, amortization of tenant improvements and leasing commissions, adjusted to remove rent straight-lining and any gains or losses on the early extinguishment of debt = **AFFO**.

In addition, since AFFO is intended to measure current and recurring cash flows, noncash write-downs of property investments due to impairment charges are usually added back too.

Noting the problems with FFO, Nareit Vice President of Financial Standards George L. Yungmann and Director of Financial Standards David M. Taube noted in the May/June 2001 issue of *Real Estate Portfolio*:

> A single metric may not appropriately satisfy the need for both a supplemental earnings measure and a cash flow measure.

They suggested using a term such as adjusted net income (ANI), which is GAAP net income prior to extraordinary items, effects of accounting changes, any results of discontinued operations, and other unusual nonrecurring items, as a supplemental

Figure 10.2
Source: Wide Moat Research.

earnings measurement. Each REIT would then be free to supplement ANI by reporting a cash flow measure such as FFO, AFFO,
CAD, or FAD. This is an interesting concept that hasn't received
the attention it deserves. So we're left with net income, FFO, and
AFFO after all.

When determining AFFO, some analysts and investors look at
actual capital expenditures incurred during a reporting period.
Others apply a long-term average to smooth out periods of unusually high or low capital expenditures. Still others try to determine a
"normalized" figure based on historical experience for the REIT over
several years. There's no "right" or "wrong" approach here, but it's
important to always compare apples to apples one way or the other.
We must always be aware of how these supplements to net income
reporting are calculated by or for each REIT. (See Figure 10.2.)

The Dynamics of FFO/AFFO Growth

One of REITs' most attractive attributes is their significant
long-term capital appreciation potential and increasing dividends.
If a REIT is viewed as having virtually no capacity to grow its FFO,
AFFO, or dividend, its shares would be bought only for yield. After

all, its dividend can be cut far too easily. As such, growth-challenged REITs normally offer higher yields than those of most bonds and preferred stocks. And their prices might be closely correlated with high-yield (or "junk") bonds.

However, investors looking for the best total returns from combined dividend yield and capital appreciation will look for REITs whose dividends aren't just safe. They should also have good long-term growth prospects. Wouldn't you rather own a REIT that pays a 4 percent return with a 5 percent average annual growth rate than one that pays 7 percent but doesn't grow at all?

Keep in mind that REIT distributions are composed of income, capital gains, and return of capital, each of which can offer tax advantages. REIT income is considered qualified business income (QBI), which is entitled to a 20% deduction as of the 2020 tax year, reducing the top tax rate from 37% to 29.6% (not including the 3.8% Medicare surcharge on all tax rates). And this is true regardless of income level, itemizing, or standard deductions. Capital gains are typically taxed at a maximum rate of 20%, while ROC is treated as a deferred capital gain.

Before REITs had become widely followed, they were often priced so cheaply that they offered the best of both worlds – a 5% yield *and* 5-6% annual growth. According to Nareit statistics, for the 40-year period through June 2019, REITs delivered an average annual total return of 11.38%.

Monthly Total Returns Through June 2019

	1 year	3 year	5 year	10 year	15 year	20 year	25 year	30 year	35 year	40 year
FTSE Nareit All Equity REITs	13.01	5.92	8.88	16.03	9.41	10.66	10.57	10.51	11.06	12.02
FTSE EPRA/Nareit Developed	8.64	5.45	5.79	$11.45	8.00	8.83	8.40	N/A	N/A	N/A
Russell 1000 (Large-Cap Stocks)	10.02	14.15	10.45	14.77	8.94	6.19	10.09	10.13	11.45	11.81
Russell 2000 (Small-Cap Stocks)	-3.31	12.30	7.06	13.45	8.15	7.77	9.26	9.29	9.83	10.92
Bloomberg Barclays US Aggregate Bond	7.87	2.31	2.95	3.90	4.27	4.93	5.50	5.99	7.21	7.32

Source: Nareit.

But some REITs are now priced more efficiently. So one with a 7% dividend yield normally suggests that investors perceive very low growth or that the shares are particularly risky.

When it comes to how these investments generate growth in FFO and AFFO (collectively referred to in the balance of this chapter, for convenience, as FFO), it's essential to look at it from a per-share basis. It does the shareholder no good if FFO grows rapidly because the REIT has issued large numbers of new shares. Such "prosperity" is meaningless – like a government printing more money in times of inflation.

In the following discussion, let's not forget that REITs must pay their shareholders at least 90% of their taxable net income each year. But, as a practical matter, most pay out considerably more than this since they normally factor in depreciation expenses when setting the dividend rate.

Since REITs can't retain much of their earnings for reinvestment, they have to find cash elsewhere to properly fund FFO growth through acquisitions or new developments. One way to do this is by selling existing assets, or they can open themselves up to joint ventures. But most of that new capital comes from selling new shares to investors – something that isn't always available or can be very expensive in terms of dilution to NAV. That's why looking for internal growth is so important.

Again, external growth through new developments, acquisitions, and the creation of ancillary revenue streams isn't always possible. There might be a lack of high-quality properties available at attractive prices, a scarcity of sufficiently profitable development opportunities, an inability to raise capital, or a high cost to such capital. Internal growth, however, is "organically" generated through existing assets, which are more under management's control.

One last note before we move on: FFO and its variants are important to measure current cash flows. But when valuing REIT stocks, many successful investors pay much more attention to estimated NAV, including whether it's been growing and will grow over time. We'll discuss that further in a later chapter. For now though, just know that a single-minded focus on FFO can lead investors astray.

Internal Growth

When a REIT increases profits from operating and managing its properties, it's enjoying internal growth. Controlling corporate overhead, interest, and other expenses is also very important in this regard. And, since internal growth rates don't depend on acquisitions, development, or raising additional capital, they tend to be stable and reliable – albeit usually in the low to mid single digits – during most economic environments.

This is where the terms "same-store sales," "revenue," and "net operating income" come into play, concepts borrowed from the retail industry. These refer to productivity from stores open for at least one year, and exclude sales from stores that have closed or from new stores, since new stores characteristically enjoy temporarily above-average sales growth. REITs report property rental revenues, expenses, and NOI on a quarterly basis, comparing them on a same-store – or more accurately, a same-property – basis. These comparisons present a good picture of how well they're doing with their owned properties over time.

Property owners, including REITs, use different tools to generate growth on a same-store basis. These tools include rental revenue increases, ancillary property revenue, upgrading tenant rolls, and upgrading or even expanding properties, as detailed below.

Rental Revenue Increases

Rental rates can be increased over time if a property is desirable to tenants. And higher occupancy rates can lead to even higher rental revenue since they give owners greater negotiating leverage with existing and new tenants alike. Nevertheless, raising rents is not always possible, and there are periods in virtually every sector's full cycle when such revenue actually falls rather than rises.

In bad economies, even raising rents slightly might be counterproductive. The hassle and cost of finding new tenants, if possible, and of properly preparing the space for them just isn't always worth it. Many other factors, such as supply and demand, space market conditions, the property's age and condition, and tenant amenities can also enhance or restrict rental revenue increases.

But most owners of well-maintained properties in markets where supply and demand are in balance will, on average and over time, continue to get rental revenue increases that at least equal to inflation. At least that's what you should expect from a REIT in general. Some will, of course, get better rental increases upon lease renewal than others. And, of course, management's leasing capabilities are also very important.

Trying to determine which REITs have better-than-average potential same-store rental revenue and NOI growth is one of the challenges – and some of the fun – of REIT investing.

How to Build Internal Growth into a Lease

Many property owners have been able to obtain above-average increases in rental revenue by focusing on tenants' needs and financial ability to pay higher effective rental rates. These methods include percentage rents, rent bumps, and expense sharing and recovery.

"Percentage-rent" clauses in retail store leases enable the property owner to participate in store revenue if it exceeds certain preset levels. For example, if a store's sales exceed $5 million in any calendar year, it would pay the landlord 3% of the excess. The extent to which lessees will sign this kind of agreement depends on property type and location, market conditions, negotiating leverage, base rent, and the property owner's reputation for maintaining an attractive environment. While this is usually applied to retail, REITs have sometimes been able to structure healthcare leases with similar considerations.

Fixed "rent bumps," meanwhile, are contractual lease clauses that provide for periodic built-in rent increases. As mentioned at the beginning of this book, these are sometimes negotiated at fixed dollar amounts or based on an index of inflation, such as the Consumer Price Index. Property owners who enter into long-term leases are often able to structure them so that the base rent increases periodically, thus providing built-in same-store NOI growth.

Then there's "expense sharing," or "cost recovery." That's a practice where each lessee pays its pro rata share of property expenses incurred by the property owner. Owners have included "cost-sharing," or common area maintenance (CAM), recovery clauses in their leases to recover rising property maintenance and sometimes even improvement expenses. These might include items such as janitorial services, security, and advertising and promotional costs.

Cost-sharing lease clauses improve NOI, and thereby FFO, while tending to smooth out fluctuations in operating expenses from year to year. The degree to which they can be used once again depends on each property's supply/demand situation, location, and similar justifications.

Property Refurbishments

Refurbishment is a skill that can separate the innovative property owner from the passive one. This ability can turn a tired mall, neighborhood shopping center, office building, or so on into a vibrant, inviting property. The upgraded and beautified asset should attract a more stable tenant base command higher rents and, for retail properties, more shoppers. The returns to the REIT property owner on such investments will often run into the double digits.

Federal Realty, a well-regarded retail REIT, has been generating outstanding returns from turning tired properties into more exciting, upscale, open-air shopping complexes. Many apartment REITs, including Mid-America Apartment Communities, and UDR Inc., have been buying apartment buildings with deferred maintenance problems or with significant upgrade potential at attractive prices, then transforming them with new window treatments and upgraded kitchens.

And Alexandria Real Estate, which focuses on the office/laboratory niche of the office market and provides space for pharmaceutical, biotech, and other life science companies, has been successful with its redevelopment strategy, often earning double-digit returns. The lesson here for investors is that REITs with innovative management teams can create value for their shareholders through imaginative property refurbishing and tenant upgrade strategies.

Capital Recycling

REITs can also sell properties with lackluster future income growth prospects, then reinvest the proceeds elsewhere. These new opportunities might include the acquisition of properties that are likely to generate higher returns. Landlords can also initiate new development projects, make stock repurchases or preferred stock redemptions, or repay high-cost debt.

REITs should "clean house" from time to time and consider which properties to keep and which to sell, using the proceeds from the sale for reinvestment in more promising opportunities or even returning it to shareholders in the form of special dividends. This strategy may still be regarded as producing internal growth, since no fresh capital is required. Or it could at least add value for shareholders.

Truly entrepreneurial management teams are always looking to improve investment returns, and sale and reinvestment is a conservative and highly effective strategy. This practice, often referred to as "capital recycling," has become popular with REIT organizations ever since the capital markets slammed shut on them in mid-1998. And many REITs used it to sell properties as the market peaked in 2006 to 2007.

Figure 10.3 is an example of capital recycling. A property might be sold at a 6% cap rate with a prospective long-term annual return

Differentiated Behavior

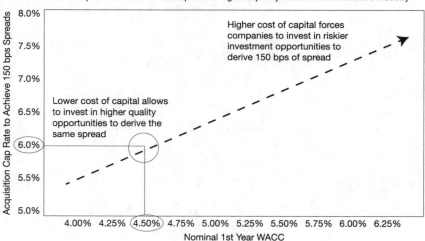

Investment Strategy: Utilizing Low Cost of Capital Advantage

Low cost of capital allows REITs to acquire the highest quality assets in the net lease industry

Figure 10.3

of 7%. The net proceeds would then be invested in another property that, with a modest investment of capital and upgraded tenant services, could provide a long-term average annual return of 8% or more after a year or two.

Funds reinvested in well-conceived and well-executed development projects can be equally profitable, as we'll discuss later. Sometimes a REIT will decide to exit an entire market if it doesn't like its long-term prospects. This can create value without requiring access to fresh capital. Most REIT management teams are always alert for new opportunities regardless.

There may be short-term costs in terms of temporary earnings dilution. Higher-quality assets that are acquired often trade at lower entry yields and cap rates than the lower-quality assets disposed of, particularly when the sale proceeds are used to pay down debt. But the long-term benefits of this strategy are typically substantial if executed with good judgment.

Technology Upgrades

COVID-19 has created an entirely new paradigm for multifamily landlords to rent their space. Due to social distancing practices, REITs like Essex Property Trust have utilized technology to showcase their sites to a single customer using multi-channel communication. Essex is now piloting its co-developed mobile leasing application, which enables customers to apply from their mobile phones while they finish their tour, even getting approved on the spot.

The company points out that "investments in technology and our Customer-Centric Operating Platform are expected to improve operating margins by 100–200 bps over the next two years."

Technology has also benefitted many self-storage landlords. Extra Space Storage, for one, touts its "Online Rapid Rental" model in which it tells prospective customers to "skip the reservation. Rent & move in now." In general, it generates strong earnings results because of its ability to utilize technology as a competitive advantage. The company has 39 million annual website views and spends over $30 million per year on digital marketing. It even employs 11 data scientists to help optimize pricing power.

There's also the office sector, where REITs are actively investing in technology to improve air quality and sanitization for healthier workplaces. And retail landlords have also benefitted from increased technology as a means to level the playing field. Simon Property Group has an e-commerce partnership with Rue Gilt Groupe that focuses on online value shopping. It also invests in next-generation commerce and retail technology through Simon Ventures.

NOI and IRR

Before we continue, let's pause to better understand net operating income. It's normally used to measure the net cash generated by an income-producing property. As such, NOI can be defined as recurring rental and other income from a property, less all operating expenses attributable to that property.

Operating expenses include real estate taxes, insurance, utility costs, property management, and sometimes recurring reserves for replacement. They don't include "corporate" items such as general and administrative expenses, interest expense, value-enhancing capital expenditures, and depreciation expense. Therefore, the term seeks to define how much cash is generated from the ownership and leasing of a commercial property.

Investors might reasonably expect NOI on a typical commercial real estate asset to grow about 2–3% annually, roughly in line with inflation, during most economic periods.

Another important term is internal rate of return (IRR). It helps calculate investors investment returns, including both returns on investment and returns of investment. It quantifies the percentage rate of return from all future cash receipts balanced against all cash investments and contributions. That way, when each receipt and con-tribution is discounted to net present value, the sum is equal to zero.

Or, to put it more simply, IRR is the real rate of return an investor expects when making the investment or, with hindsight, the rate of return obtained from the investment. Therefore, if the real estate investor requires a 10% return on a potential property, he or she won't buy it if it's believed the net present value of all future cash receipts – including any gain or loss on its eventual sale – won't likely equal or exceed 10%.

Of course, this requires some sharp-penciled calculations, including many assumptions concerning occupancy and rental rates, property expenses, growth in NOI, and what the property will be worth when sold at an assumed future date.

One of the reasons that so many real estate investors fared poorly in the early 1990s, and again in 2008 to 2010, is that the previous IRR assumptions they made were too aggressive. Perhaps the *real* value of IRR for potential acquisition opportunities isn't the resulting percentage derived from a single mathematical exercise. Rather, it comes from requiring prospective buyers to test the sensitivity of percentage returns under differing sets of performance assumptions.

They have to wonder, say, to what extent their expected IRR will be reduced if their NOI grows by only 2.5% rather than the expected 3.5%. hey have to consider what would happen if they had to sell the property at the end of their holding period at a price 5% below their purchase price.

As we've seen in this discussion, REITs' internal growth and value-creation opportunities are as numerous as their properties. In the hands of shrewd management, these options can be maximized so that results pay off for both the REIT and its investors.

External Growth

Let's assume that a widely respected REIT can obtain annual rental revenue increases slightly better than the rate of inflation of 3%. Let's also say that property expenses and overhead expense growth can be kept at less than that. And that, with modest, fixed-rate debt leverage, this REIT can increase its per-share FFO by 4 percent in a typical year.

Finally, let's assume that the well-managed REIT can achieve another 0.5% annual growth in FFO through tenant upgrades, refurbishments, and other internal means. How do we get from this 4.5% FFO growth rate to the 6–7% pace some REITs have been able to achieve quite often in the past? The answer is through *external* growth, as detailed next.

Acquisition Opportunities

The concept of acquiring additional properties at attractive initial yields with substantial NOI growth potential has been applied successfully for many years by a large number of well-regarded REITs.

For example, a REIT might raise $100 million by selling additional shares and medium-term unsecured notes. Allowing for the long-term cost of the newly issued shares and the interest costs on the debt, it might have a 7% weighted average cost of capital. The REIT would then use the proceeds to buy properties that, including initial yields, additional growth from property income increases, and some capital appreciation over time, might generate IRRs of 8%.

The net result of such transactions would be a pickup of 100 basis points over the REIT's weighted average cost of capital. We must keep in mind, however, that near-term FFO "accretion" (obtaining initial yields on a new investment that will increase per-share FFO over the near term) might be fairly easy to calculate. Yet it's much less important than finding and acquiring properties able to deliver longer-term IRRs that equal or exceed the REIT's true cost of capital. At certain times, this can be very difficult, muddying shareholder value in the process.

An effective acquisition strategy is difficult to implement if it can't raise equity capital or debt capital (when its balance sheet is already heavily leveraged or when capital markets are very tight). Furthermore, investors don't want their company to sell new equity if doing so would cause dilution to its FFO or estimated NAV. They want their REITs to patiently find the unusual acquisition opportunity at a bargain price – with the right funding to back it up.

The Cost of Equity Capital

To create value from external growth initiatives, a REIT must earn a return on any new investment that exceeds the cost of capital deployed. But what is the real cost to a REIT when it raises new capital from the issuance of shares?

There are several ways to calculate these expenses. "Nominal" cost of equity capital refers to the fact that a REIT's current cash flows (FFO or AFFO) and its asset values must be allocated among a larger number of common shares, Meanwhile, the "true" or "long-term" cost of equity capital considers such dilution over longer time periods by estimating shareholders' total return expectations on their invested capital.

Keep in mind that the cost of equity capital will rise as a REIT takes on more debt. And investors will expect higher returns to compensate for higher risk.

Yet, despite the importance of this concept, there seems to be no general agreement on how it should be calculated. As such, it's important to focus on the initial accretion to FFO from an acquisition as well as the probable longer-term IRR. Will the latter exceed the REIT's estimated weighted average cost of capital (WACC), which combines the cost of equity and the cost of debt? (For more discussion on cost of equity capital, see Appendix C.)

Even if reasonably attractive opportunities are available, REITs can't take advantage of them if their cost of capital exceeds likely returns. To use a perhaps extreme example, let's assume that "Gazelle REIT" has an aggressive business strategy and an equity capital cost of 12%. It wants to buy a package of quality properties that's expected to deliver an IRR of 7%.

Even if Gazelle finances the transaction by borrowing 50% of the purchase price at a 4% interest rate, it's probably a "no-go" from the investors' standpoint. Its WACC will be 8% (an equal blend of a 12% cost of equity capital and a 4% cost of debt capital), which exceeds the expected 7% return.

If Gazelle's cost of equity capital were 8% instead, though, the WACC would be 6%, and the deal would probably be deemed attractive.

Fortunately, calculating the cost of debt capital is fairly straightforward relative to the cost of equity capital. It's simply the interest a REIT pays for borrowed funds. Just make sure to use long-term interest rates, since drawdowns under a credit line and other forms of short-term debt must be repaid relatively quickly. Plus, they're subject to interest rate fluctuations.

Calculations should be based on rates for debt that will be outstanding for 5–10 years. Using the short-term rate would distort the picture, making it seem like a good idea for a REIT to borrow at 3% on a short-term basis and use the loan proceeds to buy properties with 6% IRR potential at a time when the cost of long-term debt is 6%. Which, for the record, it would not be.

We should also note that when professional real estate organizations like REITs acquire a property, they're often able to operate and manage it more efficiently and profitably than the prior owner. Thus, REITs often can obtain above-average internal growth from acquired properties beyond the initial expected yield through better control of expenses, even assuming no change in rents.

The largest apartment REIT, Equity Residential, often has been able to generate better profit margins than those selling apartment assets to it, and many other REITs have been able to do this as well.

I'd like to make two final points about property acquisitions:

- A REIT's weighted average cost of capital will change often with investor expectations, stock prices, borrowing costs, and other factors.
- A REIT whose shares trade in the market at a relatively high P/FFO ratio or substantial NAV premium can have a low nominal cost of equity capital yet a high true cost of equity capital. An expensive REIT stock may trade on aggressive growth assumptions with expectations to find acquisitions that boast much better-than-average investment returns. If it doesn't meet them, disappointed investors will punish it for obtaining only average returns instead.

New Developments

Until the REIT IPO boom of 1993 and 1994, very few public REITs had the capability of developing new properties from the ground up. It's hardly uncommon today, but a well-conceived development program still does stem from capital and know-how.

New developments require financing during the 12–24 months (or more) required to build them out and "stabilize" them by filling them with new tenants. Having development capabilities is a key advantage in many real estate environments, as they allow REITs to grow externally and to create value when tenant demand is strong. This may also be a time when finding good acquisitions is problematic due to high property prices.

Successful developments typically provide 7–9% initial unlevered returns on a REIT's investment when the property is stabilized, depending on the property sector. That will usually be significantly higher than returns on the acquisition of existing properties of comparable quality.

Furthermore, its NAV will be enhanced as well this way. When lower cap rates are applied to newly developed and substantially leased properties, incremental value is created. Over time, that enhances the price of the REIT's stock, development "spreads" that often approach 200 basis points.

Such development capability also allows REITs to capitalize on unique opportunities. For example, many years ago, Weingarten Realty was able to obtain a parcel of property directly across the boulevard from Houston's Galleria, one of the premier shopping complexes in America. It built an attractive new center there, which paid off nicely.

Likewise, in 2004, Macerich redeveloped the Queens Center in New York and obtained 11 percent returns on its investment. And a number of office and industrial property REITs have been able to get close to double-digit returns from developments and redevelopments at different points and places. Finally, a few REITs have even developed properties overseas, often forming partnerships or joint ventures with local real estate companies to do so.

Admittedly, there are risks involved. Leasing risk, for one, includes the possibility the landlord won't get enough tenants or enough tenants at the right rental price. This is a particular problem if the development occurs when a favorable property cycle ends abruptly or if overbuilding occurs. Plus, permanent debt financing is usually unavailable until a project is completed and substantially leased, which can take two or three years. A substantial increase in long-term interest rates during that time can reduce the projected levered return on any development project.

The bottom line is that REIT investors and management teams alike should expect substantially higher returns from new construction plans to make up for those risks. And, to be clear, it's still unclear whether the markets properly calculate that kind of daring, even from the best and brightest of development-oriented REITs.

It's often a much better idea to simply add on to existing properties that have already proven themselves to be moneymakers. The cost involved in that isn't nearly so high, yet the percentage return on invested capital might very well be. Successful expansions can be done in any property type given the place and time. So investors usually get excited when a REIT announces a "phase 2" or "phase 3" expansion. This generally means the existing property is doing well, that management had the foresight to acquire adjacent land, and that the risk-return ratio is favorable.

More External Growth Avenues

As noted earlier, a number of REITs have been able to create joint ventures with institutional partners to acquire, own, and sometimes develop properties. Although these JV structures can make a REIT's business strategy and financial structure more complex and create intra-company-related risks, they do tend to generate additional fee income streams. This can augment FFO growth and create extra value for shareholders – under the right circumstances with the right partners.

Thanks to the REIT Modernization Act, REITs can also engage in real estate–related businesses that can provide substantial additional revenues and net income. These businesses often are carried on in a taxable REIT subsidiary, and thus their profits are subject to corporate income tax. Yet they can often create shareholder value anyway, particularly if they leverage off of the REIT's inherent real estate skills.

There are certainly causes for concern in these nontraditional business decisions. They generate revenue from nonrental sources and therefore are less stable and predictable than rental revenues. In turn, that makes them more sensitive to changes in economic conditions. So investors should be careful not to value the income streams from these businesses as highly as they do income from property leases.

These nonrental businesses should be viewed as tools to create additional value and external growth for shareholders. But any tool can be used well or not at all. That's why every time a REIT goes out of its area of expertise, be sure to examine it closely according to its own merits.

11

Searching for Blue Chips

"The qualitative factors upon which most stress is laid are the nature of the business and the character of the management. These elements are exceedingly important, but they are also exceedingly difficult to deal with intelligently."

—Benjamin Graham

Many types of investment strategies can be pursued in the REIT world. You can buy and patiently hold high-quality companies over the long term. You can take more risk and go for large gains in more speculative stocks, such as very small-cap REITs. You can focus on those that are selling at deep discounts to NAV. Or you can pick and choose between the strategies depending on the stock.

Some people target REITs that have stumbled and hope for a turnaround. Others buy high-dividend yields, believing they'll somehow hold. It's all a question of one's investment preferences, return requirements, and risk aversion.

All of these approaches (or at least all but yield-chasing) can work if investors are disciplined, patient, and exercise good judgment. Ultimately, there's no consensus as to which investment style or preference works best. And a Warren Buffett–type guru of the

REIT world has yet to emerge (although Buffett himself has bought them on occasion).

But the most conservative investors – those seeking quality and safety above all else – are prone to buying blue-chip REITs. Regardless of whether that describes you personally, it's vital for all REIT investors to know what makes these investments stand out. They're the ones that set the standards all others REITs are measured by, including the alternative choices detailed next.

Growth REITs

Some see the term "growth REIT" as an oxymoron, believing that REITs can't grow per-share earnings at rapid rates by their very nature. This is an understandable perception since they can't retain such large chunks of their earnings. Yet there are times when some REITs are classified that way regardless. And such periods will undoubtedly occur again. In fact, the tech stocks we outlined before have been falling into this category for years.

Growth REITs are those that can increase their FFO at rates much faster than historical norms of 4–5% annually, perhaps even higher than 10%. This might be because a specific sector is enjoying a boom phase when rental rates and occupancies are rising rapidly. Or a specific business might be implementing a very aggressive acquisition or development program, building new properties to immediately sell or generating rapid growth from fee-based businesses.

Of course, that kind of activity often requires substantial regular infusions of new equity and debt capital. And that requires the right management team that knows how to acquire cheaply priced properties that offer strong rental and NOI growth prospects. Even with the best leadership, once those opportunities end, the REIT will be hard-pressed to meet investors' lofty expectations, and its stock price will likely decline substantially.

Several hotel REITs were in a high-growth phase in the mid-1990s, for example. Take Starwood Hotels and Patriot American Hospitality, which both enjoyed above-average internal growth while acquiring billions of dollars' worth of new hotels. Their FFOs increased rapidly, and their stocks climbed for a while as a result. But that only lasted so long. Patriot American (now Wyndham

International, and no longer a REIT) especially overextended its balance sheet, with downright disastrous results.

This isn't to say that all growth-oriented REITs end badly. Industrial examples Prologis and STAG Industrial have been growing very rapidly more recently by developing properties for Amazon and FedEx. Only time will tell how they fare in the long run, whether for better or worse. And the same goes for whenever mortgage REITs raise huge amounts of capital and make large volumes of new loans, as they sometimes do.

It's really a matter of how well they figure out when their rapid expansion will begin to slow and how well they're able to transition back into more normal trajectories.

Value or "Turnaround" REITs

If you're a value investor (like me), you know there's often a handful of REITs selling for low valuations relative to their peers or at large discounts to NAV. The reasons for this are varied, from poorly performing properties to management miscues or frightfully ugly balance sheets. There's also the chance that they simply aren't on investors' radar for some reason.

Regardless, if they're cheap enough, their stocks might be excellent short- or even long-term investments if bought at the right "turnaround" moment.

One caution on this strategy, however: It can be very difficult to know when a REIT's stock price is fully discounted, much less when it's going to turn around – if it's going to turn around at all. Again, there are exceptions to this rule, but most very cheap stocks stay that way for good.

The Virtue of Blue-Chip REITs

As I've already suggested, those who are less adventurous with their money can consider turning to the stalwarts of REITdom. Just with one caveat: There is no objective or commonly accepted definition of a "blue-chip REIT." You won't find it in Merriam-Webster's Dictionary no matter how hard you look, though I think the explanation I've compiled here should suffice.

Just like every other investment, blue-chips are subject to sector-specific ups and downs here and there. However, they deliver consistently rising growth in FFO, dividends, and asset value over reasonably long periods of time. Because they're financially strong and widely respected, they also tend to have access to additional equity and debt capital that can fuel above-average growth.

They rarely provide the highest dividend yields or even necessarily the best total returns. And they're not usually the type to trade at bargain prices. However, they are the type that provides years of 7–8% total returns, on average, with only modest risk. You see, blue-chip REITs have certain qualities that set them apart, such as:

- Outstanding proven management that's familiar with the demands of real estate ownership and operation, and the quirks of public markets
- A track record of effective deployment of available capital to create shareholder value
- Balance sheet strength and flexibility
- Sector focus and deep regional or local market expertise
- Conservative and intelligent dividend policy
- Good corporate governance
- Meaningful insider stock ownership

A blue-chip REIT doesn't have to exhibit all those attributes at once. But it will have most of them. So let's discuss that list in further detail.

The Supreme Importance of Management

Smart and capable management is what separates mere collections of properties from superior real estate–oriented businesses. By this, I mean that REITs can do reasonably well even under mediocre management just as long as their subsectors are growing. After all, rapidly rising rents and occupancy rates during any given boom cycle will generate strong internal growth for just about all property types under it.

The true test of quality comes when the going gets rough. That's when excellent property management, superior asset location, admirable leasing skills, and strong access to capital make an obvious difference. When their markets soften – meaning there are more sellers than buyers – strong companies retain their tenants at much better rates, thus minimizing cash flow erosion. They're also in better positions to take advantage of opportunities to pick up sound, well-located properties at bargain prices – that can then be put back on track to produce excellent returns for shareholders.

Summed up, superior management is adept at taking advantage of both booms and busts alike to emerge ever stronger. Without solid leaders like that, blue-chip REITs don't exist. So, when searching for them, it's important to focus on those with management teams that have built sound portfolios with only a modest amount of debt. Look for noteworthy track records of measuring risk and investing or raising reasonably priced capital to take advantage of external growth opportunities.

Other aspects to look for include internal growth efforts by upgrading properties and tenant rolls, maximizing rental revenues, and controlling operating and administrative expense growth.

Creating Value in All Types of Climates

Superior management teams know which tenants are looking for space and in which locations. So they buy accordingly, making sure that already existent lease rates make sense with more room to grow. That way, whenever tenants do leave, management can replace the old contracts with more favorable terms.

For embattled sectors such as retail and offices, the best of the best will closely monitor their tenant rosters, always looking for opportunities to replace the weak with the strong. This reduces the risk of tenant defaults, which disrupt cash flow through lost rent, the hassle of seeking new occupants, and expensive space improvements between lessees.

A well-managed REIT should never be entirely at the mercy of its tenants, no matter the economic environment. Even Covid-19 – while certainly putting dents in retail REITs' cash flows – had less of an impact on quality retail landlords than most observers expected.

The larger sector's ability to attract rosters of high-quality tenants is very important. That is particularly true of retail such as malls and neighborhood shopping centers. In a shopping center, for example, having productive tenants means higher traffic. That then means higher sales for everyone involved. And across the board, the better the lessees, the more likely they can and will renew their contracts, even after rent bumps. They might even want to expand, prompting further growth that way.

One example of a REIT that's been able to take advantage of challenging retailing environments is the net-lease subsector's Realty Income. It has an excellent long-term reputation for utilizing its impressive scale advantage and A– rated balance sheet to grow its dividend for over 26 years in a row.

Extra Growth Internally

As should be expected, even blue-chip REITs go through times when attractive acquisitions aren't easily available. Expected rates of return might be below their weighted average cost of capital, or there could simply be a lack of worthwhile development opportunities – perhaps both at the same time.

This occurred perhaps most notably in 1998–2000. Not only were real estate markets very competitive, but the resulting REIT stock prices made raising equity capital too expensive. Robert McConnaughey, managing director and senior portfolio manager of Prudential Real Estate Securities at the time, put it this way: "The low-hanging fruit has already been picked. We are no longer in an environment where anyone can find bargains, as we have been in a recovery mode for five years now."

During such periods, blue-chip REITs can still create value, though, by pursuing better-than-average internal growth. As detailed more thoroughly in Chapter 10 (and also previously in this chapter), the more attractive they can position their properties, the higher rent they can charge as some tenants inevitably leave and new ones look to come in. In the case of an apartment REIT, for instance, this could include upgrading services to include a concierge desk, community educational and enrichment programs, or cable and internet services. Perks like that can have an impressive impact.

There's no guidebook on how to improve every property possible. There's too much diversity even between the subsectors. But innovative management will always find a way to generate above-average NOI growth, which inevitably generates greater shareholder value in turn.

Of course, it doesn't hurt that most blue-chip REITs out there will already have a strong hold of key markets that stifle competitive efforts. They simply make it more difficult for competitors to come in with new development efforts. To sum it up, leaders with a strong grasp of their markets know how to "work the system" for their benefit and that of their shareholders.

The "One-Off" Deal

Exceptional access to capital and a deep understanding of one's market gives blue-chip companies a better ability to consistently expand. But it also puts them in prime positions to recognize and take advantage of once-in-a-lifetime deals.

One example of this was Vornado's majority-stake acquisition of Alexander's. The NYC-area chain had seven department stores and a 50% interest in a regional mall when it filed for bankruptcy in 1992. According to a Green Street March 1995 report, those sites – which included a full square block in Midtown Manhattan – were very valuable. So, that same month, Vornado bought a 27% stock interest in the retailer for $55 million at an estimated 20% off the prevailing market price.

Better yet, it structured the deal to earn fees for managing, leasing, and developing Alexander's real estate. The end result was Vornado increased its FFO and per-share NAV significantly and very quickly.

Home-run acquisitions can also come in the form of an occasional vacant property in an excellent location. That's what happened in 2010 when Boston Properties acquired a new but unleased building at 510 Madison Avenue in Midtown Manhattan for around $320 million. Green Street estimated that price to be below replacement cost. And it was 33% below the price paid for a similar building on Madison Avenue three years prior. Quite the steal, to say the least.

This brings me to my main point for this segment: that anyone with the necessary capital can buy real estate at market prices. But only a few can do so with such phenomenal return prospects.

Cost Control

It's always been true that low-cost providers have an edge on the competition. Add in quality, and you've got something that's even more unstoppable. This combination has never been more true than in today's highly competitive business environment.

Understanding that inside and out, the best REITs manage their properties very efficiently while also keeping overhead costs such as administration, legal services, accounting, and so forth under tight control. That way, they have the money to outbid competing buyers when new opportunities come along – and still generate highly satisfactory returns in the process. Saving just 2% on annual property management expenses amounts to $200,000 retained on a portfolio that generates $10 million in rent.

Overhead is another area that can be managed well (or wastefully). Say a REIT has no debt and owns $500 million in properties that generate unleveraged 9% NOI, or $45 million per year. If the overhead costs amount to 1% of assets, or $5 million per year, the REIT's FFO (excluding interest expense) will be $40 million, or 8% of current asset values. Yet if it can reduce those overhead costs to only 0.5%, or $2.5 million, it will generate $47.5 million and provide an 8.5% return.

Over time, that can make a major difference in providing greater long-term results to its shareholders.

Track Record of Value Creation

One of the most obvious but often neglected methods of evaluating a REIT management team is to review the company's historical performance. This means asking questions such as: Does the REIT have a long, successful record of increasing per-share FFO and NAV? Does it have a history of steady and rising shareholder dividends? How long has it been a public company, and how has it weathered various real estate cycles?

In addition, has management found ways to protect cash flow even in depressed or otherwise difficult markets? How has it invested the capital entrusted to it? And how does it truly create value for its shareholders? A REIT with a successful track record in these areas – some of which can be measured objectively – is at least on the right track to becoming a blue-chip.

We do need to be realistic, of course. Economies are cyclical, and recessions do impact tenants and therefore landlords' cash flows. When conditions are particularly severe, dividends may have to be cut to save the larger company for another day and another dollar. For instance, even Simon Property Group, Ventas, and Tanger

Outlets, three of the largest and most respected REITs in 2019, cut their dividends in 2020.

As I've said before and will say again, nothing is completely guaranteed. However, we can form an overall accurate picture by closely examining a company's track record of total returns, both on an absolute basis and in relationship to its subsector peers over a long period of time.

Over the last few decades, REITs have finally proven they can maintain successful long-term track records as public companies throughout entire real estate cycles. They've been active in pruning their portfolios at attractive prices and disciplined with respect to acquisitions. And they reacted quickly and effectively to the multitude of problems caused by major economic issues in the twenty-first century. As a result, there are now more blue-chip REITs than ever before.

Access to Capital and Its Effective Deployment

Last but not least, blue-chip REITs are defined by their access to capital and how it's deployed. As we've already shown, properly funding external growth such as acquisitions and developments is very important in determining their long-term returns to shareholders. The same goes for how a REIT chooses to allocate that money. And the better its track record, the better its ability to raise more with satisfactory results.

When markets are stable, it's reasonable to expect that a publicly traded landlord will enjoy NOI growth at or slightly above the rate of inflation, say 2–3%. And using debt leverage might enable it to obtain 3–4% FFO growth. However, if it has access to additional equity capital, it can buy more properties or pursue new developments.

This type of external growth potential can enable REITs to grow free cash flow at above-average rates, which inevitably creates value for their shareholders. Simply put, this is one of the principal reasons why many outstanding REITs report steady annual 5–6% FFO growth on average.

Certainly, obtaining capital is one thing. Using it effectively is quite another. But blue-chip REITs won't waste it by making investments at returns less than their true costs. Rather, they'll carefully consider each acquisition and development accordingly. Keep in mind that it's the spread between the investment return and the cost of capital, adjusted for risk, that's most important for investors. It isn't just the absolute levels of capital costs or investment returns.

Some investors use the term "franchise value" to describe a REIT's ability to generate returns on new opportunities that exceed its cost of capital. There are times, such as in the early 1990s, when franchise value is easy to accumulate. Outsized returns are clearly available then, oftentimes with an abundance of buying opportunities.

Conversely, the late 1990s and early years of the twenty-first century shuttered much of that. And some seasons will see certain subsectors riding high in this regard while others are forced to lay low. But blue-chip REITs use their imaginative management, value-creation strategies, and strong balance sheets to succeed one way or the other because they allocate and invest their capital wisely.

Here too, investors can identify whether a company is behaving like a blue-chip by asking a series of questions. For instance, was the recent acquisition done at a market price, or did the REIT get a great deal? What's the upside potential and prospective internal rate of return (IRR)? How is it being financed? Is management stepping outside of its field of expertise? Is it growing just for growth's sake? Could that money have been put to better use, perhaps to pay down debt?

As Clint Eastwood's character in *Magnum Force* noted, "A man's gotta know his limitations." And that admonition certainly applies to REIT management teams. You never want them to get too big for their proverbial britches.

Of course, most of the prior questions can only truly be answered in hindsight. And sometimes it can take quite some time before the answers are known. But that brings me right back to my point about looking at a company's history to better determine its future. REITs that have proven they can be trusted before are much, much more likely to prove it all over again with each new step they make.

Breaking Down the REIT Balance Sheet

(*Contributed by* Eva Steiner)

*"Ben Graham's principle of always returning to the financial
statements will keep an investor from making huge mistakes. And
without huge mistakes, the power of compounding can take over."*
—Michael Price

We're not quite done discussing blue-chip REITs yet, which
is why we need to address balance sheets. As I've already brought
up a time or two, private equity real estate buyers like to use debt
to partially finance their acquisitions. There are good reasons for
this, especially for small-scale operators. Since debt is a way to cir-
cumvent equity capital constraints, it allows owners to stretch their
equity over multiple properties, therefore lessening the risk of any
single one. Plus, interest payment deductibility creates a tax shield.

For private real estate investors, outside debt also tends to be
cheaper than outside equity. That's because the stability and predictability of those cash flows, along with its low price volatility, make real
estate a desirable collateral asset against which lenders are comfortable extending credit. Finally, so long as the property's return exceeds

the debt's interest rate, adding more debt can actually increase the equity investor's rate of return. This is known as positive leverage.

It would be tempting to conclude then that using large amounts of debt could be equally beneficial for REITs. However, unlike private real estate investors, they can access reasonably priced equity in well-functioning capital markets. Plus, they're exempt from corporate taxation, which automatically eliminates the tax-shield benefit of using debt financing. Likewise, their inability to retain large amounts of inside cash due to dividend payout requirements reduces the incentive to issue shares only when equity is overvalued.

Put together, relying too heavily on debt is much less a reward and much more a risk to REITs.

In well-functioning capital markets, there's an exact offset between higher returns and higher risk. Yes, debt is cheaper than equity. It has priority over cash flows, with equity being the residual claim. But adding it doesn't add value to a REIT because higher leverage implies a higher cost of equity capital. What matters is the overall weighted average cost of capital, which accounts for debt (D), equity (E), and the respective costs of each kind of capital (r_D and r_E). These ideas can be summarized in the equation below and in Figure 12.1:

$$\textbf{WACC} = \left[D \div (D + E) \right] \times r_D + \left[E \div (D + E) \right] \times r_E$$

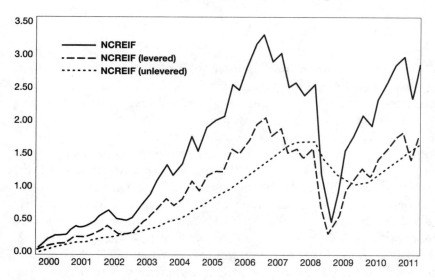

Figure 12.1

In addition to greater systematic risk exposure, there are several real-side risks associated with over-leveraging. Again, REIT investors became acutely aware of these in the Great Recession. During that period, over-leveraged entities were forced to sell properties whose values had dropped below the outstanding loan balance, often at deep fire-sale discounts. They then had to recapitalize and raise equity under very difficult market conditions.

Unfortunately, periods of rising versus falling property values can only be fully identified in hindsight. And studies suggest that real estate fund managers are no better at timing their leverage decisions than anybody else in the stock market.[1] Further studies still show that, one way or the other, highly levered REITs have substantially underperformed their less indebted peers over time. This is why I stand with Green Street's Mike Kirby, as quoted in a January 6, 2010, *Wall Street Journal* story: "At its core, commercial real estate should be an income-oriented investment . . . when you over-lever, you take away those merits."

More than a decade old or not, you can still take those words to the bank. Prudent financing strategy includes a firm commitment to maintain low leverage, mitigate refinancing risk by matching debt and asset maturity, reliance on unsecured debt as a general rule, and managing interest rate risk using fixed-rate debt.[2]

So what does a strong REIT balance sheet look like? To answer this, investors should first look at two important ratios. For one, there should only be a modest amount of debt relative to its total market cap, the total market value of its assets, or its earnings before EBITDA. For another, there should be strong coverage of the interest payments on that debt and other fixed charges from operating cash flows.

1. See Alcock, J., A. Baum, N. Colley, and E. Steiner, 2013, "The Role of Financial Leverage in the Performance of Private Equity Real Estate Funds," *Journal of Portfolio Management*, 39(5), 99–110.
2. See Riddiough, T. and E. Steiner, 2014, "Capital Structure and Firm Performance," European Public Real Estate Association (EPRA) Research Report.

Debt Ratios

Suppose a REIT has 100 million shares of common stock out-standing and its market price is $10 per share, for a total equity cap-italization of $1 billion. It also has $100 million of preferred stock outstanding and total debt of $600 million. The debt/market cap ratio can be determined by dividing its debt ($600 million) by the sum of its common equity cap ($1 billion), the preferred stock ($100 million), and the debt ($600 million). The answer is there-fore 35.3%.

$$\textbf{Debt/Market Cap Ratio} = \text{Total Debt} \div (\text{Common Stock Equity} + \text{Preferred Stock Equity} + \text{Total Debt})$$

Admittedly, a minority of analysts, including Green Street, prefers using a ratio based on estimated asset value instead of share valuation. So if a REIT has $100 million in debt and $300 million in total asset values (an estimation of the fair market values of its properties), its debt/asset value ratio would be $100 million divided by $300 million, or 33%. Here's that formula written out:

$$\textbf{Debt/Asset Value Ratio} = \text{Total Debt}/\text{Estimated Value of All Assets}$$

This method has two advantages, starting with how it's more conservative, since REITs have generally traded at market valu-ations modestly in excess of their NAVs. It also avoids rapid fluc-tuation in debt ratios, since their share prices are usually more volatile than their assets' value. Those who use it argue that leverage ratio shouldn't be subject to temporary stock price ups and downs when the price movement has nothing to do with operations or property values. At the same time, it uses estimated asset values, which is subjective – hence the reason why it's not as popular in the end.

Using total debt to asset market value, we can see that the stron-gest REITs show an average leverage ratio of 35%, whereas the weak-est are much higher at 59%.

But here's another factor to consider before you begin scooping up every asset at 35% or better. Both that ratio and debt-to-market cap can potentially provide overly rosy pictures when REIT stocks or property prices are at lofty levels. This showed in 2008 and 2009, when both fell dramatically, causing debt/market cap and debt/asset value ratios to spike. That's why we also want to look at debt to expected EBITDA over the preceding or following 12 months.

This enables investors to look at a REIT's indebtedness in the context of its free cash flow before interest payments. That will quite often be more stable than its stock price or even its aggregate property value. In which case, a debt/EBITDA ratio of 5×–7× can be considered acceptable . . . 4× or less is quite conservative . . . and above 8× should make conservative REIT investors uncomfortable.

Interest Coverage Ratios

Another way to analyze debt levels is to look at how much their EBITDA exceeds interest payments on their indebtedness, a calculation known as interest coverage ratio. For example, if "Trophy Office REIT" has annual EBITDA of $14 million and carries $100 million in debt that costs $7 million in annual interest expenses, then its interest coverage ratio would be $14 million divided by $7 million, or 2×. An interest coverage ratio significantly below that will often be cause for some concern.

Sometimes analysts also factor in other recurring financial commitments such as dividend payment obligations on outstanding preferred stock or scheduled debt repayments (fixed charges). That ratio is referred to as the fixed-charge coverage ratio and is a more conservative test. Still others look for interest or fixed-charge coverage ratios to assess a REIT's ability to service its debt obligations out of current EBITDA.

The following table presents REIT property-type sector averages of common debt ratios investors may want to consider. Based on data from Nareit at the end of Q4-19, it provides a recent reference point for REIT capital structure metrics. Note the conservative debt/market cap ratios in many of the sectors. These are caused by rising property values in the economic expansions at the time and by lessons learned from the Great Recession.

Table 12.1   U.S. Equity REIT Debt Ratios in Q4 2019

REIT Sector	Debt/Market Cap (%)	Interest Coverage (x)	Fixed Charge Coverage (x)
Office	34.0	5.97	5.84
Industrial	18.3	10.53	8.79
Retail	38.3	4.87	4.64
Residential	25.1	5.79	5.61
Diversified	40.9	2.91	2.53
Lodging	39.1	4.92	4.23
Health Care	32.2	4.21	4.21
Self-Storage	15.1	9.71	6.37
Timber	22.8	2.78	2.78
Infrastructure	35.1	2.99	2.99
Data Centers	24.8	6.45	5.77
Specialty	42.9	3.40	3.34
Total	31.4	4.88	4.59

Source: Nareit Watch June 2020.

Interest coverage, fixed-charge coverage, and debt to EBITDA ratios all avoid the difficulty of assessing leverage during periods of rapidly changing stock prices and property values. That's a definite check mark for them. However, they do end up penalizing REITs with temporarily non-revenue-producing assets such as land or properties under development. They can also unduly reward REITs that are enjoying unusually high temporary rates of return. That's why it's best to examine all the foregoing formulas when examining a prospective purchase's balance sheet.

Debt Maturity

Another crucial aspect of REITs' financing policy is the terms of their debt contracts. Of course, they hold long-lasting assets, and their debt should reflect that. (This is known as asset-liability matching.) But longer-maturity debt also reduces refinancing risk. By this I mean that, if a lender won't renew a significant loan when it comes due – and if no other source of refinancing can be found – a REIT will have to sell off assets at whatever price possible, raise new equity at very dilutive prices, or even file bank-ruptcy proceedings.

And yes, there are times that lack of lender responsivity does happen.

Longer-term debt, on the other hand, can actually be cheaper to obtain at times. That's because the cost of debt is a function of default risk, which is related to the level of leverage and the time to maturity. Longer maturities provide the borrower with more time to grow asset value and repay debt outstanding at maturity. Naturally then, blue-chip REITs should favor long-term debt.

Also naturally, investors should keep an eye on maturity dates, probably looking to each prospective buy's average debt maturity. It's also preferable for the majority of that debt to come due at least several years down the road. In short, the best of the best stagger these payments intelligently.

Term to maturity also affects debt duration. If that sounds repetitive, duration much more specifically refers to interest rate sensitivity. As debt maturity increases, so can the sensitivity of its value to the underlying interest rate . . . which brings us right to our next point.

Variable-Rate Debt

Variable-rate debt leads to significantly increased interest costs if interest rates rise. Since a large portion of a REIT's total expenses is comprised of interest expenses, substantially higher interest costs can cause a significant reduction in FFO.

So why take out such a loan to begin with? That would be because there's the chance that interest rates will decline, meaning payment amounts will too. Therefore, going that route is essentially a bet on the future course of interest rates.

Since a large portion of a REIT's total expenses is comprised of interest, substantially higher interest costs could cause a significant reduction in FFO. But interest rate shocks are especially problematic for REITs considering how their rental income almost always depends on much more predictable, gradually rising leases. Taking on fixed-rate debt is a much more balanced and even positive experience, since it improves FFO stability and therefore dividend stability as well.

Some variable-rate debt can be appropriate. For instance, REITs might want to establish short-term lines of credit that can be paid off quickly enough through such things as stock offerings; issuing longer-term, fixed-rate debt; or selling assets. And the hotel subsector, specifically, can better claim its benefits since interest rates tend to rise when the economy is strong (and vice-versa), and hotels generally perform well in strong economies.

Ipso facto, variable-rate debt can serve as a hedge against weak economies, with lower hotel receipts being partially offset by lower interest expenses. The key is the amount of it compared to, say, estimated gross asset value or market cap.

Secured Debt

As previously established, REITs tend to have significant debt capacity considering how their holdings are highly suitable as collateral. Real estate is a tangible, physical asset that's easily verifiable in court. Plus, the commercial kind's cash flows aren't terribly specific to the owner, and there's usually an active secondary market as well. This increases lenders' ability to recover their money if things go badly.

With that said, obtaining unsecured, corporate-level debt isn't always easy – which works to our benefit.

Only high-quality REITs with strong balance sheets can source significant amounts of unsecured debt. Lower-quality entities have to pledge more collateral (which they only have so much of) to finance investments. Blue-chips, however, just need their names. Lenders know they're good for it.

For these reasons, there's generally an inverse relationship between REIT quality and secured debt, and a positive relationship between firm quality and line of credit capacity.

Conservative and Consistent Dividends

A safe and growing dividend is mandatory to acquire a blue-chip label. That much should be obvious, but let's discuss it for a few paragraphs anyway, starting with AFFO.

Maintaining a modest payout ratio is good policy for two reasons: taking advantage of opportunities that come up and insuring against pitfalls. While REITs legally can't keep too much of their money, they should be saving up some amount to properly handle life's twists and turns, both positive and negative. If they're paying out too much in dividends, that means they're not in good shape to handle whatever's around the next corner.

When looking for an attractive figure here, it's best to consider free cash flow in terms of AFFO, not FFO. That's because we want to properly calculate for recurring capital expenditures, which can take quite a bite out of available money for dividend distribution – and therefore out of properly understanding what a REIT has going for it. If AFFO is \$0.95 and the dividend rate is \$0.85, the payout ratio would be 89.5% (\$0.85 ÷ \$0.95). Or we can reverse the formula to get a dividend coverage ratio of 112%.

It's important to know that payout ratios do fluctuate over time, increasing during periods when cash flow is weak. They can also go up because a company decides it doesn't make sense to be buying anything up in a given season. In that case, a higher payout ratio might actually be the most efficient use of a REIT's cash in the moment. Growth should never be forced.

Higher payout ratios therefore don't necessarily mean dividend cuts are looming. Most REITs in most environments are good at avoiding that. All the same, excessively high figures aren't something to mess around with for the simple reason that dividend cuts aren't something to mess around with. It doesn't say anything positive about a company if it can't manage its money well. That's why most blue-chips have lower dividend payout ratios.

They want to be properly prepared for whatever is coming down the road.

Corporate Governance

It might seem easy enough to shrug off REITs' board of directors. But they do matter, especially when keeping management honest, providing insider connections, and acting as a worthwhile advocate for shareholders.

Some questions to ask about a REIT's board include: Are the vast majority of directors truly independent, and willing and able to reject policies unfriendly to shareholders? And have these independent directors invested personal funds in the REIT so that they have skin in the game? If so, how much? How have they resolved issues before?

Basically, we want to see them come together with management to create structures that protect and promote shareholder positions. While this might be the least of an investor's concerns, we should still keep an eye on who's who and doing what in this regard.

It goes without saying that blue-chip REITs tend to have good, if not great, corporate governance. The more efficient the oversight, the more smoothly the business beneath it can run.

REIT Preferred Stocks

(*Contributed by* Jay Hatfield)

"The margin of safety is always dependent on the price paid. It will be large at one price, small at some higher price, nonexistent at some still higher price."

—Benjamin Graham

The legendary value investor Benjamin Graham was not a fan of preferred stock. As he once said, "Really good preferred stocks can and do exist, but they are good in spite of their investment form, which is an inherently bad one."

Graham felt as though "the typical preferred shareholder is dependent for his safety on the ability and desire of the company to pay dividends on its common stock." He believed that "preferred stock carries no share in the company's profits beyond the fixed dividend rate. Thus, the preferred holder lacks both the legal claim of the bondholder (or creditor) and the profit possibilities of a common shareholder (or partner)."

I can see why Graham was no fan since he was the quintessential value investor; he believed that they "be bought on a bargain basis or not at all." However, here I'll have to disagree with him. The way I see it, preferred stock is an attractive asset class that generally offers relatively high yields. On top of that, it provides the protection of a fixed dividend and seniority over common stock both with regard to dividends and in liquidation. Preferreds occupy a unique space between debt and equity, displaying certain attributes of both bonds and common stock at the same time.

Most of these securities have very long maturities or are perpetual. Under normal market conditions, they have lower volatility than their common counterparts. And on average, they offer much higher yields. In addition, most preferred stock is issued by large investment-grade publicly traded issuers such as banks, insurance companies, utilities, and REITs.

These companies are typically committed to maintaining strong credit metrics and ratings. So they'll usually issue common equity, reduce common dividends, or complete asset sales during recessions or business setbacks, which provides credit protection for their preferred stock.

Many investors seeking higher yields have become interested in preferred stocks, particularly in those issued by REITs. Almost all REIT preferreds are senior to the issuer's common stock and offer a fixed quarterly dividend. Unlike bonds, these shares are not guaranteed by the issuer to repay a specific amount on a specified date, and most are perpetual securities like common stock.

Furthermore, in the event of liquidation or bankruptcy, their shareholders' rights are subordinated to those of the issuer's creditors. However, they do have seniority over common stock, and common dividends cannot be paid unless preferred dividends are current. (See Figure 13.1.)

Primary Characteristics of REIT Preferred Stocks

Most REIT preferred stocks are issued with a par value of $25 per share and are typically listed on major exchanges like the NYSE. Companies often issue different series of preferred stock over time, so an issuer may have many series outstanding, each of which is referred to as an "issue." Public Storage is the largest issuer of REIT preferred stock and currently has 10 different series outstanding (as of November 2020).

Preferred Stock Benefits

Regular Income	Preferred stocks usually pay quarterly dividend or Interest payments
Senior to common stocks	Preferred stocks are senior to common stocks
Liquidity	Quoted and traded on a stock exchange
Training Flexibility	Stop orders can be used on exchange-traded preferred stocks

Figure 13.1
Source: Wide Moat Research.

The issuance of preferred stock allows REITs to raise capital without negatively impacting the company's credit ratings and without diluting common stockholders' interests. Because credit rating agencies typically assign an issuer 50% equity credit for preferred stock, REITs choose to issue preferred stock as an alternative to debt, as doing so improves credit metrics.

Most preferred dividend rates are set when the shares are first issued and remain fixed for as long as the shares are outstanding. Therefore, preferred shares have little if any appreciation potential in normal market conditions. Accordingly, holders of preferred shares won't participate in the company's earnings growth over time.

It's also important to remember that an issuer can typically redeem its preferred shares after a period of time, usually five years after issuance, at the original issue price. As a result, if interest rates fall and the issuer chooses to redeem the shares, the preferred shareholder may be deprived of an attractive, high-yielding investment.

Many REIT preferred stocks have limited liquidity, so it can be difficult to buy or sell large amounts of the stock at a time. In addition, there's often a significant spread between the bid and ask prices. Finally, in the limited cases where the issuer is acquired or goes private, preferred shareholders can be negatively affected by a lack of transparency concerning company information or by increased leverage at the newly private company.

With that said, many preferred stocks have certain shareholder protection features such as "change of control" provisions. These often allow the holder to put the security back to the issuer at par if the company is acquired or taken private.

Despite some of the drawbacks identified here, preferred stock still appeals to many investors because of its higher dividend yields compared to most common stock and corporate bonds. This, alongside preferred stock's payment priority over common stock, makes them especially attractive during times of uncertainty in the market, such as the COVID-19 pandemic.

Types of Preferred Stocks

The most prevalent type of preferred stock is fixed rate cumulative redeemable preferred stock. Many preferred stocks, however, are non-cumulative. If dividends are suspended, the issuer isn't obligated to pay the missed dividends in the future. Non-cumulative preferred stocks are favored by banks, as that feature allows for treatment as tier I capital. But they tend to be less attractive to investors due to the lack of repayment obligation.

However, with respect to preferred stock issued by regulated banks, one would expect there to be implicit credit support from regulators that would require banks to maintain credit quality by suspending share repurchases, limiting common dividends, and ensuring adequate liquidity during economic downturns.

Many preferreds convert to floating-rate coupons after five years, which provides their shareholders with some protection against rising interest rates. Also, preferred stocks may be convertible into common stock, either at the option of the holder or, in some cases, mandatorily upon maturity.

Credit Ratings and Analysis

REITs' fixed-income obligations are usually rated by credit rating agencies such as S&P, Moody's, and Duff and Phelps. These agencies use a rating scale that ranges from AAA to CCC. A rating of BBB– or above is considered "investment grade." BB+ or below, meanwhile, is "non-investment grade," otherwise referred to as "high-yield securities." Preferred stock is generally rated two notches below the issuer's unsecured bonds. For example, if a REIT's bonds is rated BBB, its preferred stock would be rated BB+.

Some investors strategically seek opportunities with REIT issuers whose unsecured bonds are investment-grade rated with preferred stock that misses that mark. In these situations, which are fairly common since most issuers target mid to low investment-grade bond ratings, the preferred stock will have an attractive yield of 5% or higher. The issuer, however, will still have excellent access to capital in either the bond market or through a sale of common or preferred stock.

As a general matter, a prudent investor seeking opportunities in the preferred stock of publicly traded REITs will focus on issuers with an equity market capitalization of $500 million or higher, and whose market value of equity is at least 3× the book value of preferred stock. This implies substantial asset coverage of the security in question.

Investors may also want to consider investing in the unrated preferreds issued by many REITs. In this case, they should review the balance sheet to ensure that leverage isn't excessive, looking for a maximum debt to total capitalization ratio of approximately 50%. They should also review the REIT's leverage in detail to determine how much debt is at the corporate level versus the asset or building level. To the extent there is a significant portion of non-recourse debt, it can provide protection during economic downturns, with certain assets that can be returned to lenders without triggering a corporate bankruptcy.

Also, investors should review the quality and diversity of the property portfolio and look to ensure that there's a pool of unpledged assets that provide asset coverage of the preferred stock portion of the capital structure. And finally, they should ensure the company has sufficient liquidity to weather a recession, either through cash balances or access to a committed bank revolver.

Unpledged assets can also be a source of liquidity for REITs, since they can be pledged to raise non-recourse mortgage debt or sold outright.

Yield to Call

When considering investing in publicly traded preferred stock, it's important to review the call provisions of the securities. For starters, don't forget that they're almost always issued with a $25 par value and are callable at par five years after the issuance date. The call price will be adjusted for any accrued dividends at the date of the call.

Consequently, it's critical to evaluate the relative yield to call of the security instead of just considering the security's current yield, which is calculated by simply taking the dividend of the security divided by its market price. When the preferred stock issue is trading above par, the yield to call will be below the current yield and could even be negative. However, when the preferred stock issue is trading below par, investors should focus on the current yield vs. the yield to call.

Because of this, investors should seek to purchase preferred securities trading below par value or at very small premiums to par, with the expectation that the preferred security may be redeemed by the issuer at par value at a future date. Investors can calculate the yield to call by using financial calculators provided by Bloomberg and others, or by using the IRR function in Excel or other electronic spreadsheets.

Interest Rate Risk

Since preferred securities have very long maturities or are perpetual, they generally have more sensitivity to interest rates than shorter-term variants. Depending on their credit rating/credit risk, however, many preferred have low or no correlation to long-term interest rates whatsoever.

With that said, most non-investment grade securities are more sensitive to changes in the stock market, which impacts investors' perceptions of default risk. An easy rule of thumb is to look at what percent of the preferred issue's yield is related to Treasuries as opposed to the percent related to credit risk or spread. For instance, if a BB-rated preferred stock has an 8% yield and the 30-year Treasury is yielding 2%, then 75% of the yield comes from the credit spread and only 25% is related to the return attributable to being a long-term or perpetual security.

Since most preferreds are either very low investment-grade or strong non-investment grade securities, they're usually positively correlated with the stock market and correlated with the

U.S. Treasury bond market. This is the opposite of what we see with investment-grade bonds, most municipal bonds, and mortgage bonds. Consequently, preferred securities can be an attractive addition to a fixed-income portfolio to hedge against rising long-term interest rates.

Stock Market Risk and Recessions

Normally, preferred stocks will have a modest correlation to the stock market. During recessions and associated stock market declines, many are likely to become more volatile and potentially even trade at steep discounts to par. The credit rating of the issue and the depth of the recession (and associated stock market drop) will determine the issue's own decline.

In a mild recession with an orderly market decline and a similar hit to long-term interest rates, investment-grade preferred securities are likely to be relatively stable. They could even appreciate slightly as diminished interest rates offset the increase in spread associated with rising default risk. Non-investment grade preferreds, however, are likely to fall significantly in line with the stock market.

In severe market declines such as the financial crisis of 2008 or the pandemic of 2020, preferreds in general declined dramatically or crashed completely as investors sought liquidity by selling most of their listed holdings. These falls from grace have proven to be excellent entry points for the asset class though, since almost all issuers of preferred stock are well-capitalized public companies that are able to preserve enterprise credit quality and maintain preferred stock distributions by reducing common dividends, issuing common or preferred equity, issuing bonds, or selling assets.

Types of Preferred Stocks

For the various reasons discussed throughout this chapter, investors generally focus on preferred stocks that are listed as $25 par value cumulative preferred. They should be aware, however, that there are other types available. Many issuers will issue $1,000 par value preferred stock, which typically isn't listed on any exchange, admittedly. Therefore, they can be difficult for retail investors to trade.

Many issuers will also issue mandatorily convertible preferred stock that typically converts to common stock after three years. It's important for investors to be aware that these are essentially a substitute for common stock, just with temporarily enhanced dividends in exchange for a reduced percentage upside. Yet they don't provide the downside protection that a non-convertible preferred stock issue does.

Taxation

REIT preferreds generally qualify for the 20% deduction offered under section 199A of the tax code. Non-cumulative preferred stock is usually classified as a qualified dividend for federal tax purposes and subject to a 20% federal personal tax rate.

In certain circumstances where the issuer has low taxable income, preferred dividends will be treated as a return of capital. All investors should, of course, consult their tax advisors prior to making investment decisions based on tax considerations.

ETFs, Mutual Funds, and Closed End Funds

Some investors may prefer to buy a diversified portfolio of preferred stocks. There are a wide variety of ETFs, mutual funds, and closed-end funds that offer diversified portfolios of preferred stocks.

These can be passive index funds or actively managed. The advantage of using managed or index funds is that the fund itself may be more liquid than an individual issue. Plus, investors reduce their single-stock risk by buying a diversified portfolio. And, in the case of an actively managed fund, they have access to professional management who address credit and call risk.

We'll discuss these categories more closely in Chapter 15.

Conclusion

REIT preferred stocks can be attractive long-term investments for many investors since most issuers are high-quality, large-capitalization companies. These companies are normally very concerned about how investors and counterparties view the credit quality of the organization. So they will take steps to ensure the credit quality of the enterprise that favor fixed-income securities.

Preferred Stock Risks

Credit Rating	Because preferred stocks are lower in the capital structure than bonds, the credit rating for preferred stocks is generally lower.
Interest Rate Fluctuation	The prices of preferred stocks are generally very sensitive to changes in interest rates. If interest rates rise, preferred stocks tend to fall.
No Dividend Guarantees	Always pay attention to the characteristics of the individual issue (unpaid coupon payments accrue to cumulative preferred stocks and lost with non-cumulative).
Call Risk	The risk that you can lose potential interest income

Figure 13.2

Investors should analyze preferred stocks carefully, however, since the call features and credit quality of these securities can affect their attractiveness dramatically. And the securities are subject to stock market risk and interest rate risk, which shouldn't be ignored. (See Figure 13.2.)

14

The Quest for Investment Value

"The combination of precise formulas with highly imprecise assumptions can be used to establish, or rather to justify, practically any value one wishes, however high, for a really outstanding issue . . . calculus [gives] speculation the deceptive guise of investment."

—Ben Graham, *The Intelligent Investor*

This chapter is my personal favorite because it's all about being an intelligent REIT investor – the main theme behind everything I teach. I learned a lot from Ralph Block when I first read his *Investing in REITs*. In fact, it was his chapter on this subject that inspired me to make my own focus what it is today.

As we've discussed a few times now in a few different ways, successful REIT investing is a marathon, not a sprint. The intelligent REIT investor will buy quality merchandise at reasonable prices, usually holding on despite annoying volatility and the various commercial real estate cycles. At the same time, our long-term returns will be higher if we add new stocks – the right stocks – to our portfolios and cull them occasionally too, taking advantage of overvalued or undervalued situations.

In other words, we want to apply something close to buy-and-hold, with intelligent caveats in place. That way, we're not unnecessarily bruised by developing trends, company missteps, and intense bouts of market volatility. Yet we don't allow ourselves to be blown about by every up and down either, buying in and out on short-term emotions rather than secular trends. This is especially true since active traders spend much more in commission costs and capital gains taxes than their more staid and steady counterparts.

To quote Benjamin Graham, "Price fluctuations have only one significant meaning for the true investor. They provide him with an opportunity to buy wisely when prices fall sharply and to sell wisely when they advance a great deal."

In order to achieve this balanced goal, we need to know how to construct and then keep a proper portfolio of worthwhile REITs. This involves recognizing when individual stocks are overpriced or underpriced according to their quality, risk profile, underlying asset values, and growth prospects. And the same holds true for evaluating the larger sector.

It shouldn't be surprising that professional investors and analysts each have their own approach. There's no general agreement on which way works best. Therefore, it's not a bad idea to understand as many of them as possible.

Real Estate Asset Values

Until the past few decades, "book value" was considered a big deal. This is simply the net carrying value of a company's assets – after subtracting its obligations and liabilities – as listed and recorded on the balance sheet. The reason why it's fallen out of favor is because plants, equipment, and inventory usually comprise only a small part of a company's value. Indeed, with very few exceptions, stocks generally trade at prices well above their book values.

Furthermore, for REITs specifically, most commercial real estate doesn't necessarily depreciate at an annual fixed rate, as I've already explained. In fact, they may do the exact opposite. As such, "intellectual capital," brand-name recognition, and "franchise value" are now generally deemed more important. Although some analysts and investors may examine private market or liquidation values, most focus on earnings and earnings growth instead.

The vast majority of today's REITs are rarely liquidated anyway. While most of them are operating companies that focus on growing their cash flows and dividends, they do own real estate with values that *can* be assessed and approximated through careful analysis. Furthermore, these fixed assets are much more liquid than, say, those of a manufacturing company or distribution network. So their market values are much less difficult to determine, with typically tighter valuation ranges, since real estate values are long-term, gradual growth vehicles.

One of the leading advocates of using net asset value to help evaluate a REIT's true worth is the previously mentioned and well-respected Green Street. It determines NAV by reviewing each company's properties by segment and location, determining an appropriate cap rate for each grouping, and applying the cap rate to a 12-month forward-looking net operating income estimate. It then adds in the estimated values of land, developments in process, equity in unconsolidated joint ventures, and an approximate assessment of fee income streams, nonrental revenue businesses, and other investments.

Quite the process, but it doesn't stop there. Next up, debts and other obligations are subtracted. Then adjustments are made for government-subsidized financing and situations where market interest rates are significantly different from what the REIT is currently paying. Finally, the dollar amount of outstanding preferred stock is deducted to calculate a per-share NAV that takes into account "in-the-money" options, operating partnership units, and convertible securities.

Obviously, Green Street recognizes that REITs should never be appraised merely at their NAVs, though. Accordingly, it derives a "warranted share value" by adding in other factors it believes could impact where they should trade. These include franchise value (i.e., management's ability to create shareholder value), balance sheet strength, corporate governance, share liquidity, and corporate overhead expense ratios. The net result is the price at which shares "should" trade when fairly valued.

Green Street also weighs REITs against each other. It doesn't deem individual stocks as cheap or expensive on an absolute basis, providing general guidelines on REIT sector valuations instead. Overall, its NAV-based approach has worked well for it, as evidenced by the firm's excellent track record of forecasting relative performance. With that said, it's clearly difficult to calculate and hardly perfect even then.

One easy takeaway, however, is that investors should ordinarily be reluctant to pay 100% or more of net asset value for a REIT that habitually destroys shareholder value, accrues excessive balance sheet risk, and/or makes poor corporate decisions. Simply stated, some deserve to trade at a discount. Conversely, a strong stock backed by a solid organization with access to capital and a proven track record of external growth and value creation could very well be worth a higher percentage.

The premiums or discounts at which a REIT may sell can be significant depending on investors' perceptions of it and the risks owning it involves. Another key factor, of course, is whether its assets' market values are expected to rise. Perhaps because of generally rising commercial real estate, the stock price and its NAV premium will rise in anticipation of those more favorable circumstances.

Investors who use this analysis should develop their own criteria for determining an appropriate premium or discount, taking into account the rate at which the REIT will grow its NAV, FFO, or AFFO relative to both its peers and a purely passive investment strategy.

Another important advantage of highlighting net asset value is it can keep investors from becoming excessively optimistic during the occasional period of unsustainable FFO growth. Take apartments from 1992 to 1994, when capital was inexpensive and there was an abundance of good-quality properties available at cap rates north of 10%. The subsector enjoyed incredible expansionary opportunities through attractive acquisitions as a result. Add in high occupancy rates and increasing rents, and FFO activity shot right up.

Analysts using non-NAV valuation models could have too easily valued these REITs at excessively high prices – perhaps not realizing that unusually attractive acquisition environments tend to dissipate quite quickly. And that's exactly what happened in 1995 and 1996 as apartment space and capital markets returned to equilibrium. Investors who bought late into that cycle never saw FFO growth live up to projections. So they saw little appreciation in their share prices for quite some time.

Considering NAV may also keep investors from giving too much credit to REITs that are levering up their balance sheets. Interest

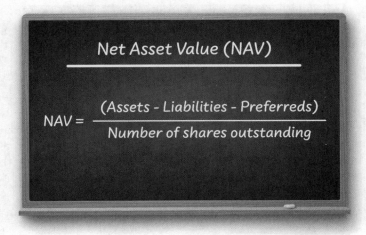

Figure 14.1
Source: Wide Moat Research.

rates on debt are usually lower than cap rates, making it easy to "buy" FFO increases . . . at least for the moment.

On the flip side, I can't overstate how carefully NAV should be calculated. It requires extensive research and attention to detail. If just the cap rates calculated are off by as little as 1%, the resulting figure will bear little resemblance to reality.

That's why U.S. investors who want a life outside of REITs have to rely on analysts' opinions on the subject. While the Financial Accounting Standards Board did seek to make these calculations easier in 2015, Europe still has a leg-up on us considering its "fair value" accounting practices. Those require companies to report estimated current real estate values instead of putting the whole onus on analysts. (See Figure 14.1.)

P/FFO Models

To reiterate, a REIT's true market value isn't based on its properties alone. Since it's also a business with enterprise value, some people prefer using assessments that better take that into consideration. If investors wanted to buy only properties, they say, they would do so directly. And if we use price-to-earnings (P/E) ratios or multiples to value and compare regular common stocks, the argument goes, we should use P/FFO or P/AFFO ratios, or multiples, for REIT stocks too.

This argument has much more appeal than it did many years ago, now that REITs really are true businesses instead of mere property portfolios. Furthermore, most brokerage firms today make extensive use of P/FFO and P/AFFO ratios. They just apply them very carefully with the understanding that they'll be based on some very arbitrary assumptions. Like NAV, they're problematic by themselves. But they can be useful when comparing REITs with each other or their own historic averages.

To understand how it works, let's take a hypothetical company: Sammydog Properties, which has an estimated FFO of $2.50 for the next 12 months. Moreover, we think it should trade at a P/FFO multiple of 15×. In that case, it would be fairly valued at $37.50. If it trades below that, it's undervalued. If it trades above, it's the opposite.

That sounds simple, but (as usual) there's more to consider before you jump wholeheartedly onto this bandwagon. For starters, remember that AFFO is a better indicator of a REIT's free cash flow. Also remember that most REITs don't report it. So the investor can either dig through various disclosure documents to construct a quarterly or annual approximation, or obtain data from outside sources.

Fortunately, most brokerage firms do issue research reports on them. Industry publications such as those from FactSet and S&P Global are also worth looking into. And Nareit provides substantial data on its website that can help approximate AFFO as well.

But even then, the problems continue. Going back to Sammydog's P/FFO ratio, how do we decide whether it should be 15 and not 12 or 20? To help determine that figure properly, price history may be a good starting point. Let's assume that, between 2019 and 2020, its average P/FFO based on expected FFO for the following year was 12. Let's assume further that Sammydog's management team, balance sheet, and business prospects have improved and that the prospects for its sector are better as well.

In that case, it might warrant a P/FFO of 14, 15, or 16 rather than 12. With "might" being the keyword. (See Figure 14.2.)

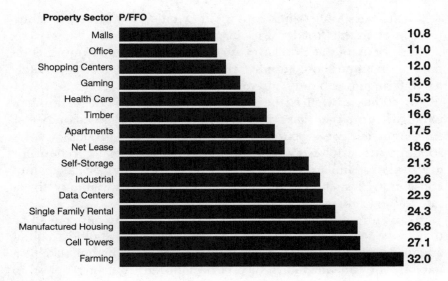

Figure 14.2
Source: Factset.

The Relevancy of Past Statistics

When constructing valuation models based on statistics that can go back many years, some people point out that the "modern REIT era" didn't begin until 1992 since there were few institutional-quality examples before then. Reasonable though that statement is, statistics from "pre-modernity" do still have relevance.

Even with the severe restrictions imposed upon them, early well-respected equity REITs can provide an accurate picture of potential returns. One might argue that, because of the higher quality of today's companies, future returns could be even better. Though that very much depends on valuation, since richer entry prices in relation to current cash flows usually mean lower future returns for any investment.

Taking that into consideration, if we think the larger market outlook for REITs is more attractive than in the past, we can use higher multiples. If we think it's less so, we can use lower ones. We also need to factor in interest rates, which have historically affected all stock prices. A 1% increase or decrease in the 10-year Treasury's yield, for instance, could equate to a similar adjustment in our REIT ratio.

Next, we should adjust our P/FFO ratio to reflect prevailing price levels in the broader stock market. If investors are willing to pay higher prices for each dollar of earnings for most other public companies, the same should apply to REITs – just adjusted appropriately for differing growth rates and risk levels.

In addition, what is the REIT in question's P/FFO ratio compared to the larger sector? How about its direct subsector peers? And, of course, we have to adjust for debt. Shares with higher levels should trade at lower P/FFO and P/AFFO multiples to account for greater risk. Similarly, other aspects of debt should be taken into consideration, including maturity and whether it's variable or fixed-rate we're dealing with.

Don't forget about cap rates in the midst of all this either. A REIT that owns 4–5% cap-rate assets (like with farming) should trade at a higher multiple than a subsector peer with 7% or higher (like cannabis). Nor can qualitative factors be ignored. A strong blue-chip REIT should have a more impressive multiple too.

There are even forward-looking and macro issues to consider. To what extent are past p/FFO ratios relevant to the period ahead? Where are prices for commercial real estate headed? What's the direction of short-term and long-term interest rates? Obviously, those last three questions require some guesswork. But they can be educated guesses nonetheless.

Despite the difficulties involved, getting appropriate pricing multiples right can be very helpful. Consider the historical example of blue-chip office landlord Boston Properties.

On October 31, 1997, it was trading at $32 at an above-average P/AFFO of 18.6× the estimated 1997 AFFO of $1.72. As it turned out, the REIT did deliver outstanding AFFO growth over the next two years, only slowing at the next office market recession. Even so, that was offset by a lower P/AFFO ratio that left the stock price to stagnate. By the end of 1999, it was only trading at $31.13, making it worth only its dividends for that period.

An in-depth evaluation of AFFO clearly would have come through then. Though, in this case, assessing its NAV premium would have done the same, since that came out to an enormous 39%! Critics can also point out how multiples that appear "too high" aren't always so, quite possibly just reflecting improving asset values and rising cash flows. And we always have to be aware of the possibility of a market bubble driving everything upward with it.

The bottom line is something I already stated: that P/FFO and P/AFFO valuation models are helpful on a comparative basis. Concluding, however, that a REIT stock is overvalued because it sells at 20× estimated 2021 AFFO when your P/AFFO model says it should sell at only 18×? Well, don't bet the farm on that one.

Discounted Cash Flow and Dividend Growth Models

Determining a net present value by discounting the sum of expected future free cash flow, or perhaps AFFO, serves as another alternative. We can obtain an approximate current value of all future free cash flows by beginning with current or 12-month forward AFFO; estimating that growth over the next 10, 20, or 30 years; and discounting the value of all future AFFOs back to the present date at an appropriate interest rate.

This does somewhat overstate value, however, since investors don't receive *all* future AFFOs as early as it implies. Shareholders receive only the REIT's cash dividend, with the rest of the AFFO retained for future growth. Nevertheless, this tool can be helpful in suggesting a fair price for a REIT on an absolute basis instead of comparatively so.

Knowing that, several methods can be used to determine the all-important assumed interest or discount rate. Consider the average cap rate of a REIT's properties adjusted for its debt leverage. If the cap rate averages 7% and there's no debt leverage at all, we can apply a 7% discount rate. The greater the debt leverage, though, the higher the discount rate. This wisely applies commercial property market valuation metrics to companies that own commercial properties, allowing cap rate movements to translate into higher or lower current valuations accordingly.

Another way to calculate it is to use a mix of private market cap rates applicable to the REIT's properties and the current yield of a very low-risk benchmark such as the 10-year U.S. Treasury, plus a "risk premium." There are various ways to determine an appropriate risk premium. But if one considers the average 6% cap rate for net-lease REITs like Realty Income against the current 10-year Treasury yield of 1.1% (as of February 2021), the investment spread of

490 basis points is at the widest of all time. So that method might be a little less than effective at the moment.

Thus, the analyst might set this portion of the discount rate formula as 10-year Treasuries + 330 basis points. (Technically, risk premiums should include a "beta" factor, which is based on each REIT's price changes relative to a broad market index.) The resulting figure can then be averaged with the prevailing private market cap rate applicable to the REIT's properties to determine an appropriate discount rate – with one extra step necessary – again adjusting appropriately for any existing debt.

One last discount rate approach is to assess the different types and degrees of risk inherent in each particular REIT, then decide what kind of total return should be earned from taking on that risk. If, for instance, you feel an 8% total return is required, you would use 8% as the discount rate. As always, higher-risk REITs with very aggressive business strategies or high debt levels require higher percentages. This method can produce more consistent valuations but with less sensitivity to property cap rate fluctuations.

Regardless of the method used to calculate it, the discount rate will make a major difference in the results. Take a REIT with an estimated first-year AFFO of $1 that's expected to increase 5% annually over 30 years. If we use a 9% discount rate, it will have a net present value of $18.56. Applying 11%, meanwhile, will give us $15.01. And 7% suggests $23.23.

After that, there's just one more hiccup to account for. Because of the peculiarities of compound interest, estimating growth rates for anything further out then five years is almost pointless. So it's probably better to estimate projected AFFO over the next half-decade and obtain its net present value by using an appropriate discount rate on it. You would then add a terminal, or residual, value by estimating AFFO in the fifth year, applying a long-term growth factor to it such as 2–3% (which may be slightly higher, depending on expected debt leverage), and then applying the discount rate to arrive at a net present value for these longer-term cash flows.

Even then, this calculation is only as good as the accuracy of future growth forecasts and the wisdom of the discount rates assigned. That's why there's also the discounted dividend growth model. Instead of starting with current or 12-month forward estimated AFFO, it begins with the dividend rate over the past

12 months. Next, it projects the current value of all future dividends over, say, 30 years, based on an assigned discount rate and an assumed dividend growth rate.

Just keep in mind that this approach can penalize REITs with low dividends compared to AFFO – unless the lower payout ratio is given extra credit with a higher assumed long-term dividend growth rate. Alternatively, you can assume faster dividend growth only over the near term, which has the benefit of only giving value to the kind of cash flow that results in dividend payments.

There's never any absolute guarantee of plugging in the correct numbers for any of these calculations. Crystal balls are currently out of stock, as they are with any other kind of investment.

We should also remember that, when assigning an appropriate discount rate, we need to consider more than just the REIT's debt. As stated before, management teams, business strategies, debt structures, corporate governance, stock liquidity, and even insider stock ownership are important aspects too. So, to some degree, you simply have to learn as you go along.

Valuing REITs as a Group

We've seen over the years that sometimes REITs can be overvalued en masse at the same time. And while they'll pay meaningful dividends regardless outside of extreme circumstances, it can be very discouraging to watch their stock prices languish or even drop for several years at a time.

National or international recessions are obviously going to affect them as much as any other business. But REIT shares can behave unimpressively even when earnings grow and property values are stable. If the original overvaluation was bad enough, it can take a while for them to recover.

For example, in October 1997, Equity Residential was trading at $50, or 13.6× estimated FFO of $3.68. Three years later, it was selling at $47, or only 9.5× its estimated FFO of $4.97. FFO growth was significant, but the stock price stagnated anyway because it was already too high.

The use of an intelligently crafted discounted AFFO growth or dividend growth model may be of some help here. When the entire REIT market is cheap, most individual REITs' current market prices will be significantly lower than their "warranted" prices, assuming our projected growth and discount rates are reasonable.

Stated another way, if we run our AFFO or growth models, only to find out that 100 of the 120 REITs we follow come out significantly undervalued, it's reasonable to start wondering if the entire sector is getting unwarranted bad press.

But that should only be a hypothesis, not an immediate conclusion. Test it out against any indications of major negative developments, both in the commercial real estate space and the larger economy. And studying REIT history can help a lot as well. For instance, knowing that they've historically provided dividend yields modestly above the 10-year Treasury (or other low-risk benchmarks) can offer valuable input for present-day evaluations.

(Incidentally, this data is available from Nareit's *REITWatch*, available at www.reit.com. The service periodically provides a graph that enables us to track such information.)

Of course, you still need to discern the reasons for any apparent discrepancies in this comparison. Current REIT dividends could be unsustainable or the Treasury might be reflecting temporary unusual conditions in the credit markets such as extreme risk aversion.

You can also use the previously mentioned method of comparing current average P/FFO or P/AFFO ratios – or NAVs – to their historical norms, just on a sector-wide level instead of company to company . . . with the same caveats in place. Don't use this as an all-calculating evaluation guide. It should be the start of your journey to a profitable conclusion or a piece of the puzzle.

Green Street, for one, considers unlevered private real estate return expectations based on existing cap rates and cash flow growth expectations. Then it does a historical comparison with yields on a bond index such as Moody's Investor Service's Baa-rated long-term listing to determine whether private real estate markets are pricing commercial real estate appropriately. Lastly, it uses REIT NAV premiums to determine whether shares have already taken into account expected movements in commercial real estate prices. (See Figure 14.3.)

Regardless of which method you ultimately choose, there will never be a substitute for detailed factual investigation and thoughtful analysis, Not on a quantitative level. Not on a qualitative one.

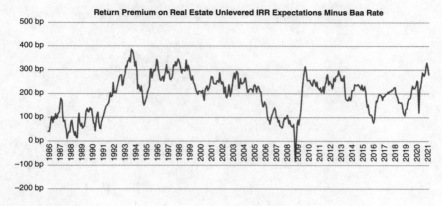

Figure 14.3
Source: Green Street.

Historical metrics tell us where we've been, not necessarily where we're going.

So while it's rarely, if ever, completely "different this time," we should also heed Peter Lynch when he said, "You can't see the future through a rearview mirror." You can only get a decent idea of it.

CHAPTER 15

Building a REIT Portfolio

"Confronted with a challenge to distill the secret of sound investment into three words, we venture the motto, Margin of Safety."

—Benjamin Graham

Before you place any buy orders, let's take a step back and seek some perspective. For instance, how much of a good thing do you want? And how much should you have?

Almost every book on financial planning and investing discusses asset allocation: how much of one's portfolio should be in stocks (domestic and international, large-cap and small-cap, growth and value, and so on), bonds, real estate, and cash. And let's not forget commodities and other "alternative investments" out there for you to consider.

Some experts say that, as we get older, we should shift more into bonds over stocks in order to reduce risk. Others recommend that our asset allocation be adjusted as needed according to economic, interest rate, and investment environments – or even one's tolerance for risk and volatility.

Personally, I don't know if there's a universally right answer. The way I see it, your proper asset mix should depend on your objectives, financial ability to absorb losses, and emotional tolerance for risk. And while this isn't a book about financial planning, here are a few thoughts about REITs' role in a diversified investment portfolio for starters.

If you have substantial spending needs over the next year or two, keeping enough cash to meet them is highly important. That's true even when bank savings and certificate of deposit (CD) rates are embarrassingly low. At least they still give you quick access to your money when you need it. Investing, on the other hand is always an uncertain venture to some degree or another, particularly over the short term.

Stock prices are affected by interest rates, inflation, corporate profits, budget deficits, the dollar's strength, world geopolitics and wars, global trade, and other situations we haven't even conceived of. And, of course, investment styles shift constantly. While solid stocks are going to perform well over the long-term, they can stagnate for years through no fault of their own.

Let's assume you have $100,000 apart from your savings that you don't think you'll need for several years. Or perhaps you have $50,000 sitting in cash in a 401(k) plan. What you do with that should depend on:

- How aggressive an investor you are (i.e., how much your pleasure from gains offsets your pain from losses)
- How comfortable you are with market volatility and fluctuating portfolio values
- How much you would have to adjust your lifestyle in the event of a possibly permanent loss in value
- How much and when you will need to withdraw annually from your portfolio investments to supplement your salary, pension, or Social Security payments
- How important a steady stream of dividend income is to you

On a long-term, total-return basis, REITs have been quite competitive with the S&P 500. But their investors should expect only moderate capital appreciation on an annual basis, consistent with moderate REIT cash flow and NAV growth. As we've already discussed, real estate is capital intensive. Plus, there are no "newest new thing" technologies that can propel their earnings upward at warp speed, with the possible exception of the cannabis subsector.

I know that Ralph Block was a strong believer that the best long-term total returns come from low-yielding REITs with higher AFFO growth as compared to higher-yielding REITs that investors consider to be "bond proxies."

Despite what many people believe, real estate ownership is usually a low-risk, modest-reward investment. So investors who wouldn't be happy with 7–8% returns shouldn't put much of their funds into REITs. All other investors, however, can apply.

Modest Risks and Sustainable Retirements

An important aspect of REIT investing is that – outside of very unusual circumstances like the 2020 shutdowns – they tend not to suffer intense declines in downturns. According to Nareit, equity REIT stocks suffered negative total returns of more than 20% in only two of the 40 years from 1971 to 2010.

As for 2020, due to COVID-19, they returned an average of –5.1%, where retail (–25%), lodging (–23.6%), and office (–18.4%) saw the greatest declines. Alternatively, the technology trifecta (we discussed in Chapter 7) saw much better returns as data centers (21.0%), cell towers (7.3%), and industrials (12.2%) benefited intensely from social distancing and the acceleration in streaming and e-commerce.

Concerning individual REITs that experience poor space markets, weakening balance sheets, or management miscues, their stocks typically decline gradually, giving investors a chance to take defensive measures. Very weak balance sheets are probably the biggest risk in this regard, but that's usually easy enough to spot and therefore easy to avoid in the first place. And often, there are other signs of risk, such as very aggressive business strategies.

Incidentally, while I generally make a habit of avoiding REITs with a history of dividend cuts, even those don't have to be lethal. One example of this is healthcare REIT Ventas, which slashed its dividend by 43% in June 2020. Yet the stock went on to perform well.

Overall, though, non-REIT common stocks have been far more sensitive to negative news. It's not unusual for an earnings shortfall, lower revenue guidance, product liability claim, rejected drug application, or competing technology to decimate "regular" share prices overnight. That's not to say REITs can't experience significant volatility, only that they're less likely to as a general rule.

Now, some financial planners advocate a large common stock weighting even for people near or in retirement. They argue that bonds don't protect retirees – who are living much longer now – from inflation. And they add that, over any significant period of time, common stocks have provided more appreciation than virtually all other types of investments.

It's hard to contradict either point at face value. But the problem with many investment theories is that they're based on long-term averages, whereas short-term situations can decimate someone's savings. Bear markets, like it or not, have a tendency to arrive when we least expect them. For retirees, for instance, many of who live off their investments, selling off stocks can wreak havoc on their income.

Owning REITs, however, provides a relatively high level of exactly that. As mentioned before, their dividend yields are fairly competitive with investment-grade bonds, as well as potential dividend increases and long-term price appreciation prospects. All put together, this makes the investor less dependent on stock prices to fund living expenses.

Looking for the "Holy Grail" Allocation

There are two asset allocation questions that need to be answered here: How should REITs be weighted relative to other investments? And how should they be weighted relative to each other?

The first one brings us right back to the five questions listed before, which can be summed up like this: It's completely up to you to decide, a frustrating answer, I know. With that said, you should never make REITs the vast majority of your investment portfolio. A fundamental principle of investing is that, over time, diversification is the key to stability of performance and preservation of capital. So investors should act accordingly, combining that knowledge with their specific needs and investment goals.

Now, there are general guidelines you can also consider. For instance, if you're simply looking for steady returns with a modest degree of risk and volatility, a REIT allocation of 15–25% of your portfolio could very well suffice. You could even adjust it from time to time according to whether the sector looks reasonably priced or not. If you're looking for higher returns though and are psychologically suited to handle the risk and volatility that goes with them, then perhaps a modest 5–10% allocation could work.

20-Year Average Annual Total Returns
November 1999 - November 2019

ML Corp/Gov't	5.22
Nasdaq Composite	7.22
S&P 500	7.49
DJ US Total Stock Market	7.93
Russell 2000 Growth	8.27
Bloomberg Barclays US Agg Credit - High Yield	8.41
S&P Utilities	10.07
Russell 2000 Value	10.65
FTSE Nareit All Equity REITs	13.94

Figure 15.1
Source: Wide Moat Research.

Based on both logic and historical precedent, I think most investors should find their REIT holdings fall somewhere in the 15–20% range. That's based on the supportable premise that these stocks can continue to deliver total returns equal to those of other asset classes with fairly low correlations to other asset classes that reduce portfolio volatility and may even increase overall investment returns. (See Figure 15.1.)

Diversification Among REITs

Moving on to the second question about REIT-specific allocation, there are plenty of property subsectors, investment characteristics, and geographic locations to consider. Much depends, of course, on the absolute level of cash you have to invest. One easy way for individual investors to diversify is through REIT mutual funds and ETFs, which we first mentioned in Chapter 13 and will discuss further in this chapter. But first, let's look at ways to diversify through individual stocks.

Six REITs would provide a minimally acceptable level of sector diversification (perhaps one in each major subsector – apartments, retail, office, and industrial – and one each in two smaller subsectors). But 8 or 10 would probably be better.

The more available investment funds you have, the more you can consider expanding into subsectors. Or you could just as easily widen your geographic focus within each subsector, perhaps adding an apartment REIT focused on the West Coast – an admittedly speculative play, as of this writing – on top of one that's national in scope. A handful of REITs also own more than one property type, so it may be logical to get additional diversification in that manner.

But be warned: Too often, diversified companies of any type turn out to be jacks-of-all-trades and masters of none, or worse.

Going back to that side note about coastal apartment REITs being speculative, there are differing opinions to consider about subsector selection. Some REIT asset managers don't try to adjust their portfolios in accordance with how much they like or dislike an asset class. They simply use "market weightings" to guide how much they put where.

For example, if data REITs make up 3% of the wider equity field, these individuals would make sure their portfolios devote 3% to the best data REITs available. The thinking behind this strategy is that REITs, like other stocks, are usually efficiently priced. So it's unrealistic to assume that anyone can consistently call which property subsectors will perform better than others.

Other investors, however, do believe they can figure out the best subsectors or property locations to own at any particular time. They'll closely examine fundamentals and overweight or underweight their subsector allocations accordingly. They'll then pursue areas where demand for space exceeds supply, where rents and occupancy rates are rising fastest, where profitable acquisition or development opportunities abound, or where some other factor seems to make the outlook for one or a few categories particularly favorable. Or they might merely emphasize those REIT subsectors where REIT stock prices look the cheapest.

This approach can be used successfully, as I've seen myself. Then again, overweighting the right subsectors can be tricky. If you're right and other investors have the same insight, it will already be factored into the stock prices. So you not only have to call the right property types at the right time; that right time has to be before the rest of the market is the wiser. Often a tall order!

Unless investors believe they can determine which subsectors will perform appreciably better than others over the next year or two, a portfolio in which each subsector is weighted in line with its share of the REIT industry makes more sense.

Still another approach to diversification is actually not to worry too much at all about subsectors or property locations. Instead, the goal is to own a package of REITs with different investment characteristics: for instance, one group with high-quality assets in major real estate markets that offer very predictable and steady growth; another trading at substantial discounts to estimated NAV or with very low p/AFFO multiples; another with above-average growth prospects; and still another with high yields, low volatility, and modest growth prospects.

Such an approach may help insulate portfolios from major price gyrations as institutional investors shift their REIT funds from one style of REIT investing to another – which they tend to do.

Which approach toward diversification is best? I'm not aware of any definitive evidence that points to one or the other, or any academic studies in general regarding this issue. There's only almost universal agreement on the need for some kind of diversification somehow.

Property Type, REITs, and Primary Locations

Apartments	Principle Locations
AvalonBay Communities	CA, CO, CN, DC, FL, MA, NJ, NY, RI, VA, WA
Camden Property Trust	CA, AZ, CO, TX, FL, GA, NC, DC
Equity Residential	CA, WA, CO, MA, NY, DC
Essex Property Trust	CA, WA (West Coast)
Mid-America Apartment Community	AL, AZ, CO, DC, FL, GA, KS, KY, MD, MS, MO, NV, NC, SC, TN, TX, VA
Shopping Centers	
Acadia Realty	NY, DE, IL, PA, VA, MN, RI, NC, ME, CT, MD, MA, AL, GA, UT, CA, NJ, IN, NM, VT, DC
Brixmor Property Group	Nationwide, heavy exposure to east coast
Federal Realty Investment	Northeast, CA, FL, IL, MI
Kimco Realty	Nationwide
Kite Realty Group	FL, NC, SC, TX, NM, NY, CT
Regency Centers	Nationwide, heavy costal presence
Retail Opportunity Investments	CA, WA, OR
Urstadt Biddle Properties	CT, PN, NY, NH
Urban Edge Properties	NY, MD, CT, NH, CA, SC
Weingarten Realty Investors	CA, WA, TX, FL, GA, SC, KY, UT, MD

Property Type, REITs, and Primary Locations

Health Care

Alexandria Real Estate	CA, WA, NC, MD, MA
CareTrust REIT	Nationwide
Physicians Realty	Nationwide
Global Medical REIT	Nationwide (Heavy exposure in TX, OH, FL)
Healthcare Trust of America	Nationwide
LTC Properties	Nationwide
Medical Properties Trust	Nationwide (International exposure: Germany, Australia, UK)
Omega Healthcare Investors	Nationwide (International exposure: UK)
Healthpeak	CA, TX, PA, WA, DC, FL, MA
Sabra Health Care REIT	Nationwide (International exposure: Canada)
Ventas	Nationwide (International exposure: Canada, UK)

Office

Boston Properties	CA, MD, DC, MA
Cousins Properties	FL, TX, NC, AZ, GA
Columbia Property Trust	CA, DC, PN, MA
Empire State Realty Trust	NY, CT
Highwoods Properties	NC, TN, GA, FL, PN, VA
Kilroy Realty	CA, WA, MI
SL Green Realty	NY, CT, KY, FL
Vornado Realty	NY, IL, and CA

Industrial

Duke Realty	CA, TX, FL, WA, IL, GA, PN, OH
EastGroup Properties	TX, FL, CA, AZ, NC, CO, GA, SC
First Industrial Realty Trust	Nationwide
Monmouth Real Estate	Nationwide
Prologis	Nationwide (International exposure: China, Germany, UK, France, Brazil)
PS Business Parks	CA, VA, TX, FL, MD, WA
STAG Industrial	Nationwide

Data Centers

CyrusOne	TX, VA, OH, NJ, AZ, NC, IL, CA
CoreSite Realty	CA, VA, IL, NJ, MA, NY, CO, DC, FL

Property Type, REITs, and Primary Locations

Digital Realty Trust	VA, CA, IL, TX, NJ, AZ (International exposure: UK, China, Japan, Germany)
Equinix	CA, VA, NJ, TX, IL, FL (International exposure: China, Japan, Germany, Italy, India)
QTS Realty	GA, VA, TX, IL, NJ, CA
Cell Towers	
American Tower	Global exposure: India, Brazil, Mexico, Nigeria, South Africa, and US
Crown Castle International	Nationwide
SBA Communications	Global exposure: Brazil, Canada, Argentina, South Aftrica, and US
Lodging	
Apple Hospitality	Nationwide
Chatham Lodging	CA, TX, VA, NY, WA, CO, FL, NH, GA, SC, DC
Host Hotels & Resorts	Nationwide (International exposure: Canada, Brazil)
Hersha Hospitality	NY, FL, CA, DC, PN, MA, WA, CT, MD, DE
Summit Hotel Properties	Nationwide
Pebblebrook Hotel	CA, MA, FL, DC, IL,OR, GA, PN, NY
Park Hotels & Resorts	Nationwide (International exposure: Germany, UK)
Sunstone Hotel Investors	CA, MA, HI, FL, NY, IL, DC, LA, MD
Net Lease	
Agree Realty	Nationwide (47 States)
Essential Properties Realty Trust	Nationwide (43 states)
Four Corners Property Trust	Nationwide (Heavy exposure in TX, FL)
National Retail Properties	Nationwide (48 States)
Realty Income	Nationwide (International exposure: UK)
Spirit Realty Capital	Nationwide (48 States)
Store Capital	Nationwide
W.P. Carey	Nationwide (International exposure: Japan, Germany, UK, France, Italy, Canada)
Gaming	
Vici Properties	11 States
MGM Growth Properties	7 States and DC
Gaming and Leisure Properties	17 States

Source: Wide Moat Research.

How to Get Started

REIT investors can choose from three basic and very different approaches toward building a REIT portfolio: do the research ourselves; rely on a professional such as a stockbroker, financial planner, or investment adviser; or buy a REIT mutual fund or ETF. Let's examine what's involved in each approach.

Doing It Yourself

The tools required to build and monitor your own REIT portfolio include a willingness to spend at least a few hours a week following the industry and monitoring your portfolio accordingly. It's without a doubt the most difficult and time-consuming method available, though many investors find it satisfying nonetheless. And, to be sure, there's something to be said for becoming a self-made expert in your own financial health.

There are several ways to stay informed about what's happening in the world of REITs. It helps to have a subscription to a REIT newsletter and/or access to REIT research reports. For example, Wide Moat Research (my company) thoroughly covers the entire sector, providing vital data plus dividends and earnings estimates. Most retail brokerage firms also provide research reports on the industry and individual companies within it. Naturally, almost all REITs themselves provide plenty of information on their websites, as does Nareit on a much more collective level.

Fortunately, understanding commercial real estate basics isn't terribly complicated once you've mastered the lingo. And REITs' business prospects don't change quickly. So DIY investing in them is perhaps less data- and research-intensive than most other common stock investing. Interested parties have access to databases (such as those provided by FactSet and Nareit), quarterly conference calls (or the resulting transcripts), and other publicly published information. The latter includes quarterly supplemental data packages, annual reports, 10-Qs, and various other filings with the SEC, all usually available on REITs' websites.

Armed with resources like those, most diligent investors can do a good job managing their portfolios. In so doing, they get to save on management fees and brokerage commissions, using discount brokers for at least some of their trades. They can also tailor their own tax-planning requirements much more personally, potentially leading to much better results overall.

Services of Information for REIT Investors

Wide Moat Research	www.widemoatresearch.com	REIT and dividend research
CBRE	www.cbre.us	news and reports on CRE
JLL	www.us.jll.com	news and reports on CRE
The Boulder Group	www.bouldergroup.com	net lease news and reports
Green Street	www.greenstreet.com	REIT investment research
Institutional Real Estate	www.irei.com	news and reports on CRE
Seeking Alpha	www.seekingalpha.com	investment research
Nareit	www.reit.com/nareit	gold mine of REIT data
NCREIF	www.ncreif.org	data and investment returns
Real Capital Analytics	www.rcanalytics.com	news and reports on CRE
Barron's	www.barrons.com	investment research
The Property Chronicle	www.propertychronicle.com	news and research on CRE
S&P Market Intelligence	www.spglobal.com	investment research
FactSet	www.factset.com	investment research
Sharesight	sharesight.com	Do-it-yourself portfolio reporting

Using a Stockbroker

Most investors understandably don't have the time and/or inclination to be so hands-on with their portfolios. And, assuming you find a good broker, there are definite advantages to this approach too. They include personally applied professional attention and much more extra time to devote to your regular job, family, friends, and maybe even a little downtime.

Obviously, a traditional brokerage's commission has to be factored in. But if you're careful to avoid excessive trading by buying up high-quality stocks and sticking with them in most cases, that can be a literally small price to pay. Some brokerage firms even offer "wrap accounts" that allow their clients to have a portion of their funds allocated to REITs invested by professional REIT portfolio managers.

Financial Planners and Investment Advisers

Financial planners can act in different capacities, with some managing and investing their clients' funds directly in specific stocks and bonds. Others prefer to use well-researched mutual funds. Still others only do the financial planning part of the process. Then there's the fact that some are paid on commissions while others charge standard fees.

Pure investment advisers generally do little or no financial planning; they specialize in investing client funds in stocks, bonds, and other securities, and make their money through annual 1–2% fees of the assets they manage. This is often determined by how much personal attention they offer, since some will take great care in individualizing each person's portfolio, taking into account their income, tax situations, and so on. Others buy and sell solely on the basis of maximizing their clients' investment gains.

REIT Mutual Funds

For those who want to take a DIY approach with as little effort as possible (not necessarily a bad thing depending on your exact situation), there's always the option of REIT mutual funds. There are more than 75 funds out there today that offer REIT-invested funds, some of which offer more than one possibility.

A list of these funds can be found on Nareit's website. And more information is available at www.morningstar.com.

Let's assume that a REIT investor wants to put 20% of a $50,000 investment portfolio into REIT stocks. In that case, the total REIT investment would be just $10,000, which would make it difficult to obtain appropriate diversification. But a REIT mutual fund can solve that problem, since most own at least 30 different REITs at once. They're run by professional fund managers who have access to REIT management teams and extensive research materials and proprietary valuation models.

Most funds are actively managed, and each utilizes a somewhat different investment strategy. Some focus almost exclusively on large-cap REITs; others try to add value with smaller names too. High current yields are important to certain ones; total returns drive the decisions of others. And some even invest in non-REIT real estate companies too. In the same way, one fund might keep real estate sub-sectors roughly in line with their benchmarks, while another ignores those market weightings.

Investors can also invest in indexed REIT funds designed to per-form in line with a particular REIT stock index. Perhaps the most well-known is the Vanguard REIT Index fund (symbol: VGSIX), which is indexed to and closely tracks the MSCI US REIT Index, less a relatively small management fee.

Most of these funds have performed pretty well relative to their benchmarks. Though that's not to say they're perfect investments. Although commissions don't apply to no-load funds, management and other fees can be sizable, typically ranging from 1% to 1.5% of total assets annually. In addition, fund investors don't receive individual attention and their tax-planning ability is limited.

In fact, they can present their investors with a large capital gains tax bill depending on the year, since any realized gains or losses are simply passed on to the individual investor. Finally, investors who reinvest dividends and capital gain distributions in additional fund shares and who trade in and out of the same fund may find it very time consuming to keep current and accurate records of their cost basis and tax information.

A Mutual Fund Alternative: ETFs

As previously acknowledged, there are quite a few "average Joe and Jane" investors out there who are limited in the amount of time and/or money they have to build their own basket of REITs. Exchange traded funds (ETFs) therefore provide an indirect ownership interest in a basket of stocks put together by a spon-soring organization and traded as a single entity on a major stock exchange.

Widely popular, their objective is to replicate the performance of a targeted group of stocks. Because they're traded as stocks, ETFs can be bought and sold during the trading day, even on margin. And because they don't employ active fund managers, management expense ratios tend to be very low.

An ETF is an easily tradable fund full of investments that fall under the same umbrella, whatever that umbrella might be. This means you get a piece of the profit across an array of companies, products, indices, or sectors, while limiting your risk. If one holding within the ETF starts to struggle, the larger fund's price should be propped up by all the other holdings.

ETFs are also popular among retail investors and financial advisers. They're simple to explain to clients, and they allow professionals to blame any negative price changes on index movements instead of their own stock-picking ability.

To be sure, an ETF will always perform in line with the index it's tied to. Plus, the adviser can charge additional fees on top of the ones directly tied to the fund itself.

It's also important to note the difference between index underperformance and underperformance from asset allocation. An ETF's portfolio can underperform due to misallocation between sectors or asset classes on the part of financial advisers. Incidentally, since there typically isn't noticeable index underperformance in an ETF's portfolio, there's less of a chance of incompetent advisers being fired.

According to David Auerbach, institutional REIT trader and co-editor of The Daily REITBeat, there were under 20 sponsors of REIT ETFs as of December 2020, most of which make more than one ETF available. They track different indices, with some being limited to specific property subsectors, others indexed to non-U.S. benchmarks (e.g., Asian and European indices), and still others using leverage to magnify performance.

Two funds, sponsored by ProShares, take short positions in REIT stocks (one of which uses leverage to magnify performance). A listing of these ETFs is available on widemoatresearch.com.

As previously noted, expense ratios for ETFs are low. For example, according to ETF Database, the expense ratio for the Vanguard Real Estate ETF (VNQ) is only 0.12% annually. (VNQ is the largest REIT ETF with assets under management of $32.45 billion as of January 2021.)

All of them are worthy of consideration if one's objective is a low-cost, index-oriented approach to REIT investing. The MSCI US REIT Index excludes mortgage REITs and REITs that don't generate most of their revenue and income from rental and leasing. It also doesn't consider REITs below a minimum size. These exclusions mean that this index could modestly outperform or underperform a broader REIT index.

According to Auerbach, the Pacer Benchmark Industrial Real Estate ETF has carved out a nice niche in its field with pure-play property-sector strategies focused on technology and logistics.

Closed-End REIT Funds

Another type of fund that's drawn interest in recent years is the closed-end REIT fund. They might own only REITs, though there are those that encompass other income-oriented stocks such as utilities or preferred stocks. Likewise, their capital structures and investment strategies can and do vary.

But two common characteristics are that they trade as stocks and, unlike conventional "open-ended" mutual funds, don't allow for shareholder redemptions or reinvestment at NAV. These features allow them to be bought and sold quickly. And shareholders don't need to be concerned about their funds having to liquidate assets in a bear market due to other shareholders bailing out.

Cynics will note that these funds are rarely liquidated regardless, even when trading at substantial discounts to their NAVs (which is true). They generate income for their sponsors even when they perform poorly. But investors do need to look closely at their structures, since many of them use investment leverage by issuing preferred stock or borrowing in the credit markets to boost investment returns. Those that do this are investing on margin; and leverage, of course, is a two-way street.

Remember that leverage increases share volatility. And those shares may perform particularly poorly when interest rates are rising. So investors need to be aware of the amount of leverage being used, how it's organized, and whether the preferred component of the fund's capital structure or the amounts borrowed are at fixed or variable rates of interest. The latter, of course, creates yet more risk for investors in these funds, particularly if exposure to rising interest rates isn't hedged.

With all that said, many small-time or non-DIY investors find that the advantages of holding REIT funds, ETFs, or closed-end funds outweigh their disadvantages. The mutual funds option is especially attractive in individual retirement accounts and 401(k) plans, where neither tax gains and losses nor cost bases are relevant.

CHAPTER 16

Investing in Global REITs

(*Contributed by* Scott Robinson)

*"The essence of investment management is the management of risks,
not the management of returns."*

—Benjamin Graham

The global landscape for real estate investing continues to flatten
with each passing day thanks to the kind of technological capabilities driving (or damaging) so many subsectors. News is now delivered faster. So are consumer staples and other products, as well as
the flow of business capital that can be managed from your desktop
or smartphone.

This globalization isn't new. It's been on the forefront of investors'
minds since at least the early 2000s. What has changed is the importance and interconnectivity of countries, regions, and – perhaps even
more importantly – cities. In many respects, this highlights how the
long-term trend of urbanization (short- or even mid-term trends
notwithstanding) is at the core of the real estate global evolution.

The industry will always ultimately be based on "local" strategies executed by regional sharpshooters. But urbanization has made those city-specific opportunities bigger and better than ever.

It's estimated that the total size of the global investable real estate market is about 80% of the total global non-real estate equity market cap. While this is a massive figure, what's more interesting is that only a fraction of this total real estate market is "institutionally owned" by such entities as pension plans, private equity funds, and REITs.

This represents a tremendous amount of opportunity to ride a long-lasting and enormous wave as other countries adopt REITs and REIT-like strategies into their own investable formats. In so doing, intrepid portfolio "travelers" can diversify their portfolios, earn competitive dividend yields, and generate enhanced returns.

Institutionalization of Real Estate

By "institutionalization of capital markets," I mean that the who's who in the capital markets has shifted from mostly individual investors to mostly larger financial institutions. Every sector of the economy seems to go through this transformation eventually. And, for the U.S. real estate landscape, it began in the early 1990s with pension funds, insurance companies, and mutual funds, in particular, getting in while the getting was good. This is still happening today with their continuing financial backing.

Now firmly into the twenty-first century, we can definitively say we're witnessing a similar trend around the world. Slowly but surely (or in significantly sized spurts of enthusiasm), REIT legislation has been adopted in country after country.

Before 2000, there were barely more than a dozen countries that had legalized their own version of REITs. Today, there are 39 (and Hong Kong), a significant increase to say the least. The vehicle, while not perfectly similar everywhere it's employed, better allows investors to allocate capital according to their individual risk appetites, regional growth prospects, and other transformational trends. (See Figure 16.1.)

Several factors have driven this "institutionalization" of real estate, most notably technology, globalization, and urbanization. If we want to make the most out of investing beyond our backyards, it's important to understand these drivers for what they're really worth.

38 Currently, 38 countries have enacted REIT legislation.	**480** The number of listed real estate companies included in the FTSE EPRA/Nareit Global Real Estate Index.	**98%** REITs comprise 98% of the headline Real Estate sector in the Global Industry Classification Standard.
79% Listed REITs account for 79 percent of the total market capitalization of the FTSE EPRA/Nareit Global Real Estate Developed Market Index.	**$1.4t** The total market capitalization of the FTSE EPRA/Nareit Global Real Estate Index.	**52%** Percent of the total market capitalization represented by non-US constituents of the FTSE EPRA/Nareit Global Real Estate Index.

Figure 16.1
Source: Nareit.

The Three Big Drivers

Technological advances have increased the integration and efficiency of the global capital markets and reduced the costs of transportation and communication. The migration of economic activity from the physical world to the digital world really only got started in the years immediately following the financial crisis. But it's expanded enormously since.

Massive amounts of digital infrastructure are required to facilitate this movement. At the risk of repeating information from previous chapters, automated transactions, smart manufacturing, smart buildings, the internet of things (IoT), and autonomous transportation are all being connected through wired and wireless networks. The information is then stored in data centers and managed through an array of consumer and enterprise applications. (See Figure 16.2.)

Globalization, meanwhile, is generally thought of in one or two ways. There's the macroeconomic context, such as the expansion of manufacturing and trade deals being made around the world. And then there's the sociocultural context, which looks at the situation through the lenses of cultural and religious immigration. However, at its core, globalization is a move to a more connected global economy through growing trade, investment, and capital capabilities.

Deregulation – the opening of those capital markets and capabilities – is one of the driving factors behind this merging that

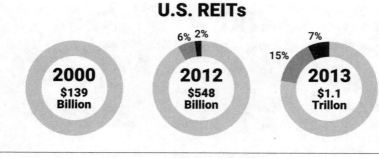

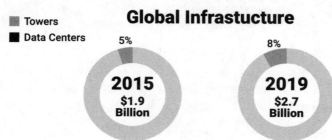

Figure 16.2

Source: Nareit, FTSE, Bloomberg, Cohen & Steers.

has, is, and no doubt will continue benefiting real estate so much. The current era of globalization has been driven by relaxed institutional constraints and regulations that generate lots of new and exciting financial exchanges. Admittedly, this regulatory liberalization has largely focused on capital, not land or labor. Yet globalization has led to an increased flow of thoughts and ideas, particularly when it comes to management and investment strategies.

Our third driving force is the combination of national and international migration away from the countryside and into city life. This can have and is having a strong impact on people's perception of real estate's worth.

Known as urbanization, it's the process through which cities grow, though even a concept as seemingly straightforward as that can be broken down into two distinct categories. New York City serves as one solid example since it experienced significant growth for at least a two-decade span. That was thanks to organic urbanization. There were free-market opportunities and other personally compelling reasons to live there that spurred that expansion. But the same results can also happen inorganically through direct or indirect regulatory processes (e.g., government incentives), such as with Shanghai through the last 20 years.

One way or the other, the United Nations estimated three years ago that 55% of the global population lived in cities – a number that was expected to grow to nearly 68% by 2050. And while current social distancing measures might put a downtick in that number temporarily, the long-term view is still looking much more urban than ever before. Consider how much economic growth this is responsible for as people move closer to intentionally or unconsciously collaborating with each other. In 2020, the World Bank said that "more than 80% of global GDP [is] generated in cities."

These trends are fairly similar across developed, emerging, and frontier markets alike, where "developed" indicates well-established capital markets, legal structures, and relatively stable currencies; "emerging" refers to those regions with up-and-coming systems in place; and "frontier" designates the potential to start building something permanent and profitable.

Cities don't all share similar economic compositions, of course. But the impact of urbanization is quite similar across the globe, resulting in a dramatic rise in living standards, increasingly complex infrastructure, and rising property valuations.

The Case for a Global Real Estate Portfolio

Knowing all that, it shouldn't be any big surprise that global real estate securities have generated competitive returns over time. Figure 16.3 compares the cumulative performance of a global real estate securities portfolio to that of a global stock portfolio from 2005 through 2020. As you can see, the global listed real estate securities delivered competitive returns with the added benefit of generating two times the amount of ongoing cash dividends for investors. (See Figure 16.3.)

Those who see the rewards as outweighing the risks cite diversification and competitive dividend yields as major motivations – both of which are valid reasons that deserve to be explored further.

When it comes to diversification, global listed real estate securities help spread risk out by lowering the correlation of holdings

Cumulative Index Performance – Gross Returns (USD)
Oct 2005–Oct 2020

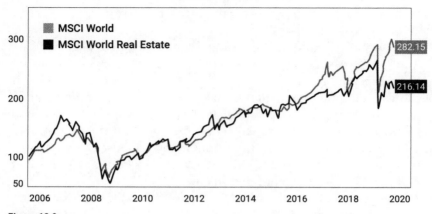

Figure 16.3
Source: Wide Moat Research.

across different markets and asset classes. Since 1990, the local listed real estate equity indices in major markets around the world have generally displayed low to moderate correlation levels with each other. This makes sense considering this chapter's previous statement that real estate growth is still locally driven.

It also shows that these individual towns and cities are different with distinct economic and property cycles. Generally speaking, most of those patterns will be supply- and demand-driven: the result of market-specific events. Consider overbuilding, which is a local issue. While every city and even large towns are bound to experience that problem from time to time, they're rarely going to be completely synchronized, if at all.

As a result, geographic diversification should decrease the risk that an average investor's real estate holdings will suffer all at once. And for those who have the time to be more hands-on with their analysis, the varying bull and bear markets offer the opportunity to take more specific advantage of these opportunities.

Last but not least, recent dividend yields offered in key listed real estate markets have been generally higher than those of respective government bonds. And due to global REITs' varying but always significant dividend payout requirements, rising cash flow from general economic growth will continue to drive them even higher – while serving as a natural hedge against rising inflation.

Defining Global Investment Opportunities

If you decide to invest in global REITs, it only makes sense you'll have to then decide where to invest – which can be more than a little overwhelming. The world is a big place with lots of REITs to choose from.

Worse yet, there are a lot of potential pitfalls out there to avoid. The planet is divided into 195 countries, after all, with more than 6,000 languages and countless legal jurisdictions. And while only about a fifth of those offer real estate investment trusts as a portfolio option, that's still a lot of room to feel overwhelmed in.

Once we start breaking this down, however, it really can become much more clear and far less complex. Once we divide this sphere by country, we can organize our opportunities further into four major regions: the Americas, Europe, Asia-Pacific, and Africa and the Middle East. These groupings aren't perfectly linked, but they do generally share compelling economic and social connectivity among them. North and South America, for example, have numerous points of socioeconomic interconnectivity.

Another way to consider the landscape is by economic development, size, capital market liquidity, and overall market accessibility. Global research and data analytics firm MSCI, for one, has a fairly straightforward way of classifying countries into the aforementioned three categories: developed, emerging, and frontier. This makes sense from a straightforward risk-assessment analysis – though it does require you to stay aware of the kind of economic growth that can bump a frontier market into an emerging one and an emerging one into a developed nation.

Risks Associated with International Investing

One of the safest ways to invest in international real estate is through multinational companies that have established operations in foreign countries. But those are relatively few and far between, which means there are additional or increased hazards to be aware of.

For starters, there are idiosyncratic risks such as differing operating strategies, corporate cultures, and financial policies. Don't automatically assume that a common focus means company 1 in country A is going to handle its business the same way as company 2 in country B.

In fact, it might be safer to assume the opposite, since almost every element of real estate can vary between any given nations. Take lease structures. Or ownership patterns. Or laws, regulations, tax structures, restrictions, economic opportunities, and so on.

Proper diversification can help smooth out these idiosyncratic issues, as does a REIT's very nature with its ability to be bought and sold quickly. But they don't eliminate them altogether. This is especially true considering how many investment analysts say that real estate carries a greater amount of idiosyncratic risk than either stocks or bonds. Because, again, it's more localized in nature, it's easier to fit into a distinct culture.

You should be equally aware of systematic risk, also known as market risk, because it's much more nationally or regionally determined. Examples include changing interest rates, inflation, and exchange rates – all of which are more difficult to diversify against. And then there's the issue of government policies, higher transaction costs (including higher brokerage commissions, potential stamp duties, levies, and clearing fees), international trading penalties, and potential problems with liquidity.

That's to say nothing about the actual act of buying these stocks. Many otherwise attractive non-U.S. real estate companies don't have American Depositary Receipts (ADRs) available that trade on U.S. indices. As such, they have to be bought in local currencies on local stock exchanges. Many global investment firms do offer professional outlets to make this juggling act easier. But, as mentioned earlier, those avenues will cost you more.

There's always going to be a give and a take to any investment decision you make. It's only a matter of whether that decision is the right one for you.

Knowing that, here's one more suggestion: For those who want to get in on the international action with as little risk as possible, you can consider closed-end funds, mutual funds, and/or ETFs (as discussed in Chapter 15) that buy into international REITs. While they're not going to offer nearly as much profit potential, the second two opportunities are especially easy and efficient for the average investor to work with.

CHAPTER 17

Management Matters

"Management changes, like marital changes, are painful, time-consuming, and chancy."

—Warren Buffett

I'm sure you've heard the phrase, "Bet the jockey, not the horse." It refers to the idea that investors should focus more on the management team than the business model.

I consider the adage to be quite true, especially in REIT-dom, where management teams are responsible for all the obligations of being a landlord – from finding a tenant to collecting the rent, taking care of repairs, and maintaining the balance sheet – and, of course, sending distributions (i.e., dividends) to investors. Stated bluntly, bad management can destroy value in a portfolio of real estate properties. Good management can add value.

I often tell people that, when you invest in a REIT, you're not only placing your "bet" on the underlying real estate. You're also putting your hard-earned money toward paying the "jockey" that's running it for you.

That's why I spend a lot of time meeting with C-suite executives, always looking for information to help me form a deeper understanding of the underlying investment strategy – and whether it allows my goals to be aligned with theirs. By that, I mean there's no conflict of interest between management and shareholders. Also, there's an independent board of directors involved and hopefully some insider ownership going on as well.

When leadership has some obvious skin in the game, you'd better believe it makes a difference in how things are run.

Remember that, as a shareholder in any company, you're helping to pay its CEO's, CFO's, and CIO's salaries. This means they owe you complete transparency regarding past earnings, acquisitions, or other pertinent information.

While there's no way they can effectively communicate with every single shareholder one-on-one, there are events where you can better interact with many of them. This includes Nareit's annual REITweek and The MoneyShow, where I'm a regular host for CEO roundtable events. I also frequently interview members of management on my podcast, *The Ground Up*. That's its whole purpose: to connect you with insider information.

In 1994, during a Berkshire Hathaway annual shareholder meeting, Warren Buffett explained how important it is to see how a manager performed. "Look at what they have accomplished," he advised, "considering what the hand was that they were dealt when they took over compared to what is going on in the industry." Those are wise words to follow.

Buffett always considers management to be a key factor on whether to buy into a stock or not. He said during the same meeting that, to learn more about a company's governance, read "about both what they've accomplished and what their competitors have accomplished," then see "how they have allocated capital over time."

In addition, review "how well they treat their owners" by reading their proxy statements. "See how they treat themselves versus how they treat [their] shareholders. . . . The poor managers also turn out to be the ones that really don't think that much about the shareholders."

As a real estate developer for over three decades, I can attest to the fact that good managers can make or break a deal. In fact, as I reflect on my experience in the private sector, it makes me realize how important management is to the success (or failure) of operating a portfolio of real estate properties.

For example, one of my tough lessons in life had to do with being a multi-unit franchisee for a global pizza chain. In addition to attempting to manage a portfolio of shopping centers and net lease buildings, I also took on the oversight of eight pizza stores in two states. If that sounds easy, let me assure you it wasn't. Not even close. And after losing close to a million dollars, I graduated with an honorary degree of hard knocks and a much clearer understanding of my "circle of competence," as Buffett calls it. I meant well, of course. But that didn't mean it ended well.

In his 1996 shareholder letter, Buffett said, "What an investor needs is the ability to correctly evaluate selected businesses. Note that word 'selected.' You don't have to be an expert on every company or even many. You only have to be able to evaluate companies within your circle of competence. The size of that circle is not very important; knowing its boundaries, however, is vital."

Thanks to that advice, and I'm sure due to my past missteps, I pay close attention to REIT management teams, always making sure they adhere to that mantra. That's why it's important to note the "pureplay" designation. REITs labeled that way are telegraphic investors that stick to their specialties. Whenever one begins to drift outside of its lane, I become skeptical, recognizing that there could be elevated risks to consider.

Personally, I tend to stay away from residential mortgage REITs for this reason. They're all externally managed, which means they have contracts with third-party businesses to perform all material operations. This includes determining the optimal use of leverage and selecting assets, which means a very good chance of picking and grabbing whatever's available. The REITs themselves are almost always large asset managers that exist to manage fee revenue, a focus that too easily leads to trouble.

Speaking of externally managed landlords, they also have to pay base management and incentive/performance fees. So it's critically important to review the terms of their contracts with these third parties. When my team and I study them, we compare all aspects of the agreement to their externally managed peers in order to try uncovering any potential conflicts of interest. This includes understanding any total return provisions and performance fee hurdles.

And for any REIT whatsoever, I pay very close attention to each one's competitive advantage, with an emphasis on two critical defensive characteristics. Quoting Buffet yet again (now from the 1995 Berkshire Hathaway annual meeting), "We're trying to find a business with a wide and long-lasting moat around it" that protects "a terrific economic castle with an honest lord in charge. . . ."

He then went on to explain ways a company can build and maintain a moat. It can happen if a business is "the low-cost producer in some area. It can be because it has a natural franchise because of surface capabilities. It could be because of its position in the consumers' mind. It can be because of a technological advantage or any kind of reason at all. . . ."

As I referenced in Chapter 10, "To create value from external growth initiatives, a REIT must earn a return on any new investment that exceeds the cost of the capital deployed." Some of the most successful ones over the last 10- and 20-year periods have been able to generate superior returns consistently because of their disciplined capital markets practices. Their management teams recognize that, in order to generate predictable profit margins, they must be low-cost providers just like Wal-Mart and Coca-Cola in their respective spaces.

Directly correlated to cost of capital advantage is scale advantage: How much bigger can they get, and what can they do with that size? In my opinion, this is one of the most important "moat metric" factors to know about when analyzing real estate investment trusts.

Remember that most of the industry's growth occurred in just the past 30 years, driven by the IPO boom of 1993 and 1994, the huge wave of secondary offerings in 1997 and 1998, and the increasing size of many REITs as time went on. Even so, the sector remains small in comparison to both the broader stock market and commercial properties. Equity REITs owned approximately $2 trillion in net real estate investments as of the end of 2020 – just 10–15% of the total value of all institutionally owned commercial real estate in the U.S.

This is all to say they have substantial growth prospects with a total market cap that could expand dramatically over the next decade. But will this actually happen? In order to hazard a guess, we need to consider two key questions: 1) Will a significant number of private real estate owners want either to become REITs or to sell their properties to them? 2) Will individual and institutional investors want to expand their REIT holdings or otherwise decide to own more commercial real estate in securitized form?

To be sure, REITs are perfectly positioned to gain market share as private property owners liquidate their holdings or utilize the upREIT tool as discussed in Chapter 3. And the highly fragmented marketplace should provide them with powerful opportunities to use their scale advantages over the next several decades. But remember their management teams must utilize costs of capital and economies of scale in the process to create shareholder value. Without those all-important additions, REITs are likely to underperform, and their investors will be disappointed.

During the Covid-19 pandemic, investors found that scale advantage especially was critical, allowing certain large, intelligently diversified REITs to grow their dividends anyway during those darkest hours. Those that weren't as expansive or well-placed, meanwhile, were forced to cut their payouts.

Smaller companies are also often unable to develop the type of extensive organizations and levels of expertise found in major corporations. So we have to ask ourselves whether a REIT might be at a competitive disadvantage if it can't afford to hire the highest-caliber employees or obtain the very best market information concerning supply and demand for properties in its market area. That lacking could affect its acquisitions, property management, financial reporting, budgeting, and forecasting.

Bigger isn't always better. And smaller isn't always riskier. But there are certain efficiencies that come more easily with substantial size, including greater bargaining power with suppliers and even tenants. Again, cost of capital is the name of the game, and better-paid leadership is often better prepared to capture that potential.

On the other hand, larger companies can find themselves relying too heavily on the superstars they hire (e.g., Warren Buffett at Berkshire Hathaway or Steve Jobs at Apple). In those cases, shareholders are at risk of any sudden departures from these outstanding individuals. It's never good for any organization to be excessively dependent on a single individual, no matter how talented.

This brings up an important side note. Management succession is a sensitive issue that is, for obvious reasons, difficult for both investors and REIT management teams to discuss. Yet it's of vital concern. Genius is tough to replace in any organization, but it's particularly tough to replace in small- and mid-cap companies like most REITs are. So REIT investors need to assess the capabilities of those who will likely be replacing them and what tools they will have at their disposal when that time comes.

Buffett put it this way (another of his 1995 meeting statements): "But we are trying to figure out . . . why is that castle still standing? And what's going to keep it standing or cause it not to be standing five, ten, twenty years from now? What are the key factors? And how permanent are they? How much do they depend on the genius of the lord in the castle?"

I haven't met Warren Buffett – yet – but when my co-author and I published the initial *Intelligent REIT Investor* in 2016, I sent him a copy. I'm not sure if he read it, but I do know that Berkshire Hathaway has since become modestly active in the REIT sector, taking an equity position in Store Capital and a debt position in Seritage Realty.

Going forward, it will be interesting to see if other large institutions follow suit in a sector that was designed for smaller investors and still serves them well. Certainly, as we addressed early on in the book, institutional investors have become more active over the last two decades. According to John Sullivan, U.S. chair and global co-chair of DLA Piper's real estate practice, there's approximately $400 billion in institutional capital ready to be invested in commercial real estate.

To me, this reiterates how important REITs continue to be as part of an asset allocation strategy – when chosen wisely. Whether you're Berkshire Hathaway or an Average Joe, investors must always insist on buying high-quality stocks. Buffett said in a 1999 *Fortune* interview that, "The key to investing is . . . determining the competitive advantage of any given company and, above all, the durability of that advantage. The products or services that have wide, sustainable moats around them are the ones that deliver rewards to investors."

Benjamin Graham, his friend and mentor, also insisted on quality, saying that "one of the most persuasive tests of high quality is an uninterrupted record of dividend payments going back over many years." That quote is one of the many reasons I'm convinced he would have approved of REITs today.

Bottom line: Today, more than ever, owning and operating commercial real estate successfully requires a proper business and a proper business mindset, no matter the subsector. Competition is fierce everywhere, but well-run organizations can often operate at lower costs and frequently enjoy more bargaining power because of their costs of capital and scale advantages, as I referenced earlier. It can't be overstated that these elements give them significant competitive edges more often than not. REITs that have both will almost assuredly attract and retain the strongest tenants because they can provide best-in-class services to them.

Although private companies can certainly build solid organizations and motivate employees and management, share liquidity makes it easier for their public counterparts to accomplish these objectives. Plus, stock options, bonuses, and purchase plans are flexible, provide liquidity, and act as effective motivational tools for employees – from the most recently hired all the way to top management. Likewise, disciplined decision making, adequate financial controls, and incisive forecasts are becoming increasingly important to publicly traded management teams as they seek to get ahead of the competition.

More recently earnings, social, and governance (ESG) issues have become items of intense interest for investors, making it increasingly important for REITs to thoroughly disclose how they're performing in each of those categories. Fortunately, this isn't an entirely new concept for them.

According to Stephen Hester, CFA and senior analyst at Wide Moat Research, several elements of ESG were already included in their regular reviews by higher-quality due-diligence officers and researchers. Admittedly, other aspects are less familiar, especially since the larger guidelines involved can and do change with society's expectations and capabilities. Its application in the REIT sector is no exception.

Leadership in Energy and Environmental Design (LEED) standards set the benchmark in sustainable building operation and design back in 1994. And by 2006, it had grown to six comprehensive systems encompassing all aspects of construction. Today, it's nine, and the challenges presented in 2020 could impact it again considering how sharply demand for improved air quality, touchless door systems, and other building enhancements have increased. Employee health and success are influenced by the buildings they work and live in, and companies will want to properly provide for their workers in this regard.

Alongside creating better buildings, companies in general are focused on building more accountable management teams. Everyone has a different vision of exactly what that entails, but the prevailing view is that more diverse viewpoints and backgrounds are necessary. As one example, the number of female CEOs at the top of Fortune 500 companies grew by 37.5% in 2019, an impressive amount, though the final figure does remain below 10%. On the other hand, 44% of non-executive director appointments to those same businesses' boards were women.

As a final point on this matter, an annual survey conducted throughout 2020 polled large institutional investors about their interest in ESG factors. It found that a full third that weren't yet using it expected to do so in the near term – with overall interest climbing three times year over year. A solid 42% already incorporate them into their portfolio construction, another record-high number. Stated simply, capital flows matter and money is flowing into ESG.

Along those lines is Jonathan Litt, CEO of Land and Buildings. A well-known REIT activist, he's pushed hard to turn around troubled REITs like Taubman Centers and Apartment Investment and Management. Litt is best known for his sometimes forceful opinion that REITs should have boards with several independent outside directors who answer to shareholders' concerns about such things as allocation of capital, expense control, and compensation programs.

These experts should also be savvy at implementing strong financial systems and controls. The stronger the organization and its financial discipline, the more efficient it will be as an owner and manager of real estate . . . and the more it should be able to increase market share relative to smaller, less well-capitalized, and less disciplined competitors.

Litt says, "The job of a REIT CEO is capital allocation: sell assets when at a discount and sell equity when at a premium. If only all CEOs and boards followed that principal, we would have a more successful industry." In the end, he's right. Many companies find that the corporate governance requirements imposed on them after they go public, while often nettlesome and costly, actually strengthen their organizations in the long run.

Others have resisted the call to move to the markets because of that burden, though, which might turn out to be the wrong choice. The way I see it, if these large private companies continue along their present path, the continuing expansion of the REIT industry will be driven by many smaller IPOs, by property acquisitions and developments (including joint ventures with institutional real estate owners), by existing REITs, and by a gradual increase in the values of REIT-held properties over time.

Considering how that should be expansive, their private counterparts could find themselves falling further and further behind.

I'll end with this thought from Graham's *Intelligent Investor.* "An investment operation is one which, upon thorough analysis, promises safety of principal and an adequate return. Operations not meeting these requirements are speculative."

While I'm more than willing to slap the "speculative" label on specific REITs when appropriate, the larger sector is filled with more than merely "adequate" returns. It offers the real chance of securing a worthwhile, enjoyable, sustainable retirement for you to enjoy, with something to pass on to your loved ones should you so choose.

That's the power of REITs . . . a power I'm proud to promote wherever I can.

Afterword

As co-founder and chairman of Kimco Realty, I've been in the real estate business for quite a while. Several decades, in fact. You can learn quite a lot in a time frame like that if you only have the drive to do so, and "drive" I have in spades.

In 1966, I joined forces with a handful of shopping center owners and real estate investors, including Martin Kimmel, to form a single entity with a single purpose: to build a real estate empire. And that's precisely what Kimco, now one of the world's largest owners and operators of neighborhood and community shopping centers, has done ever since.

That kind of reach brings profits with it, yes. Plenty of them. It offers countless opportunities to influence as well, and I appreciate every single one that comes my way. But there's a third aspect that too few people think about when contemplating running a company like Kimco.

By that, I mean human connections: the chance to meet people I would never have met otherwise.

I have a large list of such people at this point, with the late Ralph Block being one of them. I was – and still am – proud to call him a friend of mine. He was such a prolific author who wrote countless articles about REIT investing, not to mention *Investing in REITs*, a book that made such an impact it went on to be published four times.

The reason he did all that wasn't for the fame or fortune. It was because he genuinely wanted to better educate people about how to more firmly secure their financial futures. He was that kind of guy.

That's why I'm so happy to see Brad Thomas pick up his torch today. By working with Ralph's writings, updating and adding to them accordingly, Brad is continuing that goal of helping mom-and-pop investors develop or maintain solid retirements. And, since his books are required reading for more than one university course, he's educating entire classes about how far their dollars can really go.

That's the exact kind of impact Ralph would have wanted as his legacy.

As for Brad, I remember a time before I ever met him in person – perhaps 10 or even 15 years ago – when I sent him a book, Seth Klarman's *The Margin of Safety: Risk-Averse Value Investing Strategies for the Thoughtful Investor.* I knew he'd appreciate it because I sensed even then that we shared the same values, just like Ralph did.

"Investors are all too often lured by the prospect of instant millions and fall prey to the many fads of Wall Street," the Amazon book description reads. "The myriad approaches they adopt offer little or no real prospect for long-term success and invariably run the risk of considerable economic loss – they resemble speculation or outright gambling, not a coherent investment program."

But not value investing, as Klarman, Ralph, Brad, and I know. Not assessing each company for what it's really worth past the hype of high prices and fickle opinions. Not buying into quality companies at unloved prices and waiting for the masses to catch on again, giving us first-advantage price appreciation.

That's what Brad's *The Intelligent REIT Investor* does with an industry I'm privileged to be a part of. You don't have to take my word for it though: Just try putting Brad's words into practice. You'll see for yourself soon enough.

Milton Cooper

The Intelligent REIT Glossary

The following is a glossary containing some terms used frequently in the worlds of commercial real estate in general and REITs specifically. Admittedly, investors don't always interpret all of them the same way. So you will undoubtedly encounter definitions elsewhere that are somewhat different. Nonetheless, this list is meant to be as accurate and helpful as possible.

Another good resource in this regard can be found at Nareit's website: www.reit.com/IndividualInvestors/GlossaryofREITTerms.aspx

Absorption rate: The pace at which landlords are able to fill rentable space, usually as compared to existing supply. (See Gross absorption; Net absorption.)

Acquisition costs: The direct expenses involved in purchasing a particular asset, such as closing costs, brokerage fees, legal fees, title insurance, and due diligence.

Adjusted funds from operations (AFFO): Funds from operations (see FFO) minus normalized recurring expenditures that are necessary to properly maintain and lease the property (e.g., new carpeting and draperies in apartment units, leasing expenses, tenant improvement allowances) that are properly capitalized and amortized. Adjustments are also made to eliminate any rent straightlining. (See Straight-line rent.)

Amortization: The repayment of some of the principle on a loan before its term end. This cannot apply to interest-only loans, where intangible asset-related expenses are professionally recorded after net operating income (see Net operating income), or "below the (bottom) line."

Anchor tenant, or Prime tenant: A major tenant at a specific retail or office location, especially a grocery store, department store, or discount store.

Annualized return: The total return for a set period of time other than a year that's nonetheless calculated to show corresponding annual gains or losses. Different from an average since it's determined on a time-value basis; it's calculated as $(1 + \text{cumulative return}) \times (365/\text{days held}) - 1$.

Appraised value: A professional opinion on what a property is worth that's determined in one of three ways: 1) Making valuation adjustments to a property after comparing it to recent transactions for similar properties. 2) Estimating the cost of replacing it with something similar. 3) Using the property's future cash flow to analyze the capitalization rate and/or discounted cash flow.

Assessment: A property's official valuation that can then be used to determine taxes due, not to be confused with market value (see Fair-market value), which can be different.

Asset management: Efforts made to make the most out of incoming finances that drive total investment returns.

Average daily rate (ADR): A lodging industry term that divides room revenue by the number of rooms sold to measure the average amount charged per rented unit.

Base building: An office property term for basic building improvements that aren't specific to any one tenant, such as structural, mechanical, and electrical upgrades, and measures to decrease the effects of outside elements (e.g., sound pollution, temperatures, etc.).

Base rent: The initial rent that a tenant agrees to pay for the first year or established segment of time, which usually includes certain already established improvements. Depending on the lease in question, base rent can change from year to year – no matter the contract length – based on percentages, inflation, and other pre-specified calculations. Also known as "minimum rent" or "base minimum rent."

Basis points (bps): Accounting units used to describe the percentage change in a financial instrument's value or rate, with each one amounting to 0.01%.

Big-box store: A single-use retail property that may or may not be a stand-alone property. Usually between 10,000 and 100,000 square feet (but possibly more) in size, typical tenants include household names that sell electronics, appliances, books, or office supplies.

Bond proxies: A misinformed term for publicly traded REITs that offer above-average dividend yields with funds from operations, adjusted funds from operations (see Funds from operations; Adjusted funds from operations), and dividend growth rates that are expected to be very low. To be clear, though, no stock is ever an actual bond alternative.

Book cost: The historical cost of an asset along with any additional capital that was invested into it and not corrected for depreciation. Also known as "undepreciated book value."

Building classifications: A subjective way of determining commercial real estate's basic worth. Typically designated by letter, Class A buildings are usually in prime locations and either newer constructions or renovated to feature attractive "perks" that warrant higher leasing prices. Class B properties are less opportunistically placed and fitted than A examples, and C are less than B.

Building code: A set of local laws that dictate minimum construction and development requirements for real estate, from safety features to size to plumbing, roofing, and other specifications.

Build to suit: A facility constructed for a particular tenant to its specifications and for its purposes.

Capitalization rate (cap rate): The initial return a property buyer expects, told in percentage form. It's typically calculated by first estimating the net operating income (see Net operating income) that the property should bring in over the next 12 months before depreciation and interest expenses, and income taxes; then dividing that by the purchase price. Typically, higher capitalization rates correlate with greater risk or lower returns.

Capital expenditure (capex): An expense made to keep a property running properly, such as roof work or an HVAC unit replacement.

Capital improvement: A specific type of expense made to better compete against industry peers, such as adding amenities or appearance upgrades.

Carrying costs: Property taxes, interest, and similar expenses associated with assets under development.

Cash available for distribution (CAD): (See Adjusted funds from operations.)

Cash flow: In real estate, an owner's rental revenue after accounting for property-specific operating expenses such as taxes, utilities, and management – but setting aside depreciation, amortization, income taxes, and interest on any associated loans. It is sometimes interchangeably used with "net operating income" or "earnings before interest, taxes, depreciation, and amortization." (See Net operating income; Earnings before interest, taxes, depreciation, and amortization.)

Cash flow from operations: The cash left after subtracting debt service and ground lease payments from net operating income without accounting for capital expenditures (see Net operating income; Capital expenditure) or income taxes.

Commercial mortgage-backed securities (CMBS): Bonds backed by a set of commercial real estate mortgages.

Compound interest: Interest that's earned in a particular period and then added to the principal to be included in the next interest calculation due.

Consumer price index (CPI): An index that measures any fluctuations in prices associated with regular goods and services.

Convertible debt: A loan that's both secured by real property and can be converted into equity interest in that property at a set time.

Correlation: How much one investment type's price will move in line with another's. A perfect correlation of 1.0 means they should mimic each other closely. A correlation of zero means there's no noticeable pattern or connection. And a correlation of –1.0 means the two asset classes will very likely act exactly the opposite of each other.

Cost of capital: The cost involved in raising equity (common or preferred stock) or debt, often seen as an investor's expected rate of return. This should account for the dilution of the interests of the existing equity holders in the company.

Debt capital: The amount of debt on a company's balance sheet, from fixed-rate to variable-rate, any debt or debentures issued to investors, and bank credit line borrowings under a bank credit line.

Debt coverage ratio: An evaluation of projected net operating income sustainability that's calculated as net operating income (see Net operating income) divided by debt service. The higher the ratio is, the more attractive the margin of error becomes, since that means there should be sufficient cash to pay off debt as it comes due.

Debt service: The money needed to cover any outstanding loans, bonds, or mortgages.

Debt yield: Net operating income (see Net operating income) divided by the loan amount, expressed as a percentage. Higher debt yields are typically more attractive, since they indicate lower leverage and risk.

Depreciation: An asset's cost over its estimated useful life. This can only be used as a tax write-off if that asset is held for the purpose of producing income or actively and consistently used for long-term business purposes.

Discounted cash flow (DCF): An estimate of how much an investment is worth today by predicting how much it should make in the future, including the time-value of that initial money down.

Distributable net income: Net income (see Net income) as determined by generally accepted accounting principles (see Generally accepted accounting principles), that's then adjusted accordingly by adding back future income tax expenses, depreciation, and amortization. It does not, however, account for asset sales or future income tax benefits.

DownREIT: A REIT that does not own its properties directly, only a controlling interest in a limited partnership (see Limited partnership). Unlike an UPREIT (see Umbrella partnership REIT), though, it's typically formed through and with an already existing, publicly listed REIT and does not include that entity's directors or executive officers as partners.

Earnings before interest, taxes, depreciation, and amortization (EBITDA): An assessment of total cash from operations, measured by eliminating the mentioned charges.

Equity capital: Permanent capital that's been raised by selling and issuing stock with no right to repayment or redemption on the issuing company's part. This is typically common stock, though preferreds usually fall into this category as well.

Equity REIT: A REIT that either owns or has equity interest in real property.

Fair-market value: A property's value when all material facts are known to both the buyer and seller.

Funds available for distribution: (See Adjusted funds from operations.)

Funds from operations (FFO): Net income (see Net income) that doesn't account for any gains or losses from debt restructuring or property sales, but does adjust for depreciation of real property and unconsolidated entities (e.g., partnerships and joint ventures) that the REIT might own interest in.

Generally accepted accounting principles (GAAP): Terms and calculations that dictate how publicly traded companies report their profits, losses, and other aspects of their businesses.

General partner: A partner in a legally binding partnership that does not get to claim limited liability.

Gross absorption: A measure of demand that calculates how much space is leased at the beginning of a set period without calculating any space vacated after that timeframe begins. (See Absorption rate; Net absorption.)

Gross leasable area (GLA): The total amount of space in a commercial building that can be rented, along with any and all common areas. (See Net leasable area.)

Ground lease: The granted right of a landowner for a tenant to use it or a piece of it, typically for significant periods of time that are 31 to 99 years long.

Hybrid REIT: A REIT that engages in owning and renting out real property as well as writing or acquiring mortgages for real estate entities.

Internal rate of return (IRR): The annual growth rate expected from an investment, calculated by taking into account returns on investment as well as returns of investment. It balances all investment-specific actual and forecasted cash receipts against all cash contributions, though it typically doesn't assess debt leverage when applied to real estate. That way, when each entry is discounted to net present value, the sum is zero. IRR is a favorite tool of many investors, who see it as the best way to measure their returns. It is definitely superior to merely looking at current income to measure longer-term, comprehensive returns.

Interest coverage ratio: The ratio of a REIT's earnings before interest, taxes, depreciation, and amortization (see Earnings before interest, taxes, depreciation, and amortization) to total interest expenses that measures how much of the latter is covered by current cash flow.

Lessee: A person or business that signs on to rent space from a property. A tenant.

Lessor: A person or business with property that it leases out to lessees. A landlord.

Limited partnership: A business agreement between two or more parties, where a designated general partner (See General partner) acts as manager of the project and is fully liable for actions taken within that pact. The limited partner(s) involved takes a much more passive role and is only legally responsible for the amount of money he/she/it invests into the deal.

Liquidity: How easily an asset can be actively traded in the market or the amount of money that can be quickly accessed from a designated account or accounts.

Loan-to-value ratio (LTV): An assessment tool that shows the difference between a property and the amount that had to be borrowed to buy it.

Market capitalization (market cap): A company's total market value in terms of its outstanding securities and indebtedness. For example, if a REIT has 20 million shares trading at $20 each, 1 million shares of preferred stock priced at $25 each, and $100 million of debt, its market cap would be $525 million.

Master lease: An initial lease where the tenant has the right to rent out space he, she, or it is paying for under certain conditions.

Mortgage-backed security: A collection of mortgages that are first bought from a lending institution(s), then bundled and resold to investors.

Mortgage REIT: A real estate investment trust that provides financing for landlords and other real estate–related ventures by directly lending to them or through owning mortgages secured by real estate collateral.

Nareit (National Association of Real Estate Investment Trusts): The REIT industry's trade association that provides data and analysis through its website, reports, conferences, educational forums, and other platforms. It also has influence in Congress and helps to write legislation that affects REITs.

Net absorption (NA): The amount of total space that was filled at the end of a period minus what was occupied at the beginning. (See Absorption rate; Gross absorption.)

Net asset value (NAV): The estimated net current market value of a REIT's entire collection of assets – not just its properties – after subtracting at least all its liabilities and obligations from the equation. Some analysts take it a step further by marking debt up or down to reflect current interest rates.

Net leasable area: Also known as net rentable area, it measures actual floor space that will directly bring in rental revenue. As such, it normally doesn't include common areas.

Net lease: A lease that requires the tenant to pay for some aspect of the property in addition to base rent. In REIT jargon, this most often refers to a triple-net lease, where the renter handles all operating expenses, from property taxes to property insurance, maintenance, and utilities.

Net income: The resulting figure after subtracting all expenses from revenue.

Net operating income (NOI): Recurring income from a property or portfolio of properties (including rent), minus the operating expenses associated with it/them, such as repairs and maintenance, insurance, taxes, and utilities. Corporate overhead, interest expenses, unnecessary property improvements, capital expenditures, property depreciation expense, and income taxes are not included in this calculation.

Net sales proceeds: The profit made from selling an asset without factoring in marketing expenses, brokerage commissions, and closing costs.

Operating expenses: Money paid to keep a property running properly, such as for management fees, property taxes, utilities, insurance, and maintenance for common areas. It does not include income taxes, financing costs, depreciation, or principal and interest payments.

Operating partnership: For REITs specifically, a business arrangement with an UPREIT or DownREIT structure (see UPREIT; DownREIT), which holds the real property assets. In this agreement, the regular REIT typically holds the majority interest.

Operating partnership unit: A "share" in a REIT's operating partnership. (See Operating partnership.)

Passive income: The kind of income that comes from rent, royalties, dividends, and interest, or from selling securities or assets that don't require the seller to be materially involved.

Payout ratio: A REIT's annual dividend rate compared to its per-share funds from operations or adjusted funds from operations. So if FFO is $1 per share and the current dividend rate is $0.80 per share, the FFO payout ratio would be 80%. (See Funds from operations; Adjusted funds from operations.)

Price-to-earnings (P/E) ratio: A company's stock price compared to its per-share earnings. It's calculated by dividing the stock price by earnings per share on either a trailing 12-month basis or a forward-looking basis.

Rate of return: Though there are multiple forms of this that investors can calculate, it's essentially an investment's net gain or loss over a set time frame, calculated as a percentage of the original investment cost.

Real estate operating company (REOC): Typically a public company that owns, manages, and/or develops real estate but does not operate as a REIT and therefore does not have to follow any REIT requirements.

Replacement cost: The cost involved in creating a similarly functioning property, including construction, permits, and property taxes.

Reproduction cost: The cost involved in creating a complete duplicate to an already existing property down to the last detail.

Return on investment (ROI): An evaluation of how much has been or can be made on an investment. It's calculated by taking earnings before interest, taxes, and dividends, and dividing it by total invested capital. The result is then expressed as a percentage.

Revenue per available room (RevPAR): A lodging industry term that measures performance over any given amount of time and for a single property, market, business, or even the larger industry. It can be calculated in one of two ways, either by multiplying the average daily rate by the occupancy rate, or by dividing room revenue by the number of rooms available.

Sale-leaseback: A two-part transaction where a property owner sells the land to a buyer but then rents it back from that party, usually under a long-term lease.

Same-store sales: Traditionally a retail term, it compares income from stores open for at least one year, excluding any that have been closed. (New stores tend to have higher sales growth that doesn't last.) REITs have adopted the concept to better analyze their rental revenues, operating expenses, and net operating income (see Net operating income) from properties that have been owned and operated in the same fiscal period of the prior year.

Specialty REIT: A REIT that works with real estate outside of the standard property types such as offices, apartments, hospitals, retail, or industrial properties (e.g., a timber REIT or a movie theater REIT).

Straight-line rent: A way of recording rent that accurately spaces it out evenly over the course of a lease instead of recording every monthly difference.

Taxable REIT subsidiary (TRS): A corporation that's taxed at standard corporate income rates even though it's owned by a regular REIT.

Third-party management: A business arrangement that sees one party taking care of all the day-to-day property responsibilities for the actual owner (or renter).

Total return: A stock's dividend income plus capital appreciation before taxes and commissions. So if a stock rises 4% in price and provides a 4% dividend yield during a year, the total annual return would be 8%.

Umbrella Partnership REIT (UPREIT): A REIT that doesn't own its properties directly, only a controlling interest in a limited partnership that owns real estate. (See DownREIT.)

Value creation: The ability of a REIT's management team to go above and beyond standard property management to increase shareholder value over time. These actions can cover attractive property acquisitions, mergers, joint ventures, property developments, selling equity at opportune times, and refinancing debt when interest costs are low.

Contributor Biographies

Scott L. Robinson is a senior commercial real estate professional with extensive REIT, bulge-bracket, and middle-market experience in capital markets, investment banking, and credit analysis. He is a Managing Director and co-head of real estate investment banking at Oberon Securities and a Clinical Assistant Professor of Finance at the Schack Institute of Real Estate, where he is also Program Coordinator for the Finance & Investment curriculum and Director of the REIT Center. His career success as an advisor, investor, and professor is a direct result of his keen attention to details, broad economic understanding, and competitive determination.

At Oberon Securities, an NYC-based broker dealer, he oversees a team of finance professionals serving the middle-market segment. He has built a reputation for execution of capital placement, transaction structuring, and M&A/strategic advisory. Notable transactions include the recapitalization and pre-IPO advisement of Plymouth Industrial (NYSE: PLYM) and the arrangement of a programmatic, multi-tiered equity partner for a private industrial platform.

He is currently an advisor to a FinTech start-up focused on bringing algorithmic trading to the REIT and real asset sectors, and he serves on the Board of Directors of Monmouth Real Estate Investment Trust (NYSE: MNR), which he helped grow from a $200 million enterprise to its present $3,000 million total capitalization. He also served as non-executive Chairman of Full Stack Modular, a Brooklyn-based modular construction technology company. Additionally, he previously served as U.S. advisor to a technology-focused VC fund based in Hangzhou, China.

He received a Bachelor of Science with dual concentrations in Biology and Economics, and a minor in Accounting from the University of California, Riverside, and a Master of Science in Real

Estate Finance from New York University. He is also FINRA-licensed (79, 63, and 7) and a New York State Real Estate Broker.

Jay D. Hatfield is CEO of Infrastructure Capital Advisors and the portfolio manager of the InfraCap MLP ETF (NYSE: AMZA), Virtus InfraCap US Preferred Stock ETF (NYSE: PFFA), InfraCap REIT Preferred ETF (NYSE: PFFR), and a series of hedge funds. He leads the investment team and directs the company's business development. During his career, he has gained a broad perspective on the U.S. financial markets with years' experience as an investment banker, a research director and portfolio manager, and as a co-founder of an NYSE-listed company.

Prior to forming ICA, he partnered with senior energy industry executives to acquire several midstream MLPs. These companies were then merged to form what's now known as NGL Energy Partners (NYSE: NGL). NGL went public in May of 2011, and Hatfield is currently a general partner. In the years prior to forming NGL, he was a portfolio manager at SAC Capital (now Point72 Asset Management), where he focused on income securities. He joined SAC from Zimmer Lucas Partners, a hedge fund focused on energy and utility sectors, where he was head of fixed-income research.

He began his career as a CPA at Ernst & Young, and holds an MBA in Finance from the Wharton School at the University of Pennsylvania and a BS in Managerial Economics from the University of California, Davis. He is also the founder of Tutoring America, a non-profit organization dedicated to providing low-income students with supplemental tutoring services and technology to accelerate learning in both math and English language arts.

Mark O. Decker, Sr. is currently self-employed as a real estate capital markets advisor. Prior to becoming an advisor, he was Vice Chair of Bank of Montreal's U.S. Capital Markets, a position he held from 2014 to 2016. And before that, he served from 2011 to 2014 as BMO's Head of U.S. real estate investment and corporate banking.

From 2004 to 2011, he was a managing director and head of the real estate group at Robert W. Baird and Co. Inc. And he founded the real estate investment banking group at Ferris Baker Watts, Inc. in 2000. Mr. Decker began his investment banking career in 1997, when he joined Friedman, Billings Ramsey, and Co. as a managing director.

He served as President and principal spokesman of the REIT industry and its national trade association, Nareit, for twelve years from 1985 to 1997. Concurrently, he was chief staff executive of the Pension Real Estate Association (PREA) from 1985 to 1990. Before that, Mr. Decker served in the White House for Presidents Richard Nixon and Gerald Ford.

He is the 1997 recipient of the prestigious Nareit Leadership Award and holds a JD from Antonin Scalia Law School, and a BS in Education from Kent State University. He also wrote the foreword in Ralph Block's original book, *The Essential REIT, A Guide To Profitable Investing in Real Estate Investment Trusts.*

Eva Steiner is an Associate Professor of Real Estate at the Penn State Smeal College of Business, where she holds the King Family Early Career Professorship. Prior to joining Penn State, she was an Assistant Professor of Real Estate at Cornell University and at the University of Cambridge, U.K. Professor Steiner's research interests include real estate finance and economics.

Her research has been published in leading academic journals, and she regularly contributes to academic and industry seminars and conferences. Her work has been recognized through a number of international honors and awards, and has attracted sponsorship from academic and industry-related sources.

Professor Steiner is a member of the Nareit Real Estate Investment Advisory Council. She has taught real estate finance and econometrics to undergraduate and graduate students in business, real estate, and MBA programs. Professor Steiner received her BA from the University of Heilbronn, Germany, and her MPhil and PhD degrees from the University of Cambridge, U.K.

Paul E. Smithers has served as the President, Director, and CEO of Innovative Industrial Properties, Inc. (NYSE: IIPR) since its inception in 2016. Innovative Industrial Properties, Inc. is the pioneering real estate investment trust for the medical-use cannabis industry and is also the first publicly traded company on the New York Stock Exchange to provide real estate capital to do so. Innovative Industrial Properties targets medical-use cannabis facilities for sale-leaseback transactions with tenants that are licensed operators under long-term, triple-net leases.

Prior to that position, Smithers served as cofounder and chief legal officer of Iso Nano International, LLC; and before that, he was the managing partner of Smithers & Player, Attorneys at Law (1989–2013) and the law firm of Ropers Majeski (1982–1988). Much of his 33 years of legal experience has involved commercial and residential real estate transactions. He is a member of the California Bar, and a licensed California real estate broker.

Jennifer Fritzsche is CFO, Manager, and Board Member of Canopy Spectrum, a company focused on the wireless spectrum space. For 25 years before that, she served as Managing Director and Senior Equity Analyst at Wells Fargo Securities, where she focused on the telecommunication services, cable, data center, and tower sectors.

During her tenure there, Jennifer received top rankings from Institutional Investor in the communications infrastructure space in 2017, 2018, 2019, and 2020. Jennifer has made numerous media appearances and has often been a guest on Bloomberg and CNBC.

She also speaks at many of the industry and trade conferences, and often is asked to participate in many Washington, D.C., regulatory telecom seminars and events. In addition to her role at Canopy Spectrum, she is a Senior Fellow at Georgetown University's McDonough School of Business.

David Gladstone is the founder and CEO, and Chairman of the board of directors of Gladstone Capital Corporation (GOOD), Gladstone Investment Corporation (GAIN), and Gladstone Land Corporation (LAND). He is also founder of external manager Gladstone Companies and serves on the board of managers of affiliated broker-dealer Gladstone Securities, LLC.

Prior to Gladstone, he served as either Chairman or Vice Chairman of the board of directors of American Capital, Ltd. (Nasdaq: ACAS), a publicly traded leveraged buyout fund and mezzanine debt finance company, from 1997 to 2001. From 1974 to 1997, he held various positions, including Chairman and CEO with Allied Capital Corporation (NYSE: ALD), Allied Capital Corporation II, Allied Capital Lending Corporation, and Allied Capital Advisors, Inc., a registered investment adviser that managed the Allied companies. The Allied companies were the largest group of publicly traded mezzanine debt funds in the U.S. and were managers of two private venture capital limited partnerships.

From 1991 to 1997, he served either as Chairman of the board of directors or President of Allied Capital Commercial Corporation, a publicly-traded REIT that invested in real estate loans to small and medium-sized businesses, managed by Allied Capital Advisors, Inc. He managed the growth of Allied Capital Commercial from no assets at the time of its initial public offering to $385 million in assets at the time it merged into Allied Capital Corporation in 1997.

Gladstone is also a past Director of Capital Automotive REIT, a real estate investment trust that purchases and net leases real estate to automobile dealerships. He served as a Director of The Riggs National Corporation (the parent of Riggs Bank) from 1993 to 1997 and of Riggs Bank from 1991 to 1993. He served as a Trustee of the George Washington University and currently is Trustee Emeritus.

He is a past member of the Listings and Hearings Committee of the National Association of Securities Dealers, Inc. And he was the founder and managing member of The Capital Investors, LLC, a group of angel investors, where he remains a member emeritus. He holds an MBA from the Harvard Business School, an MA from American University, and a BA from the University of Virginia. Gladstone co-authored two books on financing for small- and medium-sized businesses, *Venture Capital Handbook* and *Venture Capital Investing*.

"A stock is not just a ticker symbol or an electronic blip; it is an ownership interest in an actual business, with an underlying value that does not depend on its share price."

– Benjamin Graham

Index